American Constitutional Law

The CONTEMPORARY ESSAYS Series

GENERAL EDITOR: LEONARD W. LEVY

American Constitutional Law

Historical Essays

Edited by
Leonard W. Levy

HARPER TORCHBOOKS ❦ The Academy Library
Harper and Row, Publishers, New York

To Rosalind and Richard Brown

AMERICAN CONSTITUTIONAL LAW: HISTORICAL ESSAYS

Introduction, compilation and editorial notes copyright © 1966 by Leonard W. Levy.

Printed in the United States of America.

First Edition: HARPER TORCHBOOKS, 1966
Harper & Row, Publishers, Incorporated
49 East 33rd Street, New York, N.Y. 10016

Library of Congress Catalog Card No.: 66-21601.

Table of Contents

Introduction

LEONARD W. LEVY

As beauty exists in the eye of the beholder, so American constitutional law exists in the eye of the Supreme Court. Justice Frankfurter, as if in disagreement, once remarked that the "ultimate touchstone of constitutionality is the Constitution itself, not what we have said about it." [1] The ultimate, however, is nearly as far off as the infinite. What counts is what the Supreme Court has said about the Constitution—in about three hundred and eighty volumes thus far.

The Constitution itself plays a mere secondary role in American constitutional law. When, for example, the Court had to construe the First Amendment's injunction against establishments of religion, Justice Jackson candidly observed that it was "idle to pretend that this task is one for which we can find in the Constitution one word to help us as judges to decide where the secular ends and the sectarian begins in education." [2] Justices who look to the Constitution for more than a puzzling, if majestic, phrase might just as well turn to the comic strips for all the guidance they will find on how to decide most of the great cases that involve national public policy, whether the question relates to legislative apportionment, racial segregation, the regulation of utility rates, subversive activities, the curtailment of crop production, or the seizure of steel mills. There is not a word in the Constitution about these or most of the subjects of great import with which the Court must deal. That fact, paradoxically, is a great strength of the Constitution, accounting in part for its longevity and vitality.

The members of the Philadelphia Convention of 1787, notwithstanding their enormous respect for the great John Locke, ignored his example. Locke was a dreadfully inept constitution

[1] *Graves v. N.Y.*, 306 U.S. 466, 491 (1939).
[2] *McCollum v. Board of Education*, 334 U.S. 203, 237–238 (1948).

1

maker. On the theory that written statements of fundamental law must be immutable, like the laws of the universe, in order to be eternal, Locke framed for Carolina a constitution expressly providing that "every part thereof, shall be and remain the sacred and unalterable form and rule of government for Carolina forever." As insurance, he futilely added that "all manner of comments and expositions on any part of these fundamental constitutions, or on any part of the common or statute laws of Carolina, are absolutely prohibited." [3] By contrast, the framers of the United States Constitution recognized the inevitability of change and the need for plasticity. They therefore provided for an orderly amendment procedure. They also provided for a Supreme Court whose duties —"the judicial power shall extend to all cases . . . arising under this Constitution, the Laws of the United States, and Treaties"— required it to engage in "all manner of comments and expositions."

The framers also had a genius for studied imprecision or calculated ambiguity. Their Constitution, expressed in very generalized terms, resembled Martin Chuzzlewit's grandnephew who had no more than "the first idea and sketchy notion of a face." It thereby permitted, even encouraged, nay necessitated, continuous reinterpretation and adaptation. Men trained in the common law habitually avoid minute specifications which become obsolete with a change in the particular circumstances for which they were adopted; such men tend rather to formulate principles that are expansive and comprehensive in nature. The principles themselves, not their framers' understanding and application of them, are meant to endure.

In determining "whether a provision of the Constitution applies to a new subject matter," declared Justice Stone, "it is of little significance that it is one with which the framers were not familiar. For in setting up an enduring framework of government they undertook to carry out for the indefinite future and in all the vicissitudes of the changing affairs of men, those fundamental principles which the instrument itself discloses. Hence we read its words, not as we read legislative codes which are subject to continuous revision with the changing course of events, but as the revelation of the great purposes which were intended

[3] Fundamental Constitutions of Carolina, 1669, sections 80 and 120, in Francis Newton Thorpe, ed., *The Federal and State Constitutions, Colonial Charters, and Other Organic Laws* (Washington, D.C. 1909), vol. 5, pp. 2782 and 2786.

to be achieved by the Constitution as a continuing instrument of government." [4] Thus the commerce clause applies to telestar communication, racial discrimination in motels, stolen cars, stock exchange transactions, and the wages of window washers. The Constitution, designed by an eighteenth-century rural society, serves as well today as ever, perhaps better than ever, because an antiquarian historicism that would freeze its original meanings, even if discernible, has not guided its interpretation and was not intended to. As Justice Holmes once said, "The present has a right to govern itself, so far as it can . . . Historical continuity with the past is not a duty, only a necessity." [5]

The document itself, with all amendments, clearly delineates the structure of American national government but only roughly maps the contours of power. We know unmistakably that there is to be a President whose term of office is four years; but what is "the executive power" with which he is vested? Chief Justice Marshall happily noted that the Constitution has none of the "prolixity of a legal code;" it has, rather, the virtue of muddy brevity, a mere seven thousand words, including amendments. Scarcely two percent of the verbiage possesses any significance in constitutional law. Almost without exception, these are the purposefully ambiguous words, like general welfare, due process of law, unreasonable searches, commerce among the states, liberty, equal protection, obligation of contracts, establishment of religion, necessary and proper, and direct taxes. Other words of crucial importance in constitutional law are not even in the Constitution, including clear and present danger, fair trial, war power, public purpose, separate but equal, liberty of contract, separation of church and state, interstate commerce, fair return, and police power. They are judicial glosses. In large measure we have an unwritten constitution whose history is the history of judicial review. James Beck made the point by comparing the work of the Supreme Court to that of a "continuous constitutional convention" which adapts the original charter by reinterpretation, making its duties "political in the highest sense of the word, as well as judicial." [6]

---

[4] U.S. v. Classic, 313 U.S. 299, 315–316 (1941).

[5] Oliver Wendell Holmes, Collected Legal Papers (New York, 1920), p. 139.

[6] James M. Beck, The Constitution of the United States (New York, 1922), p. 221. The phrase "continuous constitutional convention" has been used independently by other writers. E.g., Henry S. Commager, "Constitu-

The Constitution's power of survival derives also from the fact that it incorporates and symbolizes the political values of a free people. It creates a representative, responsible government empowered to serve the general welfare at the same time that it keeps the government bitted and bridled. "In framing a government which is to be administered by men over men," noted Madison in Federalist #51, "the great difficulty lies in this; you must first enable the government to control the governed; and in the next place oblige it to control itself." The Constitution deals with great powers, many of them undefined, but they are decentralized, separated and distributed, checked and balanced, limited and prohibited. At the same time, most notably through the Bill of Rights and the great Reconstruction amendments, the Constitution requires that the game shall be played freely and fairly, with the judiciary as the umpire. "The great ideals of liberty and equality," wrote Justice Cardozo, "are preserved against the assaults of opportunism, the expediency of the passing hour, the erosion of small encroachments, the scorn and derision of those who have no patience with general principles, by enshrining them in constitutions, and consecrating to the task of their protection a body of defenders." [7] Charles Evans Hughes's much quoted remark, that "the Constitution is what the judges say it is," expressed only half his thought; he added, much like Cardozo, "and the judiciary is the safeguard of our liberty and of our property under the Constitution." [8] The Lord Chancellor in *Iolanthe* might have epitomized our Constitution and Supreme Court when he humorously asserted,

> The Law is the embodiment
> Of everything that's excellent.
> It has no kind of fault or flaw,
> And I, my Lords, embody the Law.

Constitutional law is the product of the entire federal judiciary, not just of the Supreme Court. Indeed, the history of constitutional law would be as illuminating as the dark side of

---

tional History and the Higher Law," in Conyers Read, ed., *The Constitution Reconsidered* (New York, 1938), p. 231; and Robert H. Jackson, *The Struggle for Judicial Supremacy* (New York, 1941), pp. x–xi.

[7] Benjamin N. Cardozo, *The Nature of the Judicial Process* (New Haven, 1921), pp. 92–93.

[8] Charles Evans Hughes, *Addresses and Papers* (New York, 1908), pp. 139–140.

the moon without also considering the participation of the non-judicial branches of the government. The President makes constitutional history when, by simple executive order, he authorizes the internment of 70,000 American citizens of Japanese descent; or sends troops to Little Rock or Oxford, Mississippi; or ends racial discrimination in the armed forces, or in private employment under government contract, or in federally assisted housing projects; or establishes a loyalty-security program among government employees. The Congress makes constitutional history more obviously and with far greater frequency via the legislative process. Nevertheless, constitutional law is peculiarly the product of the Supreme Court. The President, Congress, and administrative agencies help make constitutional history; they even help make constitutional law, but only in the first instance. The sovereign people may even amend the Constitution itself, but unless they abolish judicial review, the Supreme Court still has the last word, for it construes not only the validity of the exercise of power by the other branches of government; it construes also the meaning of the Constitution. The point is implicit in Justice Holmes's quotation from Bishop Hoadly to the effect that the final authority to interpret the law, rather than its maker, is the real sovereign.[9]

As Tocqueville observed long ago, "Scarcely any question arises in the United States which does not become, sooner or later, a subject of judicial debate . . ." [10] Frankfurter, echoing the thought a century later, declared that most of the problems of modern society, "whether of industry, agriculture, of finance, of racial interactions or the eternal conflict between liberty and authority, become in the United States sooner or later legal problems for ultimate solution by the Supreme Court." [11] Thus trivial disputes between private litigants may be argued in terms of fundamental principles of government by judges and lawyers, and matters of the highest policy go to the courts for judgment, though the case itself may be insignificant in terms of the interest

[9] Hoadly said, "Whoever hath an absolute authority to interpret any written or spoken laws, it is he who is truly the lawgiver, to all intents and purposes, and not the person who first wrote or spoke them." Quoted in James B. Thayer, "The Origin and Scope of the American Doctrine of Constitutional Law," Harvard Law Review, vol. 7 (1893), p. 152.

[10] Alexis de Tocqueville, Democracy in America, ed. by Henry S. Commager, trans. by Henry Reeve (New York, 1947), p. 177.

[11] Frankfurter "The Supreme Court," in Sydney D. Bailey, ed., Aspects of American Government (London, 1950), p. 35.

of the immediate parties. For example, on the outcome of the claim of a Mr. Norman for $15.60 against the Baltimore and Ohio Railroad depended the financial policy of the United States, involving some one hundred billion dollars and a possible sixty percent increase in the national debt in the midst of a depression.[12] The role of the government in the economy, the relation of the individual to the state and of the states to the nation, the system of justice, and the legal standards of equality are among the subjects of our constitutional law. Its study is ennobled by an alliance with history, with statecraft, with the evolution of popular institutions of government, and with human rights.

Nearly every significant decision of the Supreme Court deals with rights or with power, whether government power or private economic power. Constitutional government is, by definition, limited government, a system of regularized restraints upon power; there is therefore an inevitable and enduring tension between the exercise of powers allegedly vested and limitations allegedly breached. In some periods in the history of constitutional law the Supreme Court tends to emphasize the affirmative aspects of power, in other periods its limitations. In each of the five periods of the Court's history, certain characteristic doctrines and precedents prevail, only to be abandoned or distinguished in a later period; as some wag once said, a distinguished case is one which is no longer distinguished. The Court also seems always to have some special interest to protect. In one period it might be the Union or the state police power; in another corporations or organized labor; in still another, radicals or the criminally accused.

The first or formative period is identified with the chief justiceship of John Marshall. When John Jay, one of his predecessors who had resigned from the Court to run for state office, declined reappointment as chief justice, he said that the Court was fatally lacking in power. Marshall took the job and no one thereafter could make the same complaint. During Marshall's long tenure of office, the Court asserted the power of judicial review, precariously over Congress and firmly over the states, establishing the supremacy of the Constitution and federal law. A partisan organ of the national government, the Court's national-

12 Perry v. U.S., 294 U.S. 330 (1935). See the discussion in Jackson, *Struggle for Judicial Supremacy*, pp. 96–103.

istic opinions conjured up the image of screaming eagles and Old Glory on the rise. Marshall also made the Court, in Max Lerner's phrase, "the strategic link between capitalism and constitutionalism." [13] His nationalism, which was both real and enduringly constructive in *McCulloch* v. *Maryland* and *Gibbons* v. *Ogden*, was more frequently a guise for the invalidation of state statutes that trenched on private property. Doctrines of vested rights, derived from extra-constitutional sources, found lodgement mainly in the contract clause.

Under Taney's chief justiceship, which was marred by the aberrational *Dred Scott* decision, the Court deviated only slightly from the course set by Marshall. Its vigorous exercise of judicial review and extension of its jurisdiction into unprecedented fields fortified the national judicial power. Less inclined to see state legislation as an assault upon the supremacy of the union, the Taney Court refused to let unused national powers serve as a rationale for the invalidation of state acts not in operative conflict with national acts. It behaved more like an impartial arbitrator between states and nation than like a strident champion of the latter. Despite some rhetoric about community rights and public welfare, property rights vested by contract were usually treated as if sacred, and corporate business was encouraged and protected. The trend, if not the tone, of decision was rather conservative.

In the third period of the Court's history, from the close of the Civil War to the 1890's, the state police power enjoyed its greatest triumphs, despite threatening judicial language which laid the groundwork for new doctrines of constitutional limitations. The contract clause, although revealed to have weaknesses, still served as the principal justification for the invalidation of much regulatory legislation. During this time the Court struck down or emasculated most of a comprehensive Congressional program for the protection of civil rights, making corporations rather than Negroes the chief beneficiary of the Fourteenth Amendment. Judicial interpretation eroded away the historic meanings of due process of law as a protection of the rights of the criminally accused, and engrafted a new economic substance to due process, making it a device for keeping man's relation to his Gold as private as possible.

[13] Lerner, "John Marshall and the Campaign of History," *Columbia Law Review*, vol. 39 (1939), p. 403. The essay is reprinted in this volume.

From 1895 to 1936, the period of "judicial supremacy," the Court acted, in Justice Brandeis's phrase, as a "superlegislature" and the due process clause was the most formidable weapon in the armory of judicial review. Brooks Adams tartly observed that the historic purpose of the federal judiciary seemed to be to "dislocate any comprehensive body of legislation, whose effect would be to change the social status." [14] Doctrines of constitutional law were arrogantly, artlessly, and inconsistently manipulated against an array of statutory reforms that sought to protect consumers, trade unions, farmers, unorganized workers, women, and children from the exploitation and abuses of business enterprise. The high-point of the Court's attempt to control public policy was reached during seventeen months of 1935–1936 in a massive and unprecedented judicial assault against a single Administration. No less than twelve acts of Congress, parts of a systematic program to combat economic and social disaster, were held unconstitutional. Public opinion, though opposed to "packing" the Court, was outraged and the Court made a timely, strategic retreat, belatedly validating Mr. Dooley's observation that it followed the election returns.

During the present period of the Court's history, the most constructive since that of Marshall, constitutional law has been modernized. Outworn and reprehensible precedents have fallen like cold clinkers through an open grate. Economic due process and doctrines constricting government powers have been junked, as has a propensity to void legislation which the judges personally dislike. Plenitude of power, both national and state, and a concept of cooperative federalism now characterize our highest public law. The authority of the government to control the economy is virtually undisputed; from New Deal to Great Society, the welfare state has been sustained. At the same time that the Court emancipated government, it vitalized the constitutional law of human rights. Cases involving free speech, the claims of the criminally accused, and equality for racial minorities now bulk largest on the Court's docket. The supreme tribunal has at last caught up with folklore: it has become the protector of civil liberties and civil rights, sometimes anticipating rather than following the election returns.

The Court is most likely, nowadays, to follow the scholarly

[14] Brooks Adams, *The Theory of Social Revolutions* (New York, 1914), p. 218.

commentators and the law reviews. Chief Justice Hughes called the journals the "fourth estate of the law." [15] Responsible, informed critics have often led the way during this period of modern constitutional law; the justices, who are sensitive readers, are also far more conscious of constitutional history and the mistakes of their predecessors. They rarely decide a case without first canvassing the journals to determine whether the issue has been discussed by some extramural authority from whom some wisdom may be gleaned. Students of constitutional law, no less than the justices themselves, must know constitutional history. Although the Court will no longer hold unconstitutional a statute fixing maximum hours for labor or prohibiting racial discrimination in public facilities, the early cases are indispensable to any understanding of current constitutional law. Modern judicial tolerance is an outgrowth of yesterday's judicial intolerance; judicial humility is the child of judicial arrogance. The essays that follow, a small sampling of some of the best that have appeared on the history of American constitutional law, enhance our understanding as citizens and students. They might even contribute to a greater degree of humility on the part of some critics who know little of history and less of the awesome responsibilities faced by our highest appellate judges.

[15] Quoted by Chester A. Newland, "Legal Periodicals and the United States Supreme Court," *Midwest Journal of Political Science*, vol. 3, (February 1959), p. 59.

1. The Founding Fathers:
A Reform Caucus in Action

JOHN P. ROCHE

EDITORIAL NOTE. *There have been many interpretations of the Constitutional Convention, and Charles Beard managed to endorse most of them, at one point or another in his career, as well as dominate any discussion of them. In The Supreme Court and the Constitution, he wrote, "It is not merely patriotic pride that compels one to assert that never in the history of assemblies has there been a convention of men richer in political experience and in practical knowledge, or endowed with a profounder insight into the springs of human action and the intimate essence of government." This estimate, which many of Beard's critics, including John P. Roche, would accept, is not necessarily inconsistent with An Economic Interpretation of the Constitution, but the tone is altogether different. The Economic Interpretation is written in a spirit that would describe the performance of a great violin virtuoso as the scraping of cats' intestines on horses' tails. Beard construed the Constitution as a conservative economic document framed by an unrepresentative minority employing undemocratic means to protect personal property interests by a central government responsive to their needs and able to thwart populistic majorities in the states.*

Since the Economic Interpretation, historians have engaged in a prolonged debate, which defies settlement, on questions raised directly or otherwise by Beard. Were the framers enlightened, disinterested statesmen, seeking to rescue—indeed, to create—a nation then dangerously drifting toward anarchy? Were they conspiratorial representatives of a rising capitalism, or perhaps the leaders of a Thermidorian reaction to the Articles of Confederation which embodied the democratic principles of the

Declaration of Independence? Was the Constitution mainly an economic or a political document? If its chief significance was political, was it the product of a clash and compromise between large and small states, or of town and tidewater against farm and frontier, or of a north-south sectionalism? Or, was the political conflict between men of nationalist principles and those devoted to states' rights; or, was an aristocratic elite pitted against the localist forces of democratic majoritarianism? If the Constitution was mainly a political document, was consensus or compromise the most significant feature in the Convention? That is, was there an agreement on certain fundamentals, such as the need for a strong centralized government that would operate on individuals, which far outweighed in importance the supposed "great" compromises, such as the Connecticut Compromise, the three-fifths rule, or the electoral college, that occupied most of the time of the delegates?

Scholars of greater sophistication than Beard continue to advance interpretations of a substantially economic-social character. Merrill Jensen, Richard Hofstadter, Forest McDonald, E. James Ferguson, Jackson T. Main, and Lee Benson, despite sharp intramural differences, have enriched our historical literature and kept a neoBeardianism at its forefront.

At the same time the works of some older constitutional scholars, chiefly Andrew C. McLaughlin and Charles Warren who saw the Federal Convention in essentially political terms, have lost little of their usefulness. Recent scholars who know more about the psychology of politics and human behavior, have written from the same perspective without the conservative bias or antimajoritarianism, and without the faint filiopietism, of McLaughlin and Warren. Cecilia Kenyon, Henry S. Commager, Robert E. Brown, and John P. Roche understand that the democratic rhetoric of antiFederalists did not often correspond with their political behavior, and that Federalist leaders could give their loyalty to a concept of national interest that transcended purse and status without compromising republican principles. Justice Holmes once said that high-mindedness is not impossible to man. "I don't readily give up the belief," he explained, "that Washington and the rest had for their dominant motive a patriotic desire to see a powerful nation take the place of squabbling states." To his credit, John P. Roche, though scarcely unfamiliar with the seamy side of political behavior, implicitly shares Holmes's view.

In the essay that follows, Roche is chiefly concerned with the political process at work in the Federal Convention. Gibbon once remarked that his experience in the Hampshire militia aided him in writing The Decline and Fall of Rome. Roche brought to a careful reading of the records of the Federal Convention a practical experience in politics, possessed by few scholars, which deepened his insights. He sees the framers mainly as masterful, professional politicians who pursued their task of radically reconstructing the American governmental system according to the prevailing rules of the game. That is, he depicts the framers as democratic politicians who were forced by political realities to water down their nationalistic objectives. They were responsible to their respective constituencies whose necessary approval, via ratification, dominated the making of the finished product. This thesis is especially striking in the light of the traditional view of the framers as men who feared and despised democracy.

Although the framers may have been democratic politicians, at least in the sense that they were responsible to the voting public, readers may question whether Roche has not mistakenly equated political realism or political pragmatism with democratic politics. His suggestive asides are sometimes overstated, as in his description of America of 1787 as a "democratic society" or of the Constitution as a "makeshift" or "patchwork" document. On balance his essay is without peer for illuminating the politics of the Convention; it is also an off-beat reflection of the "consensus" approach which now seems to characterize the work of so many historians of the United States.

THE FOUNDING FATHERS:
A REFORM CAUCUS IN ACTION

Over the last century and a half, the work of the Constitutional Convention and the motives of the Founding Fathers have been analyzed under a number of different ideological auspices. To one generation of historians, the hand of God was moving in the assembly; under a later dispensation, the dialectic (at various levels of philosophical sophistication) replaced the Deity: "relationships of production" moved into the niche previously reserved for Love of Country. Thus in counterpoint to the Zeitgeist, the Framers have undergone miraculous metamorphoses; at one time acclaimed as liberals and bold social engineers, today they appear in the guise of sound Burkean conservatives, men who in our time would subscribe to *Fortune*, look to Walter Lippmann for political theory, and chuckle patronizingly at the antics of Barry Goldwater. The implicit assumption is that if James Madison were among us, he would be President of the Ford Foundation, while Alexander Hamilton would chair the Committee for Economic Development.

The "Fathers" have thus been admitted to our best circles; the revolutionary ferocity which confiscated all Tory property in reach and populated New Brunswick with outlaws has been converted by the "Miltown School" of American historians into a benign dedication to "consensus" and "prescriptive rights." The Daughters of the American Revolution have, through the ministrations of Professors Boorstin, Hartz, and Rossiter, at last found ancestors worthy of their descendants. It is not my purpose here to argue that the "Fathers" were, in fact, radical revolutionaries; that proposition has been brilliantly demonstrated by Robert R. Palmer in his *Age of the Democratic Revolution*. My concern is with the further position that not only were they revolutionaries, but also they were democrats. Indeed, in my view, there is one fundamental truth about the Founding Fathers that *every* generation of Zeitgeisters has done its best to obscure: they were first and foremost superb democratic politicians. I suspect that in a contemporary setting, James Madison would be Speaker of the House of Representatives and Hamilton would be the *eminence grise* dominating (pace Theodore Sorenson or Sherman Adams) the Executive Office of the President. They were, with their colleagues, *political men*—not metaphysicians, disembodied conservatives or Agents of History—and as recent research into the nature of American politics in the 1780s confirms,[1] they were committed (perhaps willy-nilly) to working

[1] The view that the right to vote in the states was severely circumscribed by property qualifications has been thoroughly discredited in recent years. See Chilton Williamson, *American Suffrage from Property to Democracy, 1760–1860* (Princeton, 1960). The contemporary position is that John Dickinson actually knew what he was talking about when he argued that there would be little opposition to vesting the right of suffrage in freeholders since "The great mass of our Citizens is composed at this time of freeholders, and will be pleased with it." Max Farrand, *Records of the Federal Convention*, Vol. 2, p. 202 (New Haven, 1911). (Henceforth cited as Farrand.)

within the democratic framework, within a universe of public approval. Charles Beard and the filiopietists to the contrary notwithstanding, the Philadelphia Convention was not a College of Cardinals or a council of Platonic guardians working within a manipulative, predemocratic framework; it was a *nationalist* reform caucus which had to operate with great delicacy and skill in a political cosmos full of enemies to achieve the one definitive goal—popular approbation.

Perhaps the time has come, to borrow Walton Hamilton's fine phrase, to raise the Framers from immortality to mortality, to give them credit for their magnificent demonstration of the art of democratic politics. The point must be reemphasized; they made history and did it within the limits of consensus. There was nothing inevitable about the future in 1787; the *Zeitgeist*, that fine Hegelian technique of begging causal questions, could only be discerned in retrospect. What they did was to hammer out a pragmatic compromise which would both bolster the "National interest" and be acceptable to the people. What inspiration they got came from their collective experience as professional politicians in a democratic society. As John Dickinson put it to his fellow delegates on August 13, "Experience must be our guide. Reason may mislead us."

In this context, let us examine the problems they confronted and the solutions they evolved. The Convention has been described picturesquely as a counter-revolutionary junta and the Constitution as a *coup d'etat*,[2] but this has been accomplished by withdrawing the whole history of the movement for constitutional reform from its true context. No doubt the goals of the constitutional elite were "subversive" to the existing political order, but it is overlooked that their subversion could only have succeeded if the people of the United States endorsed it by regularized procedures. Indubitably they were "plotting" to establish a much stronger central government than existed under the Articles, but only in the sense in which one could argue equally well that

---

[2] The classic statement of the *coup d'etat* theory is, of course, Charles A. Beard, *An Economic Interpretation of the Constitution of the United States* (New York, 1913), and this theme was echoed by Vernon L. Parrington, Merrill Jensen and others in "populist" historiographical tradition. For a sharp critique of this thesis see Robert E. Brown, *Charles Beard and the Constitution* (Princeton, 1956). See also Forrest McDonald, *We the People* (Chicago, 1958); the trailblazing work in this genre was Douglas Adair, "The Tenth Federalist Revisited," *William and Mary Quarterly*, Third Series, Vol. VIII (1951), pp. 48–67.

John F. Kennedy was, from 1956 to 1960, "plotting" to become President. In short, on the fundamental *procedural* level, the Constitutionalists had to work according to the prevailing rules of the game. Whether they liked it or not is a topic for spiritualists—and is irrelevant: one may be quite certain that had Washington agreed to play the De Gaulle (as the Cincinnati once urged), Hamilton would willingly have held his horse, but such fertile speculation in no way alters the actual context in which events took place.

I

When the Constitutionalists went forth to subvert the Confederation, they utilized the mechanisms of political legitimacy. And the roadblocks which confronted them were formidable. At the same time, they were endowed with certain potent political assets. The history of the United States from 1786 to 1790 was largely one of a masterful employment of political expertise by the Constitutionalists as against bumbling, erratic behavior by the opponents of reform. Effectively, the Constitutionalists had to induce the states, by democratic techniques of coercion, to emasculate themselves. To be specific, if New York had refused to join the new Union, the project was doomed; yet before New York was safely in, the reluctant state legislature had *sua spante* to take the following steps: (1) agree to send delegates to the Philadelphia Convention; (2) provide maintenance for these delegates (these were distinct stages: New Hampshire was early in naming delegates, but did not provide for their maintenance until July); (3) set up the special *ad hoc* convention to decide on ratification; and (4) concede to the decision of the *ad hoc* convention that New York should participate. New York admittedly was a tricky state, with a strong interest in a *status quo* which permitted her to exploit New Jersey and Connecticut, but the same legal hurdles existed in every state. And at the risk of becoming boring, it must be reiterated that the *only* weapon in the Constitutionalist arsenal was an effective mobilization of public opinion.

The group which undertook this struggle was an interesting amalgam of a few dedicated nationalists with the self-interested spokesmen of various parochial bailiwicks. The Georgians, for example, wanted a strong central authority to provide military protection for their huge, underpopulated state against the Creek Confederacy; Jerseymen and Connecticuters wanted to escape from economic bondage to New York; the Virginians hoped to establish a system which would give that great state its rightful place in the councils of the republic. The dominant figures in the politics of these states therefore cooperated in the call for the Convention.[3] In other states, the thrust towards national reform was taken up by opposition groups who added the "national interest" to their weapons system; in Pennsylvania, for instance, the group fighting to revise the Constitution of 1776 came out four-square behind the Constitutionalists, and in New York, Hamilton and the Schuyler *ambiance* took the same tack against George Clinton.[4] There was, of course, a large element of personality in the affair: there is reason to suspect that Patrick Henry's opposition to the Convention and the Constitution was founded on his conviction that Jefferson was behind both, and a close study of local politics elsewhere would surely reveal that others supported the Constitution for the simple (and politically quite sufficient) reason that the "wrong" people were against it.

To say this is not to suggest that the Constitution rested on a foundation of impure or base motives. It is rather to argue that in politics there are no immaculate conceptions, and that in the drive for a stronger general government, motives of all sorts played a part. Few men in the history of mankind have espoused a view of the "common good" or "public interest" that militated against their private status; even Plato with all his reverence for disembodied reason managed to put philosophers on top of the pile. Thus it is not surprising that a number of diversified private interests joined to push the nationalist public interest; what would have been surprising was the absence of such a pragmatic united front. And the fact remains that, however motivated, these men did demonstrate a willingness to compromise their parochial interests in behalf of an ideal which took shape before their eyes and under their ministrations.

As Stanley Elkins and Eric McKitrick have suggested in a

[3] A basic volume, which, like other works by Warren, provides evidence with which one can evaluate the author's own opinions, is Charles Warren, *The Making of the Constitution* (Boston, 1928). The best brief summary of the forces behind the movement for centralization is Chapter 1 of *Warren* (as it will be cited hereafter).

[4] On Pennsylvania see Robert L. Brunhouse, *Counter-Revolution in Pennsylvania* (Harrisburg, 1942) and Charles P. Smith, *James Wilson* (Chapel Hill, 1956), ch. 15; for New York, which needs the same sort of microanalysis Pennsylvania has received, the best study is E. Wilder Spaulding, *New York in the Critical Period, 1783–1789* (New York, 1932).

perceptive essay,[5] what distinguished the leaders of the Constitutionalist caucus from their enemies was a "Continental" approach to political, economic and military issues. To the extent that they shared an institutional base of operations, it was the Continental Congress (thirty-nine of the delegates to the Federal Convention had served in Congress [6]), and this was hardly a locale which inspired respect for the state governments. Robert de Jouvenal observed French politics half a century ago and noted that a revolutionary Deputy had more in common with a non-revolutionary Deputy than he had with a revolutionary non-Deputy; [7] similarly one can surmise that membership in the Congress under the Articles of Confederation worked to establish a continental frame of reference, that a Congressman from Pennsylvania and one from South Carolina would share a universe of discourse which provided them with a conceptual common denominator vis à vis their respective state legislatures. This was particularly true with respect to external affairs: the average state legislator was probably about as concerned with foreign policy then as he is today, but Congressmen were constantly forced to take the broad view of American prestige, were compelled to listen to the reports of Secretary John Jay and to the dispatches and pleas from their frustrated envoys in Britain, France and Spain.[8] From considerations such as these, a "Continental" ideology developed which seems to have demanded a revision of our domestic institutions primarily on the ground that only by invigorating our general government could we assume our rightful place in the international arena. Indeed, an argument with great force—particularly since Washington was its incarnation—urged that our very survival in the Hobbesian jungle of world politics depended upon a reordering and strengthening of our national sovereignty.[9]

Note that I am not endorsing the "Critical Period" thesis; on the contrary, Merrill Jensen seems to me quite sound in his

[5] Stanley Elkins and Eric McKitrick, "The Founding Fathers: Young Men of the Revolution," Political Science Quarterly, Vol. 76, p. 181 (1961).

[6] Warren, p. 55.

[7] In La Republique des Camarades (Paris, 1914).

[8] See Frank Monaghan, John Jay (New York, 1935), ch. 13.

[9] "[T]he situation of the general government, if it can be called a government, is shaken to its foundation, and liable to be overturned by every blast. In a word, it is at an end; and, unless a remedy is soon applied, anarchy and confusion will inevitably ensue." Washington to Jefferson, May 30, 1787, Farrand, III, 31. See also Irving Brant, James Madison, The Nationalist (New York, 1948), ch. 25.

view that for most Americans, engaged as they were in self-sustaining agriculture, the "Critical Period" was not particularly critical.[10] In fact, the great achievement of the Constitutionalists was their ultimate success in convincing the elected representatives of a majority of the white male population that change was imperative. A small group of political leaders with a Continental vision and essentially a consciousness of the United States' *international* impotence, provided the matrix of the movement. To their standard other leaders rallied with their own parallel ambitions. Their great assets were (1) the presence in their caucus of the one authentic American "father figure," George Washington, whose prestige was enormous;[11] (2) the energy and talent of their leadership (in which one must include the towering intellectuals of the time, John Adams and Thomas Jefferson, despite their absence abroad), and their communications "network," which was far superior to anything on the opposition side;[12] (3) the preemptive skill which made "their" issue The Issue and kept the locally oriented opposition permanently on the defensive; and (4) the subjective consideration that these men were spokesmen of a new and compelling credo: *American* nationalism, that ill-defined but nonetheless potent sense of collective purpose that emerged from the American Revolution.

Despite great institutional handicaps, the Constitutionalists managed in the mid-1780s to mount an offensive which gained momentum as years went by. Their greatest problem was lethargy, and paradoxically, the number of barriers in their path may have proved an advantage in the long run. Beginning with the initial battle to get the Constitutional Convention called and delegates appointed, they could never relax, never let up the pressure. In practical terms, this meant that the local "organizations" created by the Constitutionalists were perpetually in movement building up their cadres for the next fight. (The word organization has to be used with great caution: a political organization in the United

[10] Merrill Jensen, *The New Nation* (New York, 1950). Interestingly enough, Prof. Jensen virtually ignores international relations in his laudatory treatment of the government under the Articles of Confederation.

[11] The story of James Madison's cultivation of Washington is told by Brant, *op. cit.*, pp. 394–97.

[12] The "message center" being the Congress; nineteen members of Congress were simultaneously delegates to the Convention. One gets a sense of this coordination of effort from Broadus Mitchell, *Alexander Hamilton, Youth to Maturity* (New York, 1957), ch. 22.

States—as in contemporary England [13]—generally consisted of a magnate and his following, or a coalition of magnates. This did not necessarily mean that it was "undemocratic" or "aristocratic," in the Aristotelian sense of the word: while a few magnates such as the Livingstons could draft their followings, most exercised their leadership without coercion on the basis of popular endorsement. The absence of organized opposition did not imply the impossibility of competition any more than low public participation in elections necessarily indicated an undemocratic suffrage.)

The Constitutionalists got the jump on the "opposition" (a collective noun: oppositions would be more correct) at the outset with the demand for a Convention. Their opponents were caught in an old political trap: they were not being asked to approve any specific program of reform, but only to endorse a meeting to discuss and recommend needed reforms. If they took a hard line at the first stage, they were put in the position of glorifying the status quo and of denying the need for any changes. Moreover, the Constitutionalists could go to the people with a persuasive argument for "fair play"—"How can you condemn reform before you know precisely what is involved?" Since the state legislatures obviously would have the final say on any proposals that might emerge from the Convention, the Constitutionalists were merely reasonable men asking for a chance. Besides, since they did not make any concrete proposals at that stage, they were in a position to capitalize on every sort of generalized discontent with the Confederation.

Perhaps because of their poor intelligence system, perhaps because of over-confidence generated by the failure of all previous efforts to alter the Articles,[14] the opposition awoke too late to the dangers that confronted them in 1787. Not only did the Constitutionalists manage to get every state but Rhode Island (where politics was enlivened by a party system reminiscent of

[13] See Sir Lewis Namier, *The Structure of Politics at the Accession of George III*, 2d ed. (New York, 1957); *England in the Age of the American Revolution* (London, 1930).

[14] The Annapolis Convention, called for the previous year, turned into a shambles: only five states sent commissioners, only three states were legally represented, and the instructions to delegates named varied quite widely from state to state. Clinton and others of his persuasion may have thought this disaster would put an end to the drive for reform. See Mitchell, *op. cit.*, pp. 362–67; Brant, *op. cit.*, pp. 375–87.

the "Blues" and the "Greens" in the Byzantine Empire) [15] to appoint delegates to Philadelphia, but when the results were in, it appeared that they dominated the delegations. Given the apathy of the opposition, this was a natural phenomenon: in an ideologically non-polarized political atmosphere those who get appointed to a special committee are likely to be the men who supported the movement for its creation. Even George Clinton, who seems to have been the first opposition leader to awake to the possibility of trouble, could not prevent the New York legislature from appointing Alexander Hamilton—though he did have the foresight to send two of his henchmen to dominate the delegation. Incidentally, much has been made of the fact that the delegates to Philadelphia were not elected by the people; some have adduced this fact as evidence of the "undemocratic" character of the gathering. But put in the context of the time, this argument is wholly specious: the central government under the Articles was considered a creature of the component states and in all the states but Rhode Island, Connecticut and New Hampshire, members of the national Congress were chosen by the state legislatures. This was not a consequence of elitism or fear of the mob; it was a logical extension of states'-rights doctrine to guarantee that the national institution did not end-run the state legislatures and make direct contact with the people.[16]

II

With delegations safely named, the focus shifted to Philadelphia. While waiting for a quorum to assemble, James Madison

[15] See Hamilton M. Bishop, *Why Rhode Island Opposed the Federal Constitution* (Providence, 1950) for a careful analysis of the labyrinthine political course of Rhode Island. For background see David S. Lovejoy, *Rhode Island Politics and the American Revolution* (Providence, 1958).

[16] The terms "radical" and "conservative" have been bandied about a good deal in connection with the Constitution. This usage is nonsense if it is employed to distinguish between two economic "classes"—e.g., radical debtors versus conservative creditors, radical farmers versus conservative capitalists, etc.—because there was no polarization along this line of division; the same types of people turned up on both sides. And many were hard to place in these terms: does one treat Robert Morris as a debtor or a creditor? or James Wilson? See Brown, *op. cit.*, *passim*. The one line of division that holds up is between those deeply attached to states'-rights and those who felt that the Confederation was bankrupt. Thus, curiously, some of the most narrow-minded, parochial spokesmen of the time have earned the designation "radical" while those most willing to experiment and alter the *status quo* have been dubbed "conservative"! See Cecelia Kenyon, "Men of Little Faith," *William and Mary Quarterly*, Vol. 12, p. 3 (1955).

got busy and drafted the so-called Randolph or Virginia Plan with the aid of the Virginia delegation. This was a political master-stroke. Its consequence was that once business got underway, the framework of discussion was established on Madison's terms. There was no interminable argument over agenda; instead the delegates took the Virginia Resolutions—"just for purposes of discussion"—as their point of departure. And along with Madison's proposals, many of which were buried in the course of the summer, went his major premise: a new start on a Constitution rather than piecemeal amendment. This was not necessarily revo-lutionary—a little exegesis could demonstrate that a new Con-stitution might be formulated as "amendments" to the Articles of Confederation—but Madison's proposal that this "lump sum" amendment go into effect after approval by nine states (the Arti-cles required unanimous state approval for any amendment) was thoroughly subversive.[17]

Standard treatments of the Convention divide the delegates into "nationalists" and "states'-righters" with various improvised shadings ("moderate nationalists," etc.), but these are a posteriori categories which obfuscate more than they clarify. What is strik-ing to one who analyzes the Convention as a case-study in demo-cratic politics is the lack of clear-cut ideological divisions in the Convention. Indeed, I submit that the evidence—Madison's Notes, the correspondence of the delegates, and debates on ratifi-cation—indicates that this was a remarkably homogeneous body on the ideological level. Yates and Lansing, Clinton's two chape-rones for Hamilton, left in disgust on July 10. (Is there anything more tedious than sitting through endless disputes on matters one deems fundamentally misconceived? It takes an iron will to spend a hot summer as an ideological agent provocateur.) Luther Martin, Maryland's bibulous narcissist, left on September 4 in a huff when he discovered that others did not share his self-esteem; others went home for personal reasons. But the hard core of delegates accepted a grinding regimen throughout the attrition of a Philadelphia summer precisely because they shared the Con-stitutionalist goal.

Basic differences of opinion emerged, of course, but these were not ideological; they were structural. If the so-called "states'-rights" group had not accepted the fundamental purposes of the

[17] Yet, there was little objection to this crucial modification from any quarter—there almost seems to have been a gentlemen's agreement that Rhode Island's liberum veto had to be destroyed.

Convention, they could simply have pulled out and by doing so have aborted the whole enterprise. Instead of bolting, they returned day after day to argue and to compromise. An interesting symbol of this basic homogeneity was the initial agreement on secrecy: these professional politicians did not want to become prisoners of publicity; they wanted to retain that freedom of maneuver which is only possible when men are not forced to take public stands in the preliminary stages of negotiation.[18] There was no legal means of binding the tongues of the delegates: at any stage in the game a delegate with basic principled objections to the emerging project could have taken the stump (as Luther Martin did after his exit) and denounced the convention to the skies. Yet Madison did not even inform Thomas Jefferson in Paris of the course of the deliberations [19] and available correspondence indicates that the delegates generally observed the injunction. Secrecy is certainly uncharacteristic of any assembly marked by strong ideological polarization. This was noted at the time: the *New York Daily Advertiser*, August 14, 1787, commented that the ". . . profound secrecy hitherto observed by the Convention [we consider] a happy omen, as it demonstrates that the spirt of party on any great and essential point cannot have arisen to any height." [20]

Commentators on the Constitution who have read *The Federalist* in lieu of reading the actual debates have credited the Fathers with the invention of a sublime concept called "Federalism." [21] Unfortunately *The Federalist* is probative evidence for only one proposition: that Hamilton and Madison were inspired propagandists with a genius for retrospective symmetry. Federalism, as the theory is generally defined, was an improvisation which was later promoted into a political theory. Experts on "federalism"

[18] See Mason's letter to his son, May 27, 1787, in which he endorsed secrecy as "a proper precaution to prevent mistakes and misrepresentation until the business shall have been completed, when the whole may have a very different complexion from that in which the several crude and indigested parts might in their first shape appear if submitted to the public eye." Farrand, III, 28.

[19] See Madison to Jefferson, June 6, 1787, Farrand, III, 35.

[20] Cited in Warren, p. 138.

[21] See, e.g., Gottfried Dietze, *The Federalist, A Classic on Federalism and Free Government* (Baltimore, 1960); Richard Hofstadter, *The American Political Tradition* (New York, 1948); and John P. Roche, "American Liberty," in M. Konvitz and C. Rossiter, eds., *Aspects of Liberty* (Ithaca, 1958).

should take to heart the advice of David Hume, who warned in his *Of the Rise and Progress of the Arts and Sciences* that ". . . there is no subject in which we must proceed with more caution than in [history], lest we assign causes which never existed and reduce what is merely contingent to stable and universal principles." In any event, the final balance in the Constitution between the states and the nation must have come as a great disappointment to Madison, while Hamilton's unitary views are too well known to need elucidation.

It is indeed astonishing how those who have glibly designated James Madison the "father" of Federalism have overlooked the solid body of fact which indicates that he shared Hamilton's quest for a unitary central government. To be specific, they have avoided examining the clear import of the Madison-Virginia Plan,[22] and have disregarded Madison's dogged inch-by-inch retreat from the bastions of centralization. The Virginia Plan envisioned a unitary national government effectively freed from and dominant over the states. The lower house of the national legislature was to be elected directly by the people of the states with membership proportional to population. The upper house was to be selected by the lower and the two chambers would elect the executive and choose the judges. The national government would be thus cut completely loose from the states.[23]

The structure of the general government was freed from state control in a truly radical fashion, but the scope of the au-

[22] "I hold it for a fundamental point, that an individual independence of the states is utterly irreconcilable with the idea of an aggregate sovereignty," Madison to Randolph, cited in Brant, *op. cit.*, p. 416.

[23] The Randolph Plan was presented on May 29, see Farrand, I, 18–23; the state legislatures retained only the power to *nominate* candidates for the upper chamber. Madison's view of the appropriate position of the estates emerged even more strikingly in Yates' record of his speech on June 29: "Some contend that states are sovereign when in fact they are only political societies. There is a gradation of power in all societies, from the lowest corporation to the highest sovereign. The states never possessed the essential rights of sovereignty. . . . The states, at present, are only great corporations, having the power of making by-laws, and these are effectual only if they are not contradictory to the general confederation. The states ought to be placed under the control of the general government—at least as much so as they formerly were under the king and British parliament." Farrand, I, 471. Forty-six years later, after Yates' "Notes" had been published, Madison tried to explain this statement away as a misinterpretation: he did not flatly deny the authenticity of Yates' record, but attempted a defense that was half justification and half evasion. Madison to W. C. Rives, Oct. 21, 1833. Farrand, III, 521–24.

thority of the national sovereign as Madison initially formulated it was breathtaking—it was a formulation worthy of the Sage of Malmesbury himself. The national legislature was to be empowered to disallow the acts of state legislatures,[24] and the central government was vested, in addition to the powers of the nation under the Articles of Confederation, with plenary authority wherever ". . . the separate States are incompetent or in which the harmony of the United States may be interrupted by the exercise of individual legislation." [25] Finally, just to lock the door against state intrusion, the national Congress was to be given the power to use military force on recalcitrant states.[26] This was Madison's "model" of an ideal national government, though it later received little publicity in *The Federalist*.

The interesting thing was the reaction of the Convention to this militant program for a strong autonomous central government. Some delegates were startled, some obviously leery of so comprehensive a project of reform,[27] but nobody set off any fireworks and nobody walked out. Moreover, in the two weeks that followed, the Virginia Plan received substantial endorsement *en principe*; the initial temper of the gathering can be deduced from the approval "without debate or dissent," on May 31, of the Sixth Resolution which granted Congress the authority to disallow state legislation ". . . contravening *in its opinion* the Articles of Union." Indeed, an amendment was included to bar states from contravening national treaties.[28]

The Virginia Plan may therefore be considered, in ideological terms, as the delegates' Utopia, but as the discussions continued and became more specific, many of those present began to have second thoughts. After all, they were not residents of Utopia or guardians in Plato's Republic who could simply impose a philosophical ideal on subordinate strata of the population. They were

[24] Resolution 6 gave the National Legislature this power subject to review by the Council of Revision proposed in Resolution 8.

[25] Resolution 6.

[26] Ibid.

[27] See the discussions on May 30 and 31. "Mr. Charles Pinkney wished to know of Mr. Randolph whether he meant to abolish the State Governts. altogether . . . Mr. Butler said he had not made up his mind on the subject and was open to the light which discussion might throw on it . . . Genl. Pinkney expressed a doubt . . . Mr. Gerry seemed to entertain the same doubt." Farrand, I, 33–34. There were no denunciations—though it should perhaps be added that Luther Martin had not yet arrived.

[28] Farrand, I, 54. (Italics added.)

practical politicians in a democratic society, and no matter what their private dreams might be, they had to take home an acceptable package and defend it—and their own political futures—against predictable attack. On June 14 the breaking point between dream and reality took place. Apparently realizing that under the Virginia Plan, Massachusetts, Virginia and Pennsylvania could virtually dominate the national government—and probably appreciating that to sell this program to "the folks back home" would be impossible—the delegates from the small states dug in their heels and demanded time for a consideration of alternatives. One gets a graphic sense of the inner politics from John Dickinson's reproach to Madison: "You see the consequences of pushing things too far. Some of the members from the small States wish for two branches in the General Legislature and are friends to a good National Government; but we would sooner submit to a foreign power than . . . be deprived of an equality of suffrage in both branches of the Legislature, and thereby be thrown under the domination of the large States." [29]

The bare outline of the *Journal* entry for Tuesday, June 14, is suggestive to anyone with extensive experience in deliberative bodies. "It was moved by Mr. Patterson [sic, Paterson's name was one of those consistently misspelled by Madison and everybody else] seconded by Mr. Randolph that the further consideration of the report from the Committee of the whole House [endorsing the Virginia Plan] be postponed til tomorrow, and before the question for postponement was taken. It was moved by Mr. Randolph seconded by Mr. Patterson that the House adjourn." [30] The House adjourned by obvious prearrangement of the two principals: since the preceding Saturday when Brearley and Paterson of New Jersey had announced their fundamental discontent with the representational features of the Virginia Plan, the informal pressure had certainly been building up to slow down the steamroller. Doubtless there were extended arguments at the Indian Queen between Madison and Paterson, the latter insisting that events were moving rapidly towards a probably disastrous conclusion, towards a political suicide pact. Now the process of accommodation was put into action smoothly—and wisely, given the character and strength of the doubters. Madison

[29] *Ibid.*, p. 242. Delaware's delegates had been instructed by their general assembly to maintain in any new system the voting equality of the states. Farrand, III, 574.

[30] *Ibid.*, p. 240.

had the votes, but this was one of those situations where the enforcement of mechanical majoritarianism could easily have destroyed the objectives of the majority: the Constitutionalists were in quest of a qualitative as well as a quantitative consensus. This was hardly from deference to local Quaker custom; it was a political imperative if they were to attain ratification.

III

According to the standard script, at this point the "states'-rights" group intervened in force behind the New Jersey Plan, which has been characteristically portrayed as a reversion to the *status quo* under the Articles of Confederation with but minor modifications. A careful examination of the evidence indicates that only in a marginal sense is this an accurate description. It is true that the New Jersey Plan put the states back into the institutional picture, but one could argue that to do so was a recognition of political reality rather than an affirmation of states'-rights. A serious case can be made that the advocates of the New Jersey Plan, far from being ideological addicts of states'-rights, intended to substitute for the Virginia Plan a system which would both retain strong national power and have a chance of adoption in the states. The leading spokesman for the project asserted quite clearly that his views were based more on counsels of expediency than on principle; said Paterson on June 16: "I came here not to speak my own sentiments, but the sentiments of those who sent me. Our object is not such a Governmt. as may be best in itself, but such a one as our Constituents have authorized us to prepare, and as they will approve." [31] This is Madison's version; in Yates' transcription, there is a crucial sentence following the remarks above: "I believe that a little practical virtue is to be preferred to the finest theoretical principles, which cannot be carried into effect." [32] In his preliminary speech on June 9, Paterson had stated ". . . to the public mind we must accommodate ourselves," [33] and in his notes for this and his later effort as well, the emphasis is the same. The *structure* of government under the Articles should be retained:

2. Because it accords with the Sentiments of the People
   [Proof:] 1. Coms. [Commissions from state legislatures defining the jurisdiction of the delegates]

[31] *Ibid.*, p. 250.
[32] *Ibid.*, p. 258.
[33] *Ibid.*, p. 178.

> 2. News-papers—Political Barometer. Jersey never
> would have sent Delegates under the first [Virginia]
> Plan—
> Not here to sport Opinions of my own. Wt. [What] can be
> done. A little practicable Virtue preferrable to Theory.[34]

This was a defense of political acumen, not of states'-rights.
In fact, Paterson's notes of his speech can easily be construed as
an argument for attaining the substantive objectives of the Virginia Plan by a sound political route, i.e., pouring the new wine
in the old bottles. With a shrewd eye, Paterson queried:

> Will the Operation and Force of the [central] Govt. depend
> upon the mode of Representn.—No—it will depend upon the
> Quantum of Power lodged in the leg. ex. and judy. Departments—
> Give [the existing] Congress the same Powers that you intend to
> give the two Branches, [under the Virginia Plan] and I apprehend
> they will act with as much Propriety and more Energy . . .[35]

In other words, the advocates of the New Jersey Plan concentrated their fire on what they held to be the *political lia-
bilities* of the Virginia Plan—which were matters of institutional
structure—rather than on the proposed scope of national authority. Indeed, the Supremacy Clause of the Constitution first saw
the light of day in Paterson's Sixth Resolution; the New Jersey
Plan contemplated the use of military force to secure compliance
with national law; and finally Paterson made clear his view that
under either the Virginia or the New Jersey systems, the general
government would ". . . act on individuals and not on states." [36]
From the states'-rights viewpoint, this was heresy: the fundament
of that doctrine was the proposition that any central government
had as its constituents the states, not the people, and could only
reach the people through the agency of the state government.

Paterson then reopened the agenda of the Convention, but
he did so within a distinctly nationalist framework. Paterson's
position was one of favoring a strong central government in principle, but opposing one which in fact put the big *states in the
saddle*. (The Virginia Plan, for all its abstract merits, did very
well by Virginia.) As evidence for this speculation, there is a

[34] *Ibid.*, p. 274.
[35] *Ibid.*, pp. 275–76.
[36] "But it is said that this national government is to act on individuals
and not on states; and cannot a federal government be so framed as to
operate in the same way? It surely may." *Ibid.*, pp. 182–83; also *ibid.* at
p. 276.

curious and intriguing proposal among Paterson's preliminary drafts of the New Jersey Plan:

> Whereas it is necessary in Order to form the People of the U. S. of America in to a Nation, that the States should be consolidated, by which means all the Citizens thereof will become equally intitled to and will equally participate in the same Privileges and Rights . . . it is therefore resolved, that all the Lands contained within the Limits of each state individually, and of the U. S. generally be considered as constituting one Body or Mass, and be divided into thirteen or more integral parts.
>
> Resolved, That such Divisions or integral Parts shall be styled Districts.[37]

This makes it sound as though Paterson was prepared to accept a strong unified central government along the lines of the Virginia Plan if the existing states were eliminated. He may have gotten the idea from his New Jersey colleague Judge David Brearley, who on June 9 had commented that the only remedy to the dilemma over representation was ". . . that a map of the U.S. be spread out, that all the existing boundaries be erased, and that a new partition of the whole be made into 13 equal parts." [38] According to Yates, Brearley added at this point, ". . . then a government on the present [Virginia Plan] system will be just." [39]

This proposition was never pushed—it was patently unrealistic—but one can appreciate its purpose: it would have separated the men from the boys in the large-state delegations. How attached would the Virginians have been to their reform principles if Virginia were to disappear as a component geographical unit (the largest) for representational purposes? Up to this point, the Virginians had been in the happy position of supporting high ideals with that inner confidence born of knowledge that the "public interest" they endorsed would nourish their private interest. Worse, they had shown little willingness to compromise. Now the delegates from the small states announced that they were unprepared to be offered up as sacrificial victims to a "national interest" which reflected Virginia's parochial ambition. Caustic Charles Pinckney was not far off when he remarked sardonically that ". . . the whole [conflict] comes to this": "Give N. Jersey an equal vote, and she will dismiss her scruples, and

[37] Farrand, III, 613.
[38] Farrand, I, 177.
[39] Ibid., p. 182.

concur in the Natil. system." [40] What he rather unfairly did not add was that the Jersey delegates were not free agents who could adhere to their private convictions; they had to take back, sponsor and risk their reputations on the reforms approved by the Convention—and in New Jersey, not in Virginia.

Paterson spoke on Saturday, and one can surmise that over the weekend there was a good deal of consultation, argument, and caucusing among the delegates. One member at least prepared a full length address: on Monday Alexander Hamilton, previously mute, rose and delivered a six-hour oration.[41] It was a remarkably apolitical speech; the gist of his position was that *both* the Virginia and New Jersey Plans were inadequately centralist, and he detailed a reform program which was reminiscent of the Protectorate under the Cromwellian *Instrument of Government* of 1653. It has been suggested that Hamilton did this in the best political tradition to emphasize the moderate character of the Virginia Plan,[42] to give the cautious delegates something *really* to worry about; but this interpretation seems somehow too clever. Particularly since the sentiments Hamilton expressed happened to be completely consistent with those he privately—and sometimes publicly—expressed throughout his life. He wanted, to take a striking phrase from a letter to George Washington, a "strong well mounted government"; [43] in essence, the Hamilton Plan contemplated an elected life monarch, virtually free of public control, on the Hobbesian ground that only in this fashion could strength and stability be achieved. The other alternatives, he argued, would put policy-making at the mercy of the passions of the mob; only if the sovereign was beyond the reach of selfish influence would it be possible to have government in the interests of the whole community.[44]

From all accounts, this was a masterful and compelling speech, but (aside from furnishing John Lansing and Luther Martin with ammunition for later use against the Constitution) it made little impact. Hamilton was simply transmitting on a different wave-length from the rest of the delegates; the latter adjourned after his great effort, admired his rhetoric, and then

[40] *Ibid.*, p. 255.

[41] J. C. Hamilton, cited *ibid.*, p. 293.

[42] See, *e.g.*, Mitchell, *op. cit.*, p. 381.

[43] Hamilton to Washington, July 3, 1787, *Farrand*, III, 53.

[44] A reconstruction of the Hamilton Plan is found in *Farrand*, III, 617–30.

returned to business.[45] It was rather as if they had taken a day
off to attend the opera. Hamilton, never a particularly patient
man or much of a negotiator, stayed for another ten days and
then left, in considerable disgust, for New York.[46] Although he
came back to Philadelphia sporadically and attended the last two
weeks of the Convention, Hamilton played no part in the la-
borious task of hammering out the Constitution. His day came
later when he led the New York Constitutionalists into the
savage imbroglio over ratification—an arena in which his un-
matched talent for dirty political infighting may well have won
the day. For instance, in the New York Ratifying Convention,
Lansing threw back into Hamilton's teeth the sentiments the
latter had expressed in his June 18 oration in the Convention.
However, having since retreated to the fine defensive positions
immortalized in The Federalist, the Colonel flatly denied that
he had ever been an enemy of the states, or had believed that
conflict between states and nation was inexorable! As Madison's
authoritative Notes did not appear until 1840, and there had
been no press coverage, there was no way to verify his assertions,
so in the words of the reporter, ". . . a warm personal alterca-
tion between [Lansing and Hamilton] engrossed the remainder
of the day [June 28, 1788]." [47]

IV

On Tuesday morning, June 19, the vacation was over. James
Madison led off with a long, carefully reasoned speech analyzing
the New Jersey Plan which, while intellectually vigorous in its
criticisms, was quite conciliatory in mood. "The great difficulty,"
he observed, "lies in the affair of Representation; and if this
could be adjusted, all others would be surmountable." [48] (As
events were to demonstrate, this diagnosis was correct.) When
he finished, a vote was taken on whether to continue with the
Virginia Plan as the nucleus for a new constitution: seven states
voted "Yes"; New York, New Jersey, and Delaware voted
"No"; and Maryland, whose position often depended on which

[45] Said William Samuel Johnson on June 21: "A gentleman from New-
York, with boldness and decision, proposed a system totally different from
both [Virginia and New Jersey]; and though he has been praised by every
body, he has been supported by none." Farrand, I, 363.
[46] See his letter to Washington cited supra note 43.
[47] Farrand, III, 338.
[48] Farrand, I, 321.

delegates happened to be on the floor, divided.[49] Paterson, it
seems, lost decisively; yet in a fundamental sense he and his allies
had achieved their purpose: from that day onward, it could never
be forgotten that the state governments loomed ominously in
the background and that no verbal incantations could exorcise
their power. Moreover, nobody bolted the convention: Paterson
and his colleagues took their defeat in stride and set to work
to modify the Virginia Plan, particularly with respect to its provisions on representation in the national legislature. Indeed, they
won an immediate rhetorical bonus; when Oliver Ellsworth of
Connecticut rose to move that the word "national" be expunged
from the Third Virginia Resolution ("Resolved that a *national*
Government ought to be established consisting of a *supreme*
Legislative, Executive and Judiciary" [50]), Randolph agreed and the
motion passed unanimously.[51] The process of compromise had
begun.

For the next two weeks, the delegates circled around the problem of legislative representation. The Connecticut delegation appears to have evolved a possible compromise quite early in the
debates, but the Virginians and particularly Madison (unaware
that he would later be acclaimed as the prophet of "federalism")
fought obdurately against providing for equal representation of
states in the second chamber. There was a good deal of acrimony

[49] Maryland's politics in this period were only a bit less intricate than
Rhode Island's: the rural gentry, in much the same fashion that Namier
described in England, divided up among families—Chases, Carrolls, Pacas,
Lloyds, Tilghmans, etc.—and engaged in what seemed, to the outsider,
elaborate political Morris dances. See Philip A. Crowl, *Maryland During
and After the Revolution* (Baltimore, 1943). The Maryland General Assembly named five delegates to the Convention and provided that "the said
Deputies or such of them as shall attend . . . shall have full Power to represent this State," *Farrand*, III, 586. The interesting circumstance was that
three of the delegates were Constitutionalists (Carroll, McHenry and Jenifer),
while two were opposed (Martin and Mercer); and this led to an *ad hoc*
determination of where Maryland would stand when votes were taken. The
vote on equality of representation, to be described *infra*, was an important
instance of this eccentricity.

[50] This formulation was voted into the Randolph Plan on May 30,
1787, by a vote of six states to none, with one divided. *Farrand*, I, 30.

[51] *Farrand*, I, 335–36. In agreeing, Randolph stipulated his disagreement with Ellsworth's rationale, but said he did not object to merely changing an "expression." Those who subject the Constitution to minute semantic
analysis might do well to keep this instance in mind; if Randolph could so
concede the deletion of "national," one may wonder if any word changes
can be given much weight.

and at one point Benjamin Franklin—of all people—proposed the institution of a daily prayer; practical politicians in the gathering, however, were meditating more on the merits of a good committee than on the utility of Divine intervention. On July 2, the ice began to break when through a number of fortuitous events [52]—and one that seems deliberate [53]—the majority against equality of representation was converted into a dead tie. The Convention had reached the stage where it was "ripe" for a solution (presumably all the therapeutic speeches had been made), and the South Carolinians proposed a committee. Madison and James Wilson wanted none of it, but with only Pennsylvania dissenting, the body voted to establish a working party on the problem of representation.

The members of this committee, one from each state, were elected by the delegates—and a very interesting committee it was. Despite the fact that the Virginia Plan had held majority support up to that date, neither Madison nor Randolph was selected (Mason was the Virginian) and Baldwin of Georgia, whose shift in position had resulted in the tie, was chosen. From the composition, it was clear that this was not to be a "fighting" committee: the emphasis in membership was on what might be described as "second-level political entrepreneurs." On the basis of the discussions up to that time, only Luther Martin of Maryland could be described as a "bitter-ender." Admittedly, some divination enters into this sort of analysis, but one does get a sense of the mood of the delegates from these choices—including the interesting selection of Benjamin Franklin, despite his age and intellectual wobbliness, over the brilliant and incisive Wilson

[52] According to Luther Martin, he was alone on the floor and cast Maryland's vote for equality of representation. Shortly thereafter, Jenifer came on the floor and "Mr. King, from Massachusetts, valuing himself on Mr. Jenifer to divide the State of Maryland on this question . . . requested of the President that the question might be put again; however, the motion was too extraordinary in its nature to meet with success." Cited from "The Genuine Information, . . ." Farrand, III, 188.

[53] Namely Baldwin's vote for equality of representation which divided Georgia—with Few absent and Pierce in New York fighting a duel, Houston voted against equality and Baldwin shifted to tie the state. Baldwin was originally from Connecticut and attended and tutored at Yale, facts which have led to much speculation about the pressures the Connecticut delegation may have brought on him to save the day (Georgia was the last state to vote) and open the way to compromise. To employ a good Russian phrase, it was certainly not an accident that Baldwin voted the way he did. See Warren, p. 262.

or the sharp, polemical Gouverneur Morris, to represent Pennsylvania. His passion for conciliation was more valuable at this juncture than Wilson's logical genius, or Morris' acerbic wit.

There is a common rumor that the Framers divided their time between philosophical discussions of government and reading the classics in political theory. Perhaps this is as good a time as any to note that their concerns were highly practical, that they spent little time canvassing abstractions. A number of them had some acquaintance with the history of political theory (probably gained from reading John Adams' monumental compilation *A Defense of the Constitutions of Government*,[54] the first volume of which appeared in 1786), and it was a poor rhetorician indeed who could not cite Locke, Montesquieu, or Harrington in support of a desired goal. Yet up to this point in the deliberations, no one had expounded a defense of states'-rights or the "separation of powers" on anything resembling a theoretical basis. It should be reiterated that the Madison model had no room either for the states or for the "separation of powers": effectively all governmental power was vested in the national legislature. The merits of Montesquieu did not turn up until *The Federalist*; and although a perverse argument could be made that Madison's ideal was truly in the tradition of John Locke's *Second Treatise of Government*,[55] the Locke whom the American rebels treated as

[54] For various contemporary comments, see Warren, pp. 814–818. On Adams' technique, see Zoltan Haraszti, "The Composition of Adams' Defense," in *John Adams and the Prophets of Progress* (Cambridge, 1952), ch. 9. In this connection it is interesting to check the Convention discussions for references to the authority of Locke, Montesquieu and Harrington, the theorists who have been assigned various degrees of paternal responsibility. There are no explicit references to James Harrington; one to John Locke (Luther Martin cited him on the state of nature, *Farrand*, I, 437); and seven to Montesquieu, only one of which related to the "separation of powers" (Madison in an odd speech, which he explained in a footnote was given to help a friend rather than advance his own views, cited Montesquieu on the separation of the executive and legislative branches, *Farrand*, II, 34). This, of course, does not prove that Locke and Co. were without influence; it shifts the burden of proof, however, to those who assert ideological causality. See Benjamin F. Wright, "The Origins of the Separation of Powers in America," *Economica*, Vol. 13 (1933), p. 184.

[55] I share Willmoore Kendall's interpretation of Locke as a supporter of parliamentary supremacy and majoritarianism; see Kendall, *John Locke and the Doctrine of Majority Rule* (Urbana, 1941). Kendall's general position has recently received strong support in the definitive edition and commentary of Peter Laslett, *Locke's Two Treatises of Government* (Cambridge, 1960).

an honorary president was a pluralistic defender of vested rights,[56] not of parliamentary supremacy.

It would be tedious to continue a blow-by-blow analysis of the work of the delegates; the critical fight was over representation of the states and once the Connecticut Compromise was adopted on July 17, the Convention was over the hump. Madison, James Wilson, and Gouverneur Morris of New York (who was there representing Pennsylvania!) fought the compromise all the way in a last-ditch effort to get a unitary state with parliamentary supremacy. But their allies deserted them and they demonstrated after their defeat the essentially opportunist character of their objections—using "opportunist" here in a non-prejorative sense, to indicate a willingness to swallow their objections and get on with the business. Moreover, once the compromise had carried (by five states to four, with one state divided), its advocates threw themselves vigorously into the job of strengthening the general government's substantive powers—as might have been predicted, indeed, from Paterson's early statements. It nourishes an increased respect for Madison's devotion to the art of politics, to realize that this dogged fighter could sit down six months later and prepare essays for *The Federalist* in contradiction to his basic convictions about the true course the Convention should have taken.

V

Two tricky issues will serve to illustrate the later process of accommodation. The first was the institutional position of the Executive. Madison argued for an executive chosen by the National Legislature and on May 29 this had been adopted with a provision that after his seven-year term was concluded, the chief magistrate should not be eligible for reelection. In late July this was reopened and for a week the matter was argued from several different points of view. A good deal of desultory speech-making ensued, but the gist of the problem was the opposition from two sources to election by the legislature. One group felt that the states should have a hand in the process; another small but influential circle urged direct election by the people. There were a number of proposals: election by the people, election by state governors, by electors chosen by state legislatures, by the National Legislature (James Wilson, perhaps ironically, proposed at

[56] The American Locke is best delineated in Carl Becker, *The Declaration of Independence* (New York, 1948).

one point that an Electoral College be chosen by lot from the National Legislature!), and there was some resemblance to three-dimensional chess in the dispute because of the presence of two other variables, length of tenure and re-eligibility. Finally, after opening, reopening, and re-reopening the debate, the thorny problem was consigned to a committee for resolution.

The Brearley Committee on Postponed Matters was a superb aggregation of talent and its compromise on the Executive was a masterpiece of political improvisation. (The Electoral College, its creation, however, had little in its favor as an *institution*—as the delegates well appreciated.) The point of departure for all discussion about the presidency in the Convention was that in immediate terms, the problem was non-existent; in other words, everybody present knew that under any system devised, George Washington would be President. Thus they were dealing in the future tense and to a body of working politicians the merits of the Brearley proposal were obvious: everybody got a piece of cake. (Or to put it more academically, each viewpoint could leave the Convention and argue to its constituents that it had *really* won the day.) First, the state legislatures had the right to determine the mode of selection of the electors; second, the small states received a bonus in the Electoral College in the form of a guaranteed minimum of three votes while the big states got acceptance of the principle of proportional power; third, if the state legislatures agreed (as six did in the first presidential election), the people could be involved directly in the choice of electors; and finally, if no candidate received a majority in the College, the right of decision passed to the National Legislature with each state exercising equal strength. (In the Brearley recommendation, the election went to the Senate, but a motion from the floor substituted the House; this was accepted on the ground that the Senate already had enough authority over the executive in its treaty and appointment powers.)

This compromise was almost too good to be true, and the Framers snapped it up with little debate or controversy. No one seemed to think well of the College as an *institution*; indeed, what evidence there is suggests that there was an assumption that once Washington had finished his tenure as President, the electors would cease to produce majorities and the chief executive would usually be chosen in the House. George Mason observed casually that the selection would be made in the House nineteen times in twenty and no one seriously disputed this point. The vital aspect of the Electoral College was that it got the Convention over the hurdle and protected everybody's interests. The future was left to cope with the problem of what to do with this Rube Goldberg mechanism.

In short, the Framers did not in their wisdom endow the United States with a College of Cardinals—the Electoral College was neither an exercise in applied Platonism nor an experiment in indirect government based on elitist distrust of the masses. It was merely a jerry-rigged improvisation which has subsequently been endowed with a high theoretical content. When an elector from Oklahoma in 1960 refused to cast his vote for Nixon (naming Byrd and Goldwater instead) on the ground that the Founding Fathers intended him to exercise his great independent wisdom, he was indulging in historical fantasy. If one were to indulge in counter-fantasy, he would be tempted to suggest that the Fathers would be startled to find the College still in operation —and perhaps even dismayed at their descendants' lack of judgment or inventiveness.[57]

The second issue on which some substantial practical bargaining took place was slavery. The morality of slavery was, by design, not at issue;[58] but in its other concrete aspects, slavery colored the arguments over taxation, commerce, and representation. The "Three-Fifths Compromise," that three-fifths of the slaves would be counted both for representation and for purposes of direct taxation (which was drawn from the past—it was a formula of Madison's utilized by Congress in 1783 to establish the basis of state contributions to the Confederation treasury) had allayed some Northern fears about Southern over-representation (no one then foresaw the trivial role that direct taxation would play in later federal financial policy), but doubts still remained. The Southerners, on the other hand, were afraid that Congressional control over commerce would lead to the exclusion of slaves or to their excessive taxation as imports. Moreover, the Southerners were disturbed over "navigation acts," i.e., tariffs, or special legislation providing, for example, that exports be carried

---

[57] See John P. Roche, "The Electoral College: A Note on American Political Mythology," *Dissent* (Spring, 1961), pp. 197–99. The relevant debates took place July 19–26, 1787, *Farrand*, II, 50–128, and September 5–6, 1787, *ibid.*, pp. 505–31.

[58] See the discussion on August 22, 1787, *Farrand*, II, 366–375; King seems to have expressed the sense of the Convention when he said, "the subject should be considered in a political light only." *Ibid.* at 373.

only in American ships; as a section depending upon exports, they wanted protection from the potential voracity of their commercial brethren of the Eastern states. To achieve this end, Mason and others urged that the Constitution include a proviso that navigation and commercial laws should require a two-thirds vote in Congress.

These problems came to a head in late August and, as usual, were handed to a committee in the hope that, in Gouverneur Morris' words, ". . . these things may form a bargain among the Northern and Southern states." [59] The Committee reported its measures of reconciliation on August 25, and on August 29 the package was wrapped up and delivered. What occurred can best be described in George Mason's dour version (he anticipated Calhoun in his conviction that permitting navigation acts to pass by majority vote would put the South in economic bondage to the North—it was mainly on this ground that he refused to sign the Constitution):

> The Constitution as agreed to till a fortnight before the Convention rose was such a one as he would have set his hand and heart to. . . . [Until that time] The 3 New England States were constantly with us in all questions . . . so that it was these three States with the 5 Southern ones against Pennsylvania, Jersey and Delaware. With respect to the importation of slaves, [decision-making] was left to Congress. This disturbed the two Southernmost States who knew that Congress would immediately suppress the importation of slaves. Those two States therefore struck up a bargain with the three New England States. If they would join to admit slaves for some years, the two Southern-most States would join in changing the clause which required the ⅔ of the Legislature in any vote [on navigation acts]. It was done.[60]

On the floor of the Convention there was a virtual love-feast on this happy occasion. Charles Pinckney of South Carolina attempted to overturn the committee's decision, when the compromise was reported to the Convention, by insisting that the South needed protection from the imperialism of the Northern states. But his Southern colleagues were not prepared to rock the boat and General C. C. Pinckney arose to spread oil on the suddenly ruffled waters; he admitted that:

[59] Farrand, II, 374. Randolph echoed his sentiment in different words.
[60] Mason to Jefferson, cited in Warren, p. 584.

It was in the true interest of the S[outhern] States to have no
regulation of commerce; but considering the loss brought on the
commerce of the Eastern States by the Revolution, their liberal
conduct towards the views of South Carolina [on the regulation of
the slave trade] and the interests the weak Southn. States had in
being united with the strong Eastern states, he thought it proper
that no fetters should be imposed on the power of making commercial regulations; *and that his constituents, though prejudiced
against the Eastern States, would be reconciled to this liberality.*
He had himself prejudices agst the Eastern States before he came
here, but would acknowledge that he had found them as liberal
and candid as any men whatever. (Italics added)[61]

Pierce Butler took the same tack, essentially arguing that he was
not too happy about the possible consequences, but that a deal
was a deal.[62] Many Southern leaders were later—in the wake of
the "Tariff of Abominations"—to rue this day of reconciliation;
Calhoun's *Disquisition on Government* was little more than an
extension of the argument in the Convention against permitting
a congressional majority to enact navigation acts.[63]

VI

Drawing on their vast collective political experience, utilizing
every weapon in the politician's arsenal, looking constantly over
their shoulders at their constituents, the delegates put together
a Constitution. It was a makeshift affair; some sticky issues (for

[61] August 29, 1787, Farrand, II, 449–50.
[62] *Ibid.*, p. 451. The plainest statement of the matter was put by the
three North Carolina delegates (Blount, Spaight and Williamson) in their
report to Governor Caswell, September 18, 1787. After noting that "no
exertions have been wanting on our part to guard and promote the particular interest of North Carolina," they went on to explain the basis of the
negotiations in cold-blooded fashion: "While we were taking so much care
to guard ourselves against being over reached and to form rules of Taxation
that might operate in our favour, it is not to be supposed that our Northern
Brethren were Inattentive to their particular Interest. A navigation Act or
the power to regulate Commerce in the Hands of the National Government
. . . is what the Southern States have given in Exchange for the advantages
we Mentioned." They concluded by explaining that while the Constitution
did deal with other matters besides taxes—"there are other Considerations of
great Magnitude involved in the system"—they would not take up valuable
time with boring details! Farrand, III, 83–84.
[63] See John C. Calhoun, *A Disquisition on Government* (New York,
1943), pp. 21–25, 38. Calhoun differed from Mason, and others in the
Convention who urged the two-thirds requirement, by advocating a func-
tional or interest veto rather than some sort of special majority, *i.e.*, he
abandoned the search for quantitative checks in favor of a qualitative solution.

example, the qualification of voters) they ducked entirely; others they mastered with that ancient instrument of political sagacity, studied ambiguity (for example, citizenship), and some they just overlooked. In this last category, I suspect, fell the matter of the power of the federal courts to determine the constitutionality of acts of Congress. When the judicial article was formulated (Article III of the Constitution), deliberations were still in the stage where the legislature was endowed with broad power under the Randolph formulation, authority which by its own terms was scarcely amenable to judicial review. In essence, courts could hardly determine when ". . . the separate States are incompetent or . . . the harmony of the United States may be interrupted"; the National Legislature, as critics pointed out, was free to define its own jurisdiction. Later the definition of legislative authority was changed into the form we know, a series of stipulated powers, but the delegates never seriously reexamined the jurisdiction of the judiciary under this new limited formulation.[64] All arguments on the intention of the Framers in this matter are thus deductive and a posteriori, though some obviously make more sense than others.[65]

The Framers were busy and distinguished men, anxious to get back to their families, their positions, and their constituents, not members of the French Academy devoting a lifetime to a dictionary. They were trying to do an important job, and do it in such a fashion that their handiwork would be acceptable to

[64] The Committee on Detail altered the general grant of legislative power envisioned by the Virginia Plan into a series of specific grants; these were examined closely between August 16 and August 23. One day only was devoted to the Judicial Article, August 27, and since no one raised the question of judicial review of Federal statutes, no light was cast on the matter. A number of random comments on the power of the judiciary were scattered throughout the discussions, but there was another variable which deprives them of much probative value: the proposed Council of Revision which would have joined the Executive with the judges in legislative review. Madison and Wilson, for example, favored this technique—which had nothing in common with what we think of as judicial review except that judges were involved in the task.

[65] For what it may be worth, I think that judicial review of congressional acts was logically on all fours with review of state enactments and that it was certainly consistent with the view that the Constitution could not be amended by the Congress and President, or by a two-thirds vote of Congress (overriding a veto), without the agreement of three-quarters of the states. External evidence from that time supports this view, see Charles Warren, Congress, the Constitution, and the Supreme Court (Boston, 1925), pp. 41–128, but the debates in the Convention prove nothing.

very diverse constituencies. No one was rhapsodic about the final document, but it was a beginning, a move in the right direction, and one they had reason to believe the people would endorse. In addition, since they had modified the impossible amendment provisions of the Articles (the requirement of unanimity which could always be frustrated by "Rogues Island") to one demanding approval by only three-quarters of the states, they seemed confident that gaps in the fabric which experience would reveal could be rewoven without undue difficulty.

So with a neat phrase introduced by Benjamin Franklin (but devised by Gouverneur Morris)[66] which made their decision sound unanimous, and an inspired benediction by the Old Doctor urging doubters to doubt their own infallibility, the Constitution was accepted and signed. Curiously, Edmund Randolph, who had played so vital a role throughout, refused to sign, as did his fellow Virginian George Mason and Elbridge Gerry of Massachusetts. Randolph's behavior was eccentric, to say the least—his excuses for refusing his signature have a factitious ring even at this late date; the best explanation seems to be that he was afraid that the Constitution would prove to be a liability in Virginia politics, where Patrick Henry was burning up the countryside with impassioned denunciations. Presumably, Randolph wanted to check the temper of the populace before he risked his reputation, and perhaps his job, in a fight with both Henry and Richard Henry Lee.[67] Events lend some justification to this speculation: after much temporizing and use of the conditional subjunctive tense, Randolph endorsed ratification in Virginia and ended up getting the best of both worlds.

Madison, despite his reservations about the Constitution, was the campaign manager in ratification. His first task was to get the Congress in New York to light its own funeral pyre by ap-

[66] Or so Madison stated, Farrand, II, 643. Wilson too may have contributed; he was close to Franklin and delivered the frail old gentleman's speeches for him.

[67] See a very interesting letter, from an unknown source in Philadelphia, to Jefferson, October 11, 1787: "Randolph wishes it well, & it is thought would have signed it, but he wanted to be on a footing with a popular rival." Farrand, III, 104. Madison, writing Jefferson a full account on October 24, 1787, put the matter more delicately—he was working hard on Randolph to win him for ratification: "[Randolph] was not inveterate in his opposition, and grounded his refusal to subscribe pretty much on his unwillingness to commit himself, so as not to be at liberty to be governed by further lights on the subject." Ibid., p. 135.

proving the "amendments" to the Articles and sending them on
to the state legislatures. Above all, momentum had to be maintained. The anti-Constitutionalists, now thoroughly alarmed
and no novices in politics, realized that their best tactic was
attrition rather than direct opposition. Thus they settled on a
position expressing qualified approval but calling for a second
Convention to remedy various defects (the one with the most
demagogic appeal was the lack of a Bill of Rights). Madison knew
that to accede to this demand would be equivalent to losing the
battle, nor would he agree to conditional approval (despite waver-
ing even by Hamilton). This was an all-or-nothing proposition:
national salvation or national impotence with no intermediate
positions possible. Unable to get congressional approval, he settled
for second best: a unanimous resolution of Congress transmitting
the Constitution to the states for whatever action they saw fit
to take. The opponents then moved from New York and the
Congress, where they had attempted to attach amendments and
conditions, to the states for the final battle.[68]

At first the campaign for ratification went beautifully: within
eight months after the delegates set their names to the document, eight states had ratified. Only in Massachusetts had the
result been close (187–168). Theoretically, a ratification by one
more state convention would set the new government in motion,
but in fact until Virginia and New York acceded to the new
Union, the latter was a fiction. New Hampshire was the next to
ratify; Rhode Island was involved in its characteristic political
convulsions (the Legislature there sent the Constitution out to
the towns for decision by popular vote and it got lost among
a series of local issues); [69] North Carolina's convention did not
meet until July and then postponed a final decision. This is
hardly the place for an extensive analysis of the conventions of
New York and Virginia. Suffice it to say that the Constitutionalists clearly outmaneuvered their opponents, forced them
into impossible political positions, and won both states narrowly.
The Virginia Convention could serve as a classic study in effective floor management: Patrick Henry had to be contained, and
a reading of the debates discloses a standard two-stage technique.
Henry would give a four- or five-hour speech denouncing some

[68] See Edward P. Smith, "The Movement Towards a Second Constitutional Convention in 1788," in J. F. Jameson, ed., *Essays in the Constitutional History of the United States* (Boston, 1889), pp. 46–115.

[69] See Bishop, *op. cit., passim.*

section of the Constitution on every conceivable ground (the federal district, he averred at one point, would become a haven for convicts escaping from state authority!); [70] when Henry subsided, "Mr. Lee of Westmoreland" would rise and literally poleaxe him with sardonic invective (when Henry complained about the militia power, "Lighthorse Harry" really punched below the belt: observing that while the former Governor had been sitting in Richmond during the Revolution, he had been out in the trenches with the troops and thus felt better qualified to discuss military affairs). [71] Then the gentlemanly Constitutionalists (Madison, Pendleton and Marshall) would pick up the matters at issue and examine them in the light of reason.

Indeed, modern Americans who tend to think of James Madison as a rather desiccated character should spend some time with this transcript. Probably Madison put on his most spectacular demonstration of nimble rhetoric in what might be called "The Battle of the Absent Authorities." Patrick Henry in the course of one of his harangues alleged that Jefferson was known to be opposed to Virginia's approving the Constitution. This was clever: Henry hated Jefferson, but was prepared to use any weapon that came to hand. Madison's riposte was superb: First, he said that with all due respect to the great reputation of Jefferson, he was not in the country and therefore could not formulate an adequate judgment; second, no one should utilize the reputation of an outsider—the Virginia Convention was there to think for itself; third, if there were to be recourse to outsiders, the opinions of George Washington should certainly be taken into consideration; and finally, he knew from privileged personal communications from Jefferson that in fact the latter strongly favored the Constitution. [72] To devise an assault route into this rhetorical fortress was literally impossible.

VII

The fight was over; all that remained now was to establish the new frame of government in the spirit of its framers. And who were better qualified for this task than the Framers them-

---

[70] See Elliot's Debates on the Federal Constitution (Washington, 1836), Vol. 3, pp. 436–438.

[71] This should be quoted to give the full flavor: "Without vanity, I may say I have had different experience of [militia] service from that of [Henry]. It was my fortune to be a soldier of my country. . . . I saw what the honorable gentleman did not see—our men fighting. . . ." Ibid., p. 178.

[72] Ibid., p. 329.

selves? Thus victory for the Constitution meant simultaneous victory for the Constitutionalists; the anti-Constitutionalists either capitulated or vanished into limbo—soon Patrick Henry would be offered a seat on the Supreme Court [73] and Luther Martin would be known as the Federalist "bull-dog." [74] And irony of ironies, Alexander Hamilton and James Madison would shortly accumulate a reputation as the formulators of what is often alleged to be our political theory, the concept of "federalism." Also, on the other side of the ledger, the arguments would soon appear over what the Framers "really meant"; while these disputes have assumed the proportions of a big scholarly business in the last century, they began almost before the ink on the Constitution was dry. One of the best early ones featured Hamilton versus Madison on the scope of presidential power, and other Framers characteristically assumed positions in this and other disputes on the basis of their political convictions.

Probably our greatest difficulty is that we know so much more about what the Framers *should have meant* than they themselves did. We are intimately acquainted with the problems that their Constitution should have been designed to master; in short, we have read the mystery story backwards. If we are to get the right "feel" for their time and their circumstances, we must in Maitland's phrase, ". . . think ourselves back into a twilight." Obviously, no one can pretend completely to escape from the solipsistic web of his own environment, but if the effort is made, it is possible to appreciate the past roughly on its own terms. The first step in this process is to abandon the academic premise that because we can ask a question, there must be an answer.

Thus we can ask what the Framers meant when they gave Congress the power to regulate interstate and foreign commerce, and we emerge, reluctantly perhaps, with the reply that (Professor Crosskey to the contrary notwithstanding) [75] they may not have

---

[73] Washington offered him the Chief Justiceship in 1796, but he declined; Charles Warren, *The Supreme Court in United States History* (Boston, 1947), Vol. 1, p. 139.

[74] He was a zealous prosecutor of seditions in the period 1798–1800; with Justice Samuel Chase, like himself an alleged "radical" at the time of the Constitutional Convention, Martin hunted down Jeffersonian heretics. See James M. Smith, *Freedom's Fetters* (Ithaca, 1956), pp. 342–43.

[75] Crosskey in his sprawling *Politics and the Constitution* (Chicago, 1953), 2 vols., has developed with almost unbelievable zeal and intricacy the thesis that the Constitution was designed to establish a centralized unitary state, but that the political leadership of the Republic in its forma-

known what they meant, that there may not have been any semantic consensus. The Convention was not a seminar in analytic philosophy or linguistic analysis. Commerce was commerce—and if different interpretations of the word arose, later generations could worry about the problem of definition. The delegates were in a hurry to get a new government established; when definitional arguments arose, they characteristically took refuge in ambiguity. If different men voted for the same proposition for varying reasons, that was politics (and still is); if later generations were unsettled by this lack of precision, that would be their problem.

There was a good deal of definitional pluralism with respect to the problems the delegates did discuss, but when we move to the question of extrapolated intentions, we enter the realm of spiritualism. When men in our time, for instance, launch into elaborate talmudic exegesis to demonstrate that federal aid to parochial schools is (or is not) in accord with the intentions of the men who established the Republic and endorsed the Bill of Rights, they are engaging in historical Extra-Sensory Perception. (If one were to join this E. S. P. contingent for a minute, he might suggest the hard-boiled politicians who wrote the Constitution and Bill of Rights would chuckle scornfully at such an invocation of authority: obviously a politician would chart his course on the intentions of the living, not of the dead, and count the number of Catholics in his constituency.)

The Constitution, then, was not an apotheosis of "constitu-

---

tive years betrayed this ideal and sold the pass to states'-rights. While he has unearthed some interesting newspaper articles and other material, it is impossible for me to accept his central proposition. Madison and the other delegates, with the exceptions discussed in the text *supra*, did want to diminish the power of the states and create a vigorous national government. But they were not fools, and were, I submit, under no illusions when they departed from Philadelphia that this end had been accomplished. The crux of my argument is that *political realities* forced them to water down their objectives and they settled, like the good politicians they were, for half a loaf. The basic difficulty with Crosskey's thesis is that he knows too much— he assumes that the Framers had a perfectly clear idea of the road they were taking; with a semantic machete he cuts blandly through all the confusion on the floor of the meeting to the *real* meanings. Thus, despite all his ornate research apparatus, there is a fundamentally non-empirical quality about Crosskey's work: at crucial points in the argument he falls back on a type of divination which can only be described as Kabbalistic. He may be right, for example, in stating (without any proof) that Richard Henry Lee did *not* write the "Letters from a Federal Farmer," but in this country spectral evidence has not been admissible since the Seventeenth Century.

tionalism," a triumph of architectonic genius; it was a patch-work sewn together under the pressure of both time and events by a group of extremely talented democratic politicians. They refused to attempt the establishment of a strong, centralized sovereignty on the principle of legislative supremacy for the excellent reason that the people would not accept it. They risked their political fortunes by opposing the established doctrines of state sovereignty because they were convinced that the existing system was leading to national impotence and probably foreign domination. For two years, they worked to get a convention established. For over three months, in what must have seemed to the faithful participants an endless process of give-and-take, they reasoned, cajoled, threatened, and bargained amongst themselves. The result was a Constitution which the people, in fact, by democratic processes, did accept, and a new and far better national government was established.

Beginning with the inspired propaganda of Hamilton, Madison and Jay, the ideological build-up got under way. *The Federalist* had little impact on the ratification of the Constitution, except perhaps in New York, but this volume had enormous influence on the image of the Constitution in the minds of future generations, particularly on historians and political scientists who have an innate fondness for theoretical symmetry. Yet, while the shades of Locke and Montesquieu may have been hovering in the background, and the delegates may have been unconscious instruments of a transcendent *telos*, the careful observer of the day-to-day work of the Convention finds no over-arching principles. The "separation of powers" to him seems to be a by-product of suspicion, and "federalism" he views as a *pis aller*, as the farthest point the delegates felt they could go in the destruction of state power without themselves inviting repudiation.

To conclude, the Constitution was neither a victory for abstract theory nor a great practical success. Well over half a million men had to die on the battlefields of the Civil War before certain constitutional principles could be defined—a baleful consideration which is somehow overlooked in our customary tributes to the farsighted genius of the Framers and to the supposed American talent for "constitutionalism." The Constitution was, however, a vivid demonstration of effective democratic political action, and of the forging of a national elite which literally persuaded its countrymen to hoist themselves by their own boot straps. American pro-consuls would be wise not to translate the

Constitution into Japanese, or Swahili, or treat it as a work of semi-Divine origin; but when students of comparative politics examine the process of nation-building in countries newly freed from colonial rule, they may find the American experience instructive as a classic example of the potentialities of a democratic elite.

2. John Marshall and the Campaign of History

MAX LERNER

EDITORIAL NOTE. Had the signatories of the Constitution been free agents, they would probably have proposed a national union freed from and dominant over the states, with a formidable array of powers breathtaking in scope. John Marshall bequeathed to the people of the United States what was not in the political power of the framers to give. He was the supreme framer, emancipated from a local constituency, boldly using his exalted judicial post as a stump from which to educate the country to the true meaning of the Constitution. He wrote as if words of grandeur and power and union could make dreams come true; by the force of his convictions, he seemed to will a nation into being. He remade the Constitution, giving voice to silences, clarification to ambiguities, content to omissions. And, he vitalized the inert, still malleable parchment, thrusting it on a course for "ages to come" that would make the government of the United States the supreme government in the federal system, a government of the people, by the people, for the people—Lincoln's formulation was derived from Marshall's opinion in the McCulloch case.

In that case, the Court sustained the constitutionality of a national bank chartered by Congress during the second administration of President Madison. Yet Madison himself, noting the chief justice's sweeping interpretation of the powers of Congress —"no practical limits can be assigned"—observed, "It was anticipated, I believe, by few if any of the framers of the Constitution, that a rule of construction would be introduced as broad and pliant as what has occurred." The comment by the "father of the Constitution" suggests that the orthodoxy that we now take for granted—Marshall's view of the Union—was radical in its time.

Jefferson bitterly lamented that Marshall undermined "our confederated fabric" by treating the Constitution as a thing of wax
which he twisted and shaped to his pleasure. Yet, had Jefferson's
view of the Constitution prevailed, rather than Marshall's, the
nation might have aborted; had Marshall's views of democracy
prevailed, rather than Jefferson's, the abortion might have been
shorn of its significance.

Charles Grove Haines, one of the few historians who could
write about Marshall without carrying on a love affair, acknowledged that he has been rightfully praised as a "statesman and a
constructive jurist" for his share in carving a nation out of the
disparate and discordant elements that dominated during most of
his tenure as chief justice. "Marshall's decisions and the Civil
War were the main factors in accomplishing a shift in sovereignty
from the states to the nation," wrote Haines, giving more credit
than any one man alone could merit. Yet Marshall was a great
nationalist statesman, our only judge whose distinction as a statesman derived wholly from his judicial career.

Justice Holmes once expressed the opinion "that if American
law were to be represented by a single figure, sceptic and wor-
shipper alike would agree without dispute that the figure could
be one alone, and that one, John Marshall." Yet Marshall was
and remains controversial, not the least because of his repellent
views of democracy and his contrived doctrines of vested rights.
Our foremost Jefferson scholar, blinded perhaps by loyalty to
Marshall's implacable enemy, recently expressed the most harsh
and ununderstanding estimate. The "whole tenor of his judicial
thought," wrote Julian Boyd, "was at variance with the philosophy" of McCulloch v. Maryland. "Nothing is more surely demon-
strable in the entire range of his decisions than his steady opposition to reformation, his intransigence in setting himself against
the aspirations and needs of a growing people, his narrow interpretations of the broad grants of constitutional power in support of the confined interests of a special class. Imprisoned in his
own allegiance to the Hamiltonian philosophy of government,
Marshall thus becomes in the final analysis the strict construc-
tionist, bound to the concepts of his own era. The rivets he
employed to fasten in place what he regarded as the permanent
elements of American constitutional law have in large part been
replaced."

Max Lerner's critical essay on Marshall, which follows, seems
judicious when compared to Boyd's estimate. Both are healthy

correctives to the hagiolotry that surrounds the Marshall literature. But Boyd is uncomprehending, denunciatory, and inaccu-
rate; Lerner is coldly analytical, even coldly admiring, and un-
failingly interesting. His essay bears the stigmata of the 1930's
when class interests and economic interpretation, in the fashion
of Beard and Parrington, dominated so much historical writing.
Greatly underestimating the genuine emotional and political
quality of Marshall's "vaunted nationalism," seeing it exclusively
in economic terms, Lerner concludes that "what it amounted
to was aid and tolerance for business enterprise, both on a national scale." If Lerner's thesis is exaggerated and his vision too
narrow, he nevertheless powerfully demonstrates the integral connection between constitutional law and economics. The essay
is a memorable reminder that judicial nationalism has its uses
as a patriotic smog that befogs the ulterior objectives of the judge
or the clear thinking of the historian. Yet it should be remembered that even Albert Beveridge, Marshall's admiring, apologetic
biographer, whose temples pounded rapturously when he wrote
about the nationalistic opinions, understood that they "aligned
on the side of nationalism all powerful economic forces operating through corporate organization." And it was Felix Frankfurter
who declared, "The history of American constitutional law in no
small measure is the history of the impact of the modern corporation upon the American scene."

JOHN MARSHALL AND
THE CAMPAIGN OF HISTORY

Remembering that you cannot separate a man from his place,
[I] remember also that there fell to Marshall perhaps the greatest place that ever was filled by a judge.[1]

1. THE EDUCATION OF JOHN MARSHALL
    John Marshall's first act when he became Chief Justice was
at once characteristic and ominous. He changed the established
practise, borrowed from England, by which each justice in turn
delivered his opinion on a case, and he substituted for it "the
Court" or "the unanimous Court" speaking through a single

[1] Holmes, Collected Legal Papers (1920) 269–70.

member, usually himself. He wanted to present to the world the serried ranks of a united Court. And he was for thirty-five years to cast over his associates on the bench a spell whose persuasiveness seemed to his contemporaries almost diabolical.[2] The Supreme Court had been in existence for twelve years before Marshall came on the bench. It had had three chief-justices; it contained able lawyers like Jay and Iredell; forceful personalities like James Wilson. Yet Marshall might well have said at his death that he found the Supreme Court a straggling group of lawyers and left it an institution and a power.

The shambling but iron-willed Richmond lawyer who was to preside over the Supreme Court from 1801 to 1835 did not seem earmarked by fate to play his great role. He was a frontier boy, born in 1755 on a small backwoods farm in western Virginia, but of good proprietary stock.[3] His education was a frontier education; its economic horizon was bounded by the self-sufficient backwoods plantation; his moral ideas were those inculcated by upright parents, based on self-improvement and steeled by the rigors of their venture. On his father's side he came of humble stock, but his father was a sturdy competent person who stood out in the backwoods counties, served in the Virginia Legislature and on his death left his children large stretches of land.[4] On his mother's side he came of country gentry and tolerably high Scottish nobility.

A consciousness of property and of the owning classes as the basis of social order came quite easily to the alert mind of a normal boy, descended of proprietary stock and brought up in a high-minded home. On the frontier the educational agency was not the school but the family. Marshall's formal schooling throughout his life amounted to less than two years, including

2 "It will be difficult to find a character of firmness enough to preserve his independance on the same Bench with Marshall": Jefferson to Madison, May 25, 1810, 9 *Jefferson's Writings* (Ford ed. 1892) 275. And Attorney General Rodney, referring to the defection of Justice Johnson, thought to be a staunch Republican, wrote in a letter to Jefferson, "You can scarcely elevate a man to a seat in the Court of Justice before he catches the leprosy of the Bench." Letter of Oct. 31, 1808; cf. 1 Warren, *Supreme Court in United States History* (1924) 336. The experience with Joseph Story was to prove as bitter as any in this respect. Story, a Republican, practically became Marshall's *alter ego*. Marshall's personal mastery over the Court was, however, challenged toward the end of the 1820's; *Ogden v. Saunders*, 12 Wheat. 213 (U.S. 1827) marks a break.

3 1 Beveridge, *Life of John Marshall* (1916) 3–19.

4 *Id.* at 166, n. 7.

a year with a family tutor. He imbibed every homily that an idealistic family environment could impress on him—of law and order, of moral uprightness, personal loyalty and sturdy independence, of respect for authority and the identification of authority with respectability. Being self-taught he developed the resourcefulness and the wide sweep that often characterize self-taught people, but also their narrow self-confidence and dogmatism. To this was added an innate sense of purpose and an unruffled consciousness of stature that were to make of him the dominating personality so magnetic to friends and terrifying to opponents. His very insulation from formal teaching cut him off from influences that might otherwise have crashed through the shell of his self-sufficiency—separated him from the effective if rare mind of the mature teacher or the iconoclasm of fellow-students. He never outgrew his provincialism. He never acquired the cosmopolitan tastes of a Jefferson or a Franklin. For the English mind, with its dour insularity, he had some liking. But he found himself ill at ease in French thought.

His reading was family-selected and re-enforced the compulsions of property and authority. By the age of twelve he had copied out Pope's *Essay on Man* and knew most of it from memory. At seventeen he read Blackstone's *Commentaries* assiduously with his father, who had subscribed to the volume less on his own account than that of his son. During the debates on the ratification of the Constitution he studied carefully the *Federalist Papers*, and we know him to have been greatly influenced by Hamilton's reasoning. While he was practising law at Richmond he read, as did every fervent Federalist, Burke's *Reflections on the French Revolution*, and in his *Life of Washington* he reproduces an essentially Burkian view of the impact of Jacobin ideas on the American mind.[5] Marshall was not a man of extensive reading, although Story assures us in his *Memoirs* of his friend that he cared a good deal for literature and we know that later in life he liked Jane Austen's novels.[6] But while his genius was not bookish, the three English writers he read in his formative years left an unmistakable mark on his thinking.

[5] This did not prevent him, however, from giving in this same *Life* a realistic description of the conflicts involved in the formation of the Constitution. See Beard, *Economic Interpretation of the Constitution* (1921) 295–9.

[6] 1 *Joseph Story, Life and Letters*, edited by William Story (1851) 505–6, Marshall to Story, Nov. 26, 1826.

That they did so is of some moment. Pope's poem has a political content: it "depicts the universe as a species of constitutional monarchy";[7] from it Marshall could get his individualistic psychology, of a world ruled by egoism restrained by reason; his sense of "general laws" as governing human conduct; and an ethical bolstering for his authoritarian conservatism ("whatever is, is right"). Blackstone was of the tough and crabbed English tradition of a tenacious concern for property. He was the legal theorist of a landed aristocracy that felt its power slipping and sought to retain its hold by entrenching itself behind legal earthworks. As for Burke, he was a gigantic figure whose genius it was to translate a morbid hatred of change into undying political theory, and whose defense of the existing order was more compact of passion than any revolutionary attack upon it could be. In these writers—poet, lawyer, political theorist—was stored up the heritage of conservative English thought which was to pass through Marshall's mind into the fabric of American constitutional law.

In such an education the Revolutionary War was a curious interlude, a sort of shadow-play in which Marshall went gallantly through all the motions of a minor young hero, experienced Valley Forge, and came home to Virginia to be idolized by the girls. Marshall was young when the war came and scarcely more than stripling when it was ended. He had caught up the revolutionary contagion with the sensitive energies of youth; but he was quickly responsive to the ebbing of the revolutionary fervor in the leaders whom he followed—men like Washington and Hamilton, who were his archetypal heroes. It was natural in the turbulent years of the Confederation that he should, with them, be dismayed at the agrarian unrest; natural that he should be alarmed at the prospect of a military revolution becoming a social revolution—or worse, a Jacquerie; natural that he should be anxious for the creation of a strong constitutional government to keep it within bounds; natural that he should become a Federalist although a Virginian; natural, later in life, that he should repudiate "the wild and enthusiastic notions" of his youth and wonder that he should ever have entertained them.[8]

His political career up to the time he became Chief Justice was solid and eventful if not distinguished. He settled in Rich-

[7] Corwin, *John Marshall*, 12 *Dict. Am. Biog.* 316.

[8] Marshall was, of course, not alone in this respect. The phenomenon of revolutionist turned pillar of society is a familiar one.

mond to practise law; became a member of the Virginia Legislature; fought valiantly for the Constitution in the Virginia ratifying convention; served a term in Congress; went to France on the unfortunate but eventually highly publicized X Y Z mission; was a member of John Adams' ill-starred cabinet, serving in the last years as Secretary of State and working heroically to rally the remnants of the badly beaten and demoralized Federalist forces. For a time it looked as if Marshall were only a second-string Federalist politician, caught like the other Federalists in a blind alley of history.

He had much in common with them. His class roots were theirs, although his disarming democratic ways, casting a spell over his biographers, have tended to obscure that fact. He was outwardly the frontiersman—a charming, gangling Virginian, rustic and unpretentious in his manner, simple in his tastes, careless and even unkempt in his clothes. An entire mythology has grown up around all the little tender and mildly heterodox ways in which the great Chief Justice half-outraged and half-titillated his friends by forgetting the dignity of his position. Remove this surface and we might with entire clarity view Marshall as we view Fisher Ames or Alexander Hamilton—as a conscious and clean-cut representative of the owning class, the aristocratic temperament and English political theory. Marshall, it is true, was no New England Brahman or New York fashionable. But he was actually a man of substance, with a deep personal and psychological stake in property. He stood heir, by descent, to a long proprietary tradition; he grew up accustomed to regard himself one of the possessors of the earth; he continued this tradition, bought huge landed properties, and was always up to his neck in suits over land titles.[9] By marriage too he had become related to landowners, speculators, and financiers. His business and political connections were with the men of funds and funded income, the lawyers and *rentiers*, the landowners and speculators, the shipbuilders, the merchants and manufacturers. Marshall's habits were molded in the back country of Virginia and among the impoverished farmers who made up Washington's ragged little army at Valley Forge; but his social theory was fashioned among the lawyers at Richmond, and the wealthy planters who travelled there to litigate land titles, and the Brahmans and

[9] *Gustavus Myers, History of the Supreme Court* (1912) 231–41, 270–2, 278–82.

tie-wigs of the New England financial aristocracy with whom
Marshall threw in his political fortunes. You have here only
the lag that you will find in many a man between his boyhood
conditionings and his manhood maturities. The boyhood patterns
linger on, outliving their utility or even their congruity, like the
college-boy folkways in the chairman of a finance board, or a
debutante whimsy in a dowager of fifty.

In several respects Marshall's career was a good preparation
for his work on the Supreme Court. His political experience did
him no harm: like Taney after him, he illustrated the general
rule that the great justices have also been skillful politicians. He
gained a sense of political realities and an adroitness in manipu-
lating them. As the ranking member of the cabinet during the
last demoralized years of the Adams administration, he practically
ran the government and the campaign of 1800 as well. He grew
accustomed to handling large political issues in an audacious way,
he mastered the technique of the devious attack and the strategic
retreat, he learned the grand manner in politics. His talents were
long in maturing. They proved substantial rather than brilliant.
He was at his best, as he showed both on the French mission
and in the Adams cabinet, in a small group where he could
bring to bear the massive influence of his personality.

Much has been made of Marshall's nationalist feeling, especially by his biographer, Senator Beveridge, who uses it to pattern
Marshall's entire career. For others as well it seems to be the
far-off divine event toward which, as toward a fatality, the whole
of Marshall's life moved. The logic goes somewhat as follows:
Marshall as a boy lives in a backwoods region immune against
the fierce localism of the Virginia planters; Valley Forge burns
into his consciousness the heroic character of the national effort;
in the Virginia ratifying convention his zeal for national unity
is whetted by the attacks upon it and the hazardous margin
by which it is saved; as a member of the French mission he is
stirred to the depths by the contempt of Talleyrand for a weak
and divided American nationality; as Secretary of State he bears
the brunt of foreign negotiations, feeling keenly our inferior
bargaining and coercive power; finally as Chief Justice he wel-
comes the chance to strengthen the Constitution as the symbol
of national power against the claims of state sovereignty.

The pattern does not lack persuasiveness. In fact, it is a
tribute to the ultimate triumph of Marshall's nationalism that
we, who think and write in the shadow of it, accept it so un-

questioningly as the rationale of his career. Coleridge once remarked that "every original writer must create the taste by which
he is appreciated." Thus also every great figure in the history
of political thought helps create the institutional and intellectual
climate in which his thinking comes to be ratified.

Nevertheless we must not conclude that nationalism was the
primum mobile of Marshall's being. It must be remembered that
he was to show himself, on the bench, the best of the Federalist
strategists. And nationalism, however fatefully it may have been
rooted in his personality, was above all good strategy. Marshall
learned this primarily from his experience on the X Y Z mission.[10] He came home to find himself a national hero, toasted
everywhere. The French had insulted our national pride, and the
insult was skilfully publicized by the Federalists. Marshall learned
that the common man, who would not respond to Federalist
aristocratic theory, would respond to the same property interests
when they were clothed in the rhetoric of the national interest.[11]
It was a crucial discovery and Marshall was to make the most of
it on the judicial front, where in the name of nationalism he was
to fight the battles of the propertied groups.[12]

Nor must we be confused by Marshall's apparent libertarianism. That too, like his nationalism, was probably sincere
enough. Marshall carried over the English constitutional tradition. He thought of himself as a fighter for liberty, and drew
his inspiration from the struggle against Tudor and Stuart despotism. There is in every man, even the inveterate Tory, a desire
to associate himself with some ringing defiance, to attempt a

[10] The mission itself was a curious one; it was sent over in 1796 by a
Federalist administration to the French revolutionary government to protest
against French depredations on American commerce and iron out treaty
difficulties. Marshall was a curious choice for such a mission; he thought
the French revolution criminal, French diplomacy diabolical, and Jacobin
ideas anarchistic. He went because his land litigation had left him in financial straits, and the twenty thousand he got were, in his own phrase, a
"Godsend." The mission was foredoomed to failure. Talleyrand's foxlike
tactics met their match in Marshall's stubbornness and conspicuous honesty.
The French open bid for a bribe proved a boomerang.

[11] " 'Millions for Defense but not a cent for Tribute' is one of the
few historic expressions in which Federalism spoke in the voice of America.
Thus the Marshall banquet in Philadelphia June 18, 1798, produced that
slogan of defiant patriotism which is one of the slowly accumulating American maxims that have lived." 2 *Beveridge, Life of John Marshall* (1916)
348-9.

[12] See Section 4, *infra*, "The Uses of Nationalism."

Promethean struggle against the unjust ruling divinities. Marshall saw himself in combat against the legislative and executive tyranny of Jeffersonian democracy, and he must be accorded his vision of himself. He was full of forebodings about the future; his letters throughout his judicial career breathe a dark pessimism.[13] It was his fate to come to the fore in the councils of the Federalist party in the declining years of the Adams administration. He must be seen symbolically as the dying Federalist who, out of the reckless strength of that dying, made the way safe for the path of American capitalism.

When John Adams in those fateful closing days of his administration looked about at the political terrain, he saw the Federalists defeated and fleeing everywhere before the new legions of Jeffersonian democracy. Only the judiciary remained. The Federalists "have retired into the judiciary as a stronghold," wrote Jefferson in what has become a famous prediction, "and from that battery all the works of republicanism are to be beaten down." [14] There can be no doubt that Jefferson saw clearly. And there can be little doubt that Marshall was a party to the Federalist councils and plans. Happily for the Federalists the Chief-Justiceship of the Supreme Court fell vacant. When Adams sought one man after another to fill it, he was playing perhaps unwittingly with American destiny. When finally he told Marshall that nothing remained but to send his name to the Senate that destiny was fulfilled.[15] For Marshall, able as he was, never really found himself until he reached the Court. And the Court

[13] As early as 1800 Marshall wrote to Otis, "There is a tide in the affairs of nations, of parties, of individuals . . . I fear that of real Americanism is on the ebb." 2 Beveridge 515. And as late as 1833, "Marshall could not free his mind of the despondency that had now settled upon him. . . . He was sure to refer to the woeful state of the country and the black future it portended." 4 Beveridge 575. See also Story, Life and Letters (1851) 172–3.

[14] 4 The Works of Thomas Jefferson, edited by H. A. Washington (1884) 424–5: Letter to John Dickinson, Dec. 19, 1801.

[15] It had for some time been believed that Marshall did not know of President Adams's intention to appoint him until he received formal notice. This was Beveridge's view. But a recently discovered letter of Marshall to Story in 1827, An Autobiographical Sketch by John Marshall, written at the request of Joseph Story, edited by John Stokes Adams (1937) p. 30, gives a different picture. Adams first asked Jay, whose Federalism could be trusted. On Jay's refusal, Paterson was considered. But Marshall relates that Adams said "I shall not nominate him." Then, after a moment's hesitation, "I believe I must nominate you [Marshall]." "I was pleased as well as surprised," Marshall writes, "and bowed in silence."

was where he belonged. The task before him was an unusual one, but he brought an unusual equipment. For his mind was not that of the great lawyers of history, with their heavy erudition, their tortuousness, their narrow legalism, but the mind of a man of action with its powerful concentration on a single purpose. He had mastered the art of finality. He possessed a large resourcefulness in the service of a singular tenacity of purpose. He was to be a magnificent dictator, dwarfing and uniting his colleagues, polarizing around himself as a dominant personality the forces that were later to be institutionalized in judicial review.

He seems miraculously to have turned up in history just at the point where a rising capitalism most needed him. So near a miracle does this seem that I am ready to pardon Senator Beveridge his four volumes of ecstasy and hosannas. Yet Justice Holmes seemed nearer the truth. "A great man," he said of Marshall, "represents . . . a strategic point in the campaign of history, and part of his greatness consists of his being there." [16] Marshall's role was to effect a nexus between the property interests under an expanding industrialism and the judicial power under a federal system of government. He was to be the strategic link between capitalism and constitutionalism. And for occupying that position in the campaign of history his education and the nature of his mind fitted him superbly. Rarely in American history has the exterior tension of events been matched so completely by an interior tension of preparation and purpose on the part of the exactly right man.

2. COUNTER-REVOLUTION AND JUDICIAL SUPREMACY

There was a grim irony in the fact that Thomas Jefferson, riding the crest of the revolutionary wave of 1800, was sworn into office by John Marshall, his arch-enemy and the arch-enemy of his doctrine. That tense moment represented the climax of one struggle—the political-economic struggle between Federalists and Republicans, and the beginning of another—the judicial-economic struggle between the vested interests and the common man.

The owning classes were in a panic. Their defeat at the polls made it imperative for them to draft their best leadership for the crucial judicial battles to come. Marshall had been designated for the most strategic post. In 1798 he had refused to become an Associate Justice of the Court; in 1801, when the Federalists

[16] Holmes, Collected Legal Papers (1920) 267–8.

had been ousted both from the Presidency and Congress, he had
no choice as a party-man but to accept the Chief-Justiceship. The
necessity he yielded to was the last-ditch necessity of the Federalist propertied groups. And as soon as he was on the Court
he moved swiftly to his purpose. "The Democrats," he wrote to
Pinkney on the morning of the inauguration, and the solemnity
of the occasion should have made him weigh his words, "the
Democrats are divided into speculative theorists and absolute
terrorists. With the latter I am disposed to class Mr. Jefferson." [17]
This version of Mr. Jefferson seems to have influenced the historians as well, for the early part of Marshall's incumbency is
generally characterized as "Jefferson's attack on the Judiciary." [18]
In reality it may with fully as much justice be called the judiciary's attack on Jefferson. Marshall's appointment was only part,
if the most important part, of an extended Federalist plan embracing the passage of the Judiciary Act of 1801, the creation
of new judgeships, and the eventual affirmation of the power
of judicial review.

Jefferson was no inconsiderable opponent. He had a well-
disciplined party machine, he controlled mass opinion, and he
was himself a supple and seasoned warrior in this sort of battle.
For all his revolutionary talk he was no revolutionist. He had
come into office on a popular landslide. The enemy was beaten
and demoralized. Yet his Inaugural Address was an admixture of
sweetness and light, and breathed a honied humility. "We are
all Federalists," he said, "we are all Republicans." But before
he had been half a year in office he had determined to change
his tone. Charles Beard found among the Jefferson manuscripts
the last draft of his message to Congress in December 1801 before the final revision.[19] It included a statement of the doctrine
of the separation of powers in as sharp a form as was to be found
in the Kentucky resolutions; the right of each branch of the
government to interpret the Constitution after its best lights;
his intent to declare the Sedition laws of the previous administra-

[17] 3 *Beveridge* 11.
[18] This seems to apply to Federalist and non-Federalist historians alike.
It is true, of course, of 3 *Beveridge*, c. 2, "The Assault on the Judiciary."
But it is a bit surprising in Corwin, *John Marshall and the Constitution*
(1919), which devotes Chapter III to "Jefferson's War on the Judiciary";
and even more surprising in the pro-Jeffersonian Claude G. Bowers, who
in his *Jefferson in Power* (1936) calls Chapter XIII "Jefferson Attacks the
Federal Judiciary."
[19] Beard, *Economic Origins of Jeffersonian Democracy* (1915) 454–5.

tion unconstitutional and void. While admitting that the Supreme Court as a coordinate branch could check the power of the other branches of government, the message would nevertheless have denied that the Court had the exclusive right of construing the Constitution.[20] Jefferson had already signed this draft when at the last moment he lost heart, struck out the entire passage, and wrote in the margin for posterity: "This whole passage was omitted as capable of being chicaned, and furnishing something to the opposition to make a handle of." [21] Henry Adams, writing before this draft of the message was known, nevertheless lays the blame for Marshall's victory on Jefferson himself and the fact that he faltered in his determination to crush his most dangerous opponent. He might, writes Adams,[22] have had Congress declare the Alien and Sedition laws unconstitutional; he might have asked for an annulment of the dangerous Section 25 of the Judiciary Act of 1789. He might even, although that would have been more risky, have had a constitutional amendment passed giving the judges a fixed tenure of years—four or six—renewable by the President and the Senate. In fact, this was the suggestion that Jefferson finally made, desperate and defeated, four years before he died, when he understood more fully the extent of Marshall's victory.[23]

Not daring the larger plan, Jefferson dared the lesser. He moved to have Congress repeal the Judiciary Act of February 13, 1801, which had reorganized the lower federal courts, creating additional circuit judgeships and filling them with staunch Federalists. He could count on a congressional majority. He could count even more on popular opinion, which was already militantly aroused against the highly partisan charges by the judges to the jury in cases involving the Sedition Act. It must be remembered that the excesses of the French Revolution had produced an anti-Radical scare, and that the Federalists had sought in the Alien and Sedition acts to use that scare as an instrument against Jeffersonianism. The victory of Jefferson at the polls showed how crude the Federalist tactic had been. The Jeffersonians now

[20] Corwin has called this the "political" or "departmental" doctrine of judicial review, as against Marshall's "juristic" doctrine. See his *Court Over Constitution* (1938) 5–7.

[21] See Appendix A of *Beveridge* for complete text of this paragraph.

[22] 1 *History of the United States During the Administration of Jefferson and Madison* 258–9.

[23] Jefferson to W. T. Barry, July 2, 1822, in his *Works*, edited by H. A. Washington, vol. 7, p. 255–7.

moved along two lines to undo the work of the Federalists. They
sought the repeal of the Judiciary Act, and they moved for the
impeachment of the more blatantly partisan judges. The first
line of action reached its climax in the "Great Judiciary Debate"
in the Senate, in January 1802; the second in the impeachment
proceedings against Justice Chase in January and February of
1805. Between these two came the memorable decision in Marbury v. Madison [24] in 1803.

The Great Judiciary Debate of 1802 furnished the stage setting for Marbury v. Madison. The problem of judicial review was
no new problem when Marshall came on the scene. It had been
quietly volcanic since colonial times. The Federalists, fearing the
majority sentiment, had hitherto not dared face the issue. Seeing
themselves swept out of power, however, by the "revolutionary"
wave of 1800, there was nothing for them to do but fall back
on their last line of defense. Of Jefferson it may be said that he
did not so much fear the judiciary as hate the Federalists. He saw
that the Federalists had retreated behind judicial entrenchments,
had passed a last-minute act reorganizing the judiciary, had created new circuit judgeships and filled them with the biggest
diehard Republican-haters they could find in the country.[25] When
he saw this, he knew what he wanted. He proceeded to move
for the repeal of the act and the offices. John Taylor of Carolina,
the official philosopher of the Jeffersonian party, furnished him
with a proper rationalization. It is true, he said, writing to Breckenridge of Kentucky, the leader of the Jeffersonian forces in the
Senate, that the Constitution guarantees judicial tenure during
good behavior. But that means only so long as the office itself
exists.[26] Which Gouverneur Morris, with Federalist unkindness,
rephrased as follows: "You shall not take the man from the office
but you may take the office from the man; you may not drown
him, but you may sink his boat under him." [27]

All of which on both sides, in the face of the actual vote-

24 1 Cranch 137 (U. S. 1803).

25 For the list of appointees, see Frankfurter and Landis, The Business
of the Supreme Court (1928) 21, n. 56. Among them were Richard Bassett
of Delaware, Jeremiah Smith of New Hampshire, Oliver Wolcott of Connecticut, Philip Barton Key of Maryland, whose partisan feeling was well known.
Charles Lee and Jared Ingersoll, also distinctly partisan, declined appointments. See Beard, Economic Origins of Jeffersonian Democracy (1915) 103.

26 Letter of Taylor to Breckenridge, Dec. 22, 1801, quoted in 3 Beveridge 607.

27 11 Annals of Congress 39 (1802).

counting, was only talk. In the debate the Federalists for the first
time in our history openly and insistently claimed for the judiciary the final and exclusive power of interpreting the Constitution; some of the Republicans restated the extreme states'-rights
doctrine of the Kentucky Resolution, others steered shy of discussion. The Federalists did the best talking, but the Republicans
had the votes. The act was repealed and the stage was set.

The stage was set, but not even the Federalist claque could
have forseen the brilliance and audacity with which their leading
actor would play his part. John Marshall hated Jefferson as he
hated no other man in the world: but he respected his strength.
Jefferson had talked soft in his Inaugural, but he was willing to
use the Big Stick and was obviously moving to dislodge the
Federalists from the judiciary. Congress had repealed the Federalist act of reorganization; and, as if to twist the knife in the
wound, had provided also that the Supreme Court was not to
meet until February of the following year (1803). To be sure,
Jefferson might have increased the Supreme Court and packed it
with Republicans, and had refrained: but there was already talk
of impeaching some of the more extreme Federalist judges. Marshall had to move swiftly and with daring. The Marbury case
gave him his chance.

The case of poor Marbury (if he was poor Marbury; he may
merely have been acting as a Federalist stooge)[28] was raked by
the cross fires of Federalist and Republican *Machtpolitik*.[29] Marshall was faced at once by an opportunity and a dilemma. It was
a God-sent chance which he had—to administer a rebuke to
Jefferson, assert officially the judicial power that the Federalists
had claimed in the debates, and place the judiciary in a position
of control. This was the strategic moment: not to use it would
be tantamount to defeat. Yet how use it to advantage? If Mar-

[28] See Corwin, *Doctrine of Judicial Review* (1914) 4; Ernst, *The Ultimate Power* (1937) 227–30; Bowers, *Jefferson in Power* (1936) 165.

[29] Marbury, a small-time Federalist politician, was one of John Adams's
"midnight appointments" as justice of the peace for the District of Columbia. The appointment had been ratified by the Senate, the commission had
been signed and sealed; everything had been done to give William Marbury
his petty office and eternal obscurity except one thing—the commission had
not been delivered. It had been left on the desk of Secretary of State John
Marshall, who was too busy being the Poo-Bah of the Adams government
to follow the affairs of William Marbury. Now Marbury was seeking from
the Supreme Court a writ of mandamus commanding the Secretary of State,
James Madison, to give it up.

shall denied Marbury's claim to his office it would be an admission of judicial powerlessness. But if he upheld it, Jefferson (through Madison) would simply refuse to comply. He might say what Jackson is reputed to have said thirty years later, "John Marshall has made his decision, now let him enforce it," [30] and thus make Marshall and the Court a laughing-stock.

Marshall solved his problem. By a maneuver he managed to administer a public spanking to the administration, assert judicial supremacy, yet leave Jefferson helpless to strike back. Marbury's commission, he said, was a valid one; even without the delivery of the document he had a vested right in it which it was the function of "a government of laws and not of men" to protect; having a right, he had also a remedy, which was mandamus. But the Supreme Court, by its reading of the Constitution, could issue such a writ only where it has appellate and not original jurisdiction; and Section 13 of the Judiciary Act of 1789 which sought to confer original jurisdiction on the Court was therefore unconstitutional.

It mattered little to Marshall that if his conclusion was valid and the Court had no jurisdiction, everything before it was superfluous—a vast *obiter dictum* that was sheer political maneuver. It mattered little to him that none of the opposing counsel had argued that the section of the Judiciary Act was unconstitutional, and that in order to declare it so he had to wrench it beyond all principles of statutory interpretation. He was setting the classic example of what has since come to be called "judicial statesmanship." He made each of his purposes play in superbly with the others. He had disarmingly picked a portion of a Federalist statute to declare unconstitutional; and he had picked one beyond the reach of the Executive—one whose application depended upon the judiciary itself. There was, moreover, a movement afoot in the Jeffersonian Congress to capitalize on the popular feeling against the lower Federal judges, and abolish the lower courts entirely, parceling out their functions among the Supreme Court and the state courts.[31] Marshall sought

[30] Whether Jackson actually said this is now extremely doubtful. See 4 *Beveridge* 551. It was Horace Greeley, in his *American Conflict*, vol. 1, p. 106, who attributed the remark to him. See *Marquis James, Andrew Jackson, Portrait of a President* (1937) 304–5.

[31] See 1 *Warren, The Supreme Court in United States History* (revised ed. 1926) 218–222, who feels that this movement arose "from the very concrete fear lest the decisions of the Federal Courts might be adverse to the land laws and landholders of Virginia and Kentucky."

to quell this movement by asserting the finality of the Supreme Court's decisions on all matters of jurisdiction. There is no point in blaming him. It was the formative period of the American political structure, when every important move was decisive for later power configurations. Legalisms did not count: what counted was the daring, decisive coup.

From a legalistic standpoint alone, *Marbury v. Madison* has a nightmarish fascination. If ever the history of the Court is written with the proper cosmic irony, here will be the cream of the jest. Upon this case, as legal precedent, rests the power of judicial review. Yet every part of its reasoning has been repudiated even by conservative commentators and by later Supreme Court decisions, which none the less continue to exercise the power it first claimed. "Nothing remains of *Marbury v. Madison*," writes Professor J. A. C. Grant,[32] "except its influence." Everything else has been whittled away. But its influence continues to grin at us from the Cimmerian darkness like the disembodied smile of the Cheshire cat.

It remains to ask how much *Marbury v. Madison*, and through it Marshall, contributed to judicial review. Marshall did not originate it, nor did he single-handedly succeed in establishing it beyond all dislodgement. There are historians who give too much credit both to the originality and the decisiveness of his achievement. There are precedents for judicial review, both in the colonial and the English decisions, that stretch into the shadowy past. As for reasoning, Marshall's argument added nothing substantial to the argument of the Federalists in the Great Debate of 1802. Ultimately, the whole of the theory may be found in No. 78 of the *Federalist*, written by Hamilton; in fact, much of Marshall's entire career may be summed up as a process of reading Hamilton's state papers and dissertations into the Constitution. And yet his having translated these ideas into judicial action is Marshall's decisive achievement.

As for the permanence of his work, I find much in Louis B. Boudin's forceful contention that judicial review as we know it is primarily a post-Civil War creation, and that *Marbury v. Madison* decided only the Court's power to determine its own jurisdiction.[33] And yet the permanence of Marshall's work is not to be

[32] J. A. C. Grant, *Marbury v. Madison* (1929) 23 *Am. Pol. Sci. Rev.* 673, 681.

[33] 2 *Boudin, Government by Judiciary* (1932) 230–1. See also Corwin, *Court Over Constitution* (1938) 65–8. Corwin argues that while Marshall

judged wholly in legalistic terms. The influence of the case
went far beyond its strict legal effect. Everything that the Court
drew upon after the Civil War in completing judicial review is
already to be found in Marshall's opinion. Marshall found judicial review a moot question: he left it an integral part of the
constitutional fabric. And while the Court did not again use
judicial review against Congress ("national" judicial review) until
the Dred Scott case, more than half a century later, it was because
in all economic matters the property interests favored expanding
the national power. Where judicial review was used effectively
during this period was against state power ("federal" judicial
review). In these decisions the reasoning of Marbury v. Madison
and the increased strength and prestige of the Supreme Court
worked powerfully. Marshall's role in this entire process was to
give judicial review a foothold, use it for the immediate interests
of the capitalism of his day, tie it up with the powerful appeal
of nationalism, and entrench it where a later stage of capitalism
could take it up and carry it further for its own purposes.

Marshall's decision has been described as a revolutionary
coup. That it was daring and ultimately decisive there can be
little doubt. But it would be a mistake to see it as an isolated
act, or to see Marshall's whole policy apart from the orientation
of his class. Marshall's decision was the high point of a counter-
revolutionary movement that stretched back to the Constitutional
Convention. The wheelings and turnings of Federalists and Republicans were not only the maneuverings of propertied groups
and the agrarian-labor masses for salvaging or hemming in the
consequences of the Revolution: they were part of a world-wide
movement of social struggle fought out in France and England
as well as in America. For the history of this period can be
written adequately only if it is seen as world history.[34]

Marshall and his fellow-Federalists (and Marshall was by no
means the most extreme) viewed the Republicans as Jacobins,
Jefferson as Robespierre, and his letter to Mazzei as the sure

---

made broad assertions as to the scope of the Court's power of judicial
review, he uses among other arguments as to its finality the judges' oath
to support the Constitution. This, Corwin points out ingeniously, would
seem to make an ever stronger case for the President's final power of constitutional interpretation.

[34] Marcus L. Hansen has stressed a similar point with respect to frontier
history. See Sources of Culture in the Middle West, edited by D. R. Fox
(1934) 103–10. I feel that it applies equally here.

mark of the Antichrist.[35] Jefferson, on the other hand, considered the Federalists oligarchs and despots, and he feared Marshall's implacability and cunning. He was exasperated that his victory at the polls should be frustrated by the judiciary. He never forgot that the Federalist judges had used the bench as hustings for election speeches.[36] His attempt to impeach these judges fell through: but it was a characteristic part of the political tactics of the day, as was also the united front that Federalist bench and bar offered—a united front so complete that it was difficult for the government to find counsel to prosecute the impeachments.[37] It was class against class.

The whole situation was made far graver by the danger of war, either with England or France, and the threats of treason. War was one thing that Jefferson meant to avoid; his inaugural addresses and his annual messages are filled with eulogies of peace and of the joys of reproduction.[38] Jefferson felt the American borders were being menaced by foreign invasion and internal disaffection. The Burr conspiracy was to prove how close that danger was, and the Burr trial proved how determined the Federalists were to embarrass the administration: while Marshall's own behavior was clearly partisan,[39] Jefferson's moves behind the scenes were obviously those of a man determined to get a conviction.

Thus the first six years of Marshall's term—1801–1807—witnessed the battle of two giants in a setting of world revolution and counter-revolution. The Alien and Sedition laws (previously), the Judiciary Act, the Marbury decision, and the decision in the

[35] "The morals of the author of the letter to Mazzei," wrote Marshall, "cannot be pure." Marshall to Hamilton, Jan. 1, 1801, in 6 Works of Alexander Hamilton, edited by J. C. Hamilton (1850) 501–3.

[36] Judge Pickering of New Hampshire was a known drunkard, and his eccentricities bordered on insanity. Justice Chase of Maryland delivered from the bench tirades against Republican principles and practices that would have graced the speeches of President Dwight of Yale, who had brooded so deeply upon what the Republicans might do in the future, that he had convinced himself they had done so in the present.

[37] Ambassador Dodd, with his eye probably on the similar united front of the American Bar Association today against the New Deal, pointed out this fact in his letter to some Senators, published in the New York Times, May 12, 1937, p. 4.

[38] 1 Henry Adams, History of the United States of America (1891) 200–13, 249, 250–8.

[39] Ex parte Bollman, 4 Cranch 75 (U. S. 1807). See Corwin, John Marshall and the Constitution (1919) 108–14.

Burr case were the Federalist moves; the victory of 1800, the repeal of the Judiciary Act, the attempt to impeach Chase and the Burr trial were the Jeffersonian moves. Out of the whole melée there emerged as the great and enduring result the enunciation of the power of judicial review.

3. LAND CAPITALISM AND MERCHANT CAPITALISM

In Marshall's day the great threat to the property interests lay in the action of the state legislatures. Since colonial times the state legislatures had been the standing enemy of the creditor and moneyed class—they had even in colonial times sought to control business; they had been centers of focal infection, threatening both the ratification of the Constitution and the dominance of the moneyed groups in the new government. They had an unseemly habit of being responsive to the economic plight of the common man.[40] What was needed now was a way of using judicial review to keep them in check.

Marshall found the answer in the "obligations of contract" clause in the Constitution:[41] he seized upon it, brought in a "higher law" theory to give a moral afflatus to sanctity of contract, and ended by creating the doctrine of vested rights as an implied limitation on state powers. To do this he had to stretch contract far beyond its contemporary meaning, but he was equal to the task. Sir Henry Maine once said that the progress of society

[40] The role of the states as centers of American radicalism has tended to become obscured by the constitutional controversy over states' rights and centralization. But the states' rights theory must be viewed as growing out of this tendency toward local radicalism. For the state legislatures expressed the localist feeling in each state as against the financial centers, and agrarian feeling as against industrial development. The pull of industry and the spread of communications prevented the growth of any real regionalism or autonomy; but the states' rights doctrine represents the desire for it. From Daniel Shays to the Non-Partisan League and the Farm Holiday Association the states have been the nuclei of populist and progressive sentiment, and of the radical theory of Jefferson, John Taylor, Madison, Jackson, and Bryan. It is only recently that they and the states' rights theory associated with them have become refuges of capitalism and, in Beard's phrase, "wards of the Supreme Court." See my unsigned editorial, Who Owns States' Rights? (1936) 142 Nation 632.

[41] "No state shall . . . pass any . . . law impairing the obligation of contracts." Art. I, § 10, ¶ 1. For a full discussion of the history of the clause and its constitutional interpretation, see Wright, The Contract Clause of the Constitution (1938).

is from status to contract: [42] if that is true, Marshall must rank as one the great heroes of humanity, for he gave contract a sanctity overriding every consideration of public policy or economic control. Next to judicial review itself this conception of contract —broadened into a doctrine of "vested rights" [43]—is probably the most important invention in the history of the Court. It dominated the constitutional scene up to the Civil War, both in state and federal courts; it served as a model after which later doctrines of implied limitations on state power, such as due process of law and freedom of contract, could be fashioned.

The first of the contract cases [44] to stir attention, *Fletcher v. Peck*, [45] has been described as "a corner-stone of legal structure laid in mud." [46] Behind it is one of the most malodorous episodes in American history—that of the Yazoo land frauds. The Georgia Legislature of 1796, in what Beveridge has described as a "saturnalia of corruption," disposed of a strip of Indian land half the size of New England, comprising most of the present states of Alabama and Mississippi, to a land speculating company for about a cent and a half an acre. Every legislator except one had received a large bribe of land stock which could be disposed of for cash. The scandal broke; the people of Georgia, in a fury, wrote a new constitution, elected a new legislature and rescinded the

[42] *Maine, Ancient Law.* (1906 ed.) 165. For a discussion of this famous generalization, around which storms of controversy have raged, see K. Smellie, *Sir Henry Maine* (1928) 8 *Economica* 64–94. Maine valued Marshall's work highly and was deeply influenced by it. In his *Popular Government* (1885) p. 248, he calls the Marshall contract decisions "the bulwark of American individualism against democratic impatience and socialistic fantasy."

[43] Corwin is more responsible than anyone else before Wright for tracing the history of this doctrine. See his *A Basic Doctrine of American Law* (1913) 12 Mich. L. Rev. 247–76, and *The Doctrine of Due Process of Law before the Civil War* (1911) 24 Harv. L. Rev. 366–85, 460–79. See also Haines, *The Revival of Natural Law Concepts* (1930) c. 4; and my own article, *Vested Interests* (1934) 15 Encyc. Soc. Sci. 240–3. Wright, *The Contract Clause of the Constitution* (1938) n. 40, includes the vested rights doctrine in its discussion of the history of the contract clause.

[44] The first important one, Calder v. Bull, 3 Dall. 386 (U. S. 1798) involved the interpretation of the ex post facto clause.

[45] 6 Cranch 87 (U. S. 1810).

[46] Morgan, *New England and the Yazoo Land Frauds, 1795–1814* (1914) 9 *Americana* 324, 325. This is easily the best discussion of the political and social context of the case, and a brilliant piece of writing. See also Haskins, *The Yazoo Land Companies* (1891); Corwin, *John Marshall and the Constitution* (1919); Wright, *The Contract Clause of the Constitution* (1938) 29–34.

corrupt act. But meanwhile the speculators had sold their stock
to purchasers in New England and the Middle States. The latter
proceeded to attack the legality of the rescinding act, and made
many unsuccessful attempts in Congress to get compensation.
Finally, on the basis of an opinion prepared by Alexander Hamilton,[47] they contrived an obviously trumped-up suit and brought
it before the Supreme Court. Joseph Story, later to become
Marshall's *fidus Achates* on the Court, represented the New
England speculators; but it is a safe guess that the opposing attorney did not trouble himself to present too formidable an
argument.[48]

Marshall's decision is breath-taking. He ignored the obvious
collusion by which the case had been brought before the Court.
He held that the Court could not concern itself with the alleged
corruption of the Georgia Legislature, thereby inaugurating the
Supreme Court tradition of maintaining when convenient a de-
cent ignorance of events outside the Court. What counted was
that the sovereign state of Georgia had, through the original
legislative grant, entered into a contract the obligation of which
could not be impaired by another act. As against the legislature's
power to rescind its own act, Marshall argued that there was a
higher moral duty to stand by the sanctity of contract. That
moral duty flowed both from the specific sanctity of vested rights
under a contract, and from more general considerations of "the
nature of society and of government" which prescribed limits to
the legislative power. Thus a decision which had started by
throwing moral considerations out of the window ended by admitting them again through the back door.

It is not difficult to say why the framers of the Constitution
inserted the "obligations of contract" clause. They had been
distressed by the state legislation repudiating debts and placing
moratoria on their payment, by paper currency legal tender laws,
by installment and commodity payment laws. They were an-
noyed even more by "special acts," through which the legislatures
had intervened in pending lawsuits and set contracts aside. To
meet this problem of moratoria and other debtor relief laws, they

[47] This opinion will be found reprinted in *Wright, op. cit. supra,* at 22.
[48] Story's brief is summarized in 6 Cranch 115–125, Martin's at 6 Cranch
115 (U. S. 1810). Justice Johnson raised the question of collusion in his
concurring opinion, but Marshall did not. Beveridge guesses that the reason
why Johnson, a Jefferson appointee, did not press the matter more strongly
was that Madison wanted the ruling that Marshall favored.

counted on a sound and plentiful monetary supply, which would
be achieved by giving the federal government a monopoly of
coinage. But, as if to make doubly sure, they adopted also, at the
motion of Rufus King, a clause probably suggested by the contract clause in the recently enacted Ordinance of 1787. The interesting thing is that the contract clause got little enthusiasm in
the discussions at the Convention, but seems to have been the
product mainly of an agreement within the Committee on Style.
In the discussions attending ratification there was not much
clarity about the meaning of the clause, except for a general agreement that it referred only to private contracts.[49] The prevalent
notion of contract at the time was a far narrower one than at
present. In fact, contract as a basic concept of law was not developed until the period between the 1830's and 1860's.[50] Little
was thought about the contract clause until in 1796 Alexander
Hamilton, retained as counsel by the New England purchasers of
the land stock, submitted an opinion that for Georgia to rescind
its act was a violation of the contract it had by implication entered into not to rescind the act.

This was the reasoning Marshall adopted, in a halting and
hesitant way. His argument is even more rickety than that in
Marbury v. Madison. He ignored what was the common understanding that the contract clause applied to private and not public contracts, and that it applied only when an obligation had
been undertaken under a contract which the law protected and
which had not yet been fulfilled. But having determined to assert his principle, Marshall went the whole way, and brought
already executed public contracts within the scope of constitutional protection. He ignored also the fact that it was an established principle of the English common law that a legislature
could rescind an act when fraud was involved, and the fact that
British Parliaments had done so repeatedly.

Despite its logical weakness, however, Marshall's decision
takes on meaning in the economic context of the day. Gambling
in land values represented the principal financial activity in ex-
pansionist America at the turn of the nineteenth century, before
industrialism came to overshadow everything else. Some of the

---

[49] We are indebted to Wright, *op. cit. supra,* at 6–79, for an excellent treatment of the history of the enactment of the clause in the
Constitution. He blasts effectively the tradition that James Wilson was responsible for it.

[50] Isaacs, *John Marshall on Contracts* (1921) 7 Va. L. Rev. 413.

most prominent men of the day had been involved in the Yazoo
land scandal, including James Wilson, an Associate Justice of the
Supreme Court, who was up to the neck in the business: "When
the deal was consummated," says Beveridge, "the Justice held
shares to the amount of at least three-quarters of a million
acres." [51] Nor is this surprising. America was still an agrarian nation at the time, living by the soil and hoping to build its heaven
from the soil. For the common people land meant a livelihood; for
the landed squirearchy it meant a social position and a way of life;
for a large intermediate group it meant easy profits. "Stock-job-
bing" in land was much moralized over, and was considered one
of the evils of the day; but it was an evil that involved wide
circles in its participation. The great families of the day were
landowning families, who had obtained their titles in some cases
through fraud and in most cases through privilege. But their
seigneurial estates could not be run profitably in the North with
free labor; so they had turned to land speculation, where their
political influence and their social and financial connections
would be of account. The "aristocracy of patronage and paper,"
as John Taylor of Carolina termed the new banking and financial
group,[52] also found in land speculation a source of revenue. The
fever spread to the workers in the northern cities; in fact, many
of the people who had bought the Yazoo stock had invested the
savings of a lifetime.

Land ate itself into the fiber of the period: but it was a
speculative fiber that was involved. The economic fluctuations up
to the Civil War were largely to be the history of land booms
and land bubbles. The organization of the Yazoo land deal,
in fact, foreshadowed the methods of later corporate promoting.
The legislature was bought by "gifts" of stock; the promoters
granted themselves large stock melons for promotion; northern
men were hired as decoys in marketing the stock, and were paid
by stock "gifts." [53] This was agrarian capitalism, but it was the
sort that was the spearhead of the emerging industrial capitalism.
Marshall's decision was thus not merely the decision of a man
who knew land and loved land—in whose circles of friendship

[51] 3 *Beveridge* 548, n. 5. Corwin's article on Wilson in the *Dictionary
of American Biography* is worth reading. It is interesting, incidentally, that
even Jefferson and Madison winked at the Yazoo affair.

[52] John Taylor, *An Inquiry into the Principles and Policy of the Government of the United States* (1814) 15.

[53] For a good description of the investment fever and the financing
methods, see Morgan, *op. cit. supra* note 46.

land-speculation was the breath of life. It was also a decision in harmony with the progress of an exploitative merchant capitalism.

One other phase deserves mention. At the time the case of *Fletcher* v. *Peck* was being fought out, Marshall was himself involved in land litigation. Sometime between 1794 and 1800 he had bought from the heirs of Lord Fairfax their claims to two or three million acres of Virginia land between the Rappahannock and the Potomac: these lands had been granted by Charles II in 1673 and had been taken back by Virginia after the Revolution and parceled out to returning soldiers as homesteads. The same had happened to the claims of the Penn heirs in Pennsylvania and the Granville heirs in North Carolina. Marshall, before he became Chief Justice, acting with his brother and Robert Morris —whom William E. Dodd, the Virginia historian, has called "a shameless speculator of Philadelphia"—[54] bought the Fairfax claims and carried the litigation time and time again to the Virginia Supreme Court, which decided unanimously against him. After he became Chief Justice, the case was carried to the Supreme Court. The issue involved in both cases was the same: the power of a state legislature to revoke a grant made by a previous sovereign body. The principle invoked was the same— sanctity of contract as overriding legislative sovereignty. When Marshall was deciding the case of the Yazoo land frauds, he was in effect setting a precedent for the decision of his own case. When that case came up for decision in 1813, as *Fairfax's Devisee* v. *Hunter's Lessee*,[55] Marshall quite properly refrained from sitting on it. The opinion of the Court was written by Justice Story, who had been one of the counsel for the land speculators in the re-argument of *Fletcher* v. *Peck*, and it was an opinion upholding the claim of the Marshall brothers on essentially the same grounds as the Yazoo case.[56]

I am not urging a personal interpretation of Marshall's land decisions. Marshall was a man of stubborn integrity. He would undoubtedly have ruled as he did in *Fletcher* v. *Peck* even if his

[54] See the letter from Ambassador Dodd to Senators Glass and Bulkley, mentioned *supra* note 37. See also his *Chief Justice Marshall and Virginia, 1813–1821* (1907) 12 *Am. Hist. Rev.* 776.

[55] 7 Cranch 603 (U. S. 1813).

[56] Nine months after Story handed down the decision in 1813, Spencer Roane and the other judges of the Virginia Court of Appeals unanimously refused to obey the Supreme Court's ruling. Jefferson in a letter to Roane (Oct. 12, 1815) approved of Roane's action. 9 *Writings* (Ford. ed. 1892) 530–2. The case reappeared in the Supreme Court as Martin v. Hunter's Lessee, 1 Wheat. 304 (U. S. 1816). Again Story reiterated his first decision.

own land speculations were not concerned. But the fact that
even he was involved in such speculations shows how deeply the
substance of the issues reached to the economics of the period,
how directly it was part of its ethos And as the frontier of settlement moved further west and south after the Louisiana Purchase,
the principle of *Fletcher* v. *Peck* and *Fairfax's Devisee* v. *Hunter's
Lessee* was extended to the land claims of speculators based on
flimsy and often corrupt Spanish titles.[57] In *United States* v.
Arredondo,[58] *Chouteau* v. *United States*,[59] and *Soulard* v. *United
States*,[60] an exceedingly liberal interpretation was placed by the
court on the power of Spanish officials to grant land deeds regardless of the written limitations of their authority, and on the
validity of the titles based on those deeds. The result was that
the bribing of officials and the forging of deeds became a common method of obtaining land titles, and the Supreme Court in
accordance with its principle of not examining the ethics behind
a contractual grant of a sovereign gave those titles authenticity.

Marshall and his Court felt no doubt that in thus placing
the sanctity of contract above every adventitious consideration
of policy or ethics they were encouraging economic stability.[61]
Actually they were encouraging the reckless development of
American economic resources and the flagrant corruption of state
politics which were to characterize the opening of the American
continent throughout the nineteenth century.[62]

[57] Nelles and King, *Contempt by Publication in the United States*
(1928) 28 *Columbia Law Rev.* 401–31; Myers, *History of the Supreme
Court* (1912) 326–49, 419–20, 425.

[58] 6 Pet. 691 (U. S. 1832).

[59] 9 Pet. 137 (U. S. 1835).

[60] 10 Pet. 100 (U. S. 1836).

[61] There may have been some such consideration in his mind in the
decision of New Jersey v. Wilson, 7 Cranch 164 (U. S. 1812) in which an
agreement by the state to exempt land from taxation was held to be a contract within the meaning of the clause. Yet, although in short-run terms
it may seem desirable to the business mentality to limit the taxing power of
the state, it is very doubtful whether that adds to economic stability. The
number of instances in which New Jersey v. Wilson was invoked during
the rest of the nineteenth century to throw the cloak of the law around
tax exemption cases whose nakedness would otherwise have been revolting,
may have added to the speculative *elan* of capitalist expansion, but could
not have added to economic stability.

[62] For Veblen's analysis of this "American Plan of Seizure and Conversion," see his *Absentee Ownership* (1923) c. vii, *The Case of America*,
especially § v, "The Timber Lands and the Oil Fields."

The *Dartmouth College*[63] decision is one of the most famous that Marshall handed down. The little New Hampshire college, established in 1769 to educate and Christianize the Indians, found itself in 1815 without any Indians but with a Christian college community split to the center by a cleavage that ranged Congregationalist Federalists against non-Congregationalist Jeffersonians. The issue, as could have happened only in New England where politics was theology and theology politics, was fought out in a bitter state campaign. The Republicans won both the governorship and the legislature, and they proceeded in 1816 to pass an act amending the college charter, increasing the number of trustees and thus taking control away from the Federalist Old Guard. Jefferson, from his Monticello retreat, applauded: to do otherwise, he wrote, would be to hold "that the earth belongs to the dead and not to the living." [64] The case was fought out before the highest court in New Hampshire, which held the law valid, on the ground that the college was a public corporation, devoted to public purposes, and that its charter could therefore be amended as public policy shifted. *Fletcher v. Peck*, it was held, did not apply; that related only to legislative grants involving the property rights of individuals, and not to grants of power for public purpose.

The case went to the Supreme Court, where it was argued with eloquence for the college by Daniel Webster, at that time (at thirty-seven) reaching the height of his powers. Every schoolboy knows Webster's reputed eloquent plea ("it is, Sir, as I have said, a small college. Yet there are those who love it") and how Marshall, whom the Yazoo land scandals had left cold, found his own eyes suffused with tears as Webster, overcome by the emotion of his words, wept.[65] But few schoolboys know that the case had ultimately less to do with colleges than with business corporations; that sanctity of contract was invoked to give them immunity against legislative control; and that business enterprise

[63] Trustees of Dartmouth College v. Woodward, 4 Wheat. 517 (U. S. 1819). For further discussion, see Wright, *The Contract Clause of the Constitution* (1938) 39–46, citing the literature.

[64] Letter to Governor William Plumer, July 21, 1816, in *Writings of William Plumer*, edited by A. Peabody (1857) 440–1.

[65] This is probably apocryphal. Professor Goodrich of Yale, who attended the trial, told the story to Rufus Choate, in whose biography it appears. See Fuess, *Daniel Webster* (1930). Although Webster's speech was a great example of forensic art, Hopkinson seems to have delivered the better argument.

in America has never nad more useful mercenaries than the tears
Daniel Webster and John Marshall are reputed to have shed so
devotedly that March day in Washington in 1818.

The mechanics by which the decision was arrived at are almost as interesting as the decision itself. After the argument the
judges found they could not agree. The case was continued. Webster, who had ways of knowing, guessed that at least three of the
seven judges were safe. Justice Livingston was crucial. Since he
leaned heavily on the advice of Chancellor Kent of New York,
whose learning was as well known and almost as greatly admired
as his conservatism, steps were taken to argue Kent out of his
view that the New Hampshire court was right in holding the
college a public corporation. There were letters, whisperings, con-
ferences. When Court met again the following February, Marshall read the opinion of four of the judges. It held that the
charter was a contract, that it was a "private" contract in the
sense that the trustees represented the original grantees, whose
vested rights to the money and effort they had put up had to be
protected; that no one would give money to found a "private
eleemosynary institution" such as the college was unless he could
be certain that the charter that was granted him in return for his
money would run in perpetuity.[66]

There were holes in the argument, especially where Marshall
agreed that Parliament, which granted the charter, could legally
(not morally) have amended or revoked it, and that with the
Revolution the state of New Hampshire had succeeded to the
sovereignty. Marshall's sustained assurance, however, could bridge
any gap in logic. While his opinion did not even mention *Fletcher
v. Peck* (the concurring opinions of Story and Washington did),
that case was assumed. What the *Dartmouth College* decision
did was to apply *Fletcher* v. *Peck* to corporate charters. The
question of whether they were public or private was actually of
small moment historically, whatever may have been its importance
in the case itself: for, once it was clear that a charter was a contract within the meaning of the contract clause, the exemption
of public contracts could not have exempted the charters of busi-

[66] Marshall wrote the court opinion upholding the charter as a contract, 4 Wheat. 518 (U. S. 1819). Justices Washington and Story wrote
concurring opinions, 4 Wheat. 518, 654, 666, mostly supplying the legal
learning Marshall's opinion lacked. Justice Johnson concurred with Marshall.
Justice Livingston acquiesced in all the opinions. Justice Duval dissented
without opinion.

ness corporations from the operation of the rule.[67] What was important was the ruling that a charter of incorporation was a contract: this Marshall scarcely discussed, although Story and Washington did; yet this was the new impetus given to the extension of the contract clause, and it was in this sense that the *Dartmouth* decision went a step beyond *Fletcher* v. *Peck*.

A step beyond it not only in constitutional terms, but in economic terms as well. *Fletcher* v. *Peck* threw the protection of vested rights around the capitalism of land speculation, and allowed it to operate on any terms it chose. The *Dartmouth College* case did the same for corporate business enterprise. I am not speaking in terms of specific intent. The corporation in Marshall's day was not the unit of business enterprise and was not to become so until after the Civil War; although it may be said in qualification that already it was not entirely unimportant, and that it was to become increasingly important with the grant of charters for turnpikes, canal companies, railroads, bridge construction companies.[68] In its consequences the decision operated to make an initial grant of power, of tax exemption,[69] of government lands a permanent one. Later developments, principally Chief Justice Taney's decision in the *Charles River Bridge* case,[70] have stripped the decision of some of its starkness. Taney ruled that while charters are contracts, they must be strictly construed in favor of the public interest, and no power exercised that was not expressly granted in them.[71] State legislatures also learned

[67] This of course excludes business corporations having the direct character of public utilities which might be argued to come within the scope of public contract.

[68] See 2 *Davis, Essays in the Earlier History of American Corporations* (1917) cc. 3, 4, 5.

[69] For an earlier case involving tax exemption specifically, see New Jersey v. Wilson, 7 Cranch 164 (U. S. 1812), cited *supra* note 60. But see also Providence Bank v. Billings, 4 Pet. 514 (U. S. 1830), where Marshall limited his own doctrine of tax immunity, along much the same lines of strict construction of a charter that Taney was to follow in the *Charles River Bridge* case, *infra*.

[70] Proprietors of Charles River Bridge v. Proprietors of Warren Bridge, 11 Pet. 420 (U. S. 1837).

[71] This doctrine of strict construction of corporate charters is one of the elements principally responsible for the reputation of liberalism that the Taney Court has had. Actually, as Wright well points out, *The Contract Clause of the Constitution* (1938) 62–3, the Taney Court on the whole continued the tradition of the Marshall Court with respect to the contract clause, and with respect also to the protection of property rights. There

how to insert "reservation clauses" into constitutions and statutes —provisions reserving to themselves the right to "alter, amend, or repeal" the charters they granted.[72] But the overmastering fact is that the *Dartmouth* case set up an inviolability of corporate charters that has had slowly to be qualified, instead of starting at the opposite pole with a rule of legislative discretion and control. And by putting all the burdens on the original wording of the charter, it encouraged a tie-up between corporate interests and legislative greed that has been one of the peculiar marks of the American capitalist spirit.

The contract cases made Marshall the best hated man in the country. State bankruptcy laws, squatter laws, tax laws fell under the interdict of "vested rights." The decision which aroused the bitterest feeling was *Sturges* v. *Crowninshield*,[73] ruling that a state bankruptcy act violated the contract clause as it applied to contracts already entered into ("retrospective"). Marshall's opinion, however, sought to go further and apply this even to contracts made after the passage of the law. This was too much even for Marshall's usually obedient colleagues, and acting in response to a storm of popular protest they repudiated this obiter dictum eight years later in *Ogden* v. *Saunders*.[74] Marshall, however, held out to the end. For once he found himself a solitary dissenter. His dissenting opinion in this case gives the clearest statement of his whole philosophy of contract as the basis of the doctrine of vested rights: it breathes a weird Rousseauist natural-rights mysticism, and represents perhaps the most explicit statement we have of the transcendental sources of sanctity of contracts which he finds to be "original and pre-existing principles," "anterior to, and independent of society." [75] The obligation of contract, he says is a moral obligation, dictated by reason or nature.

was not, however (at least until the *Dred Scott* case) the same imperialistic expansion of the judicial power as in Marshall's Court, and there was a less blatant and more sophisticated approach to the protection of property rights. The Taney Court will form the subject of a forthcoming chapter by the author.

[72] See *Wright*, op. cit. supra, at 168–172, citing the cases. Wright's judgment is worth quoting, that "the general adoption of this reservation in one form or another has, with the possible exception of the rise of due process, been the principal factor in the decline of the contract clause." *Id.* at 169.

[73] 4 Wheat. 122 (U. S. 1819).

[74] 12 Wheat, 213 (U. S. 1827).

[75] 12 Wheat. 213, 345 (U. S. 1827).

In short, in the words of a commentator, "it is not the state that gives validity and force to the contract, but, conceivably, a contract which gives validity and force to the state." [76]

Marshall was clearly riding an obsession. His primary drive was to protect private property from governmental encroachment. His struggle against the powers of the state legislatures was an instrument for this purpose.[77] But the pursuit of even a secondary objective over a long period of time may transform it eventually into an independent objective. States' rights finally became Marshall's bugbear. He came to believe that every concession to the states' regulatory power sapped the Constitution. He began his Supreme Court tenure in the shadow of Jeffersonian democracy: he ended it in the shadow of Jacksonian democracy. Increasingly his letters and conversation were filled with dark forebodings about the future.

Yet he had done his work. Vested rights remained an operative doctrine in state judicial review until the Civil War, especially in such industrial states as New York. And after the Civil War, the due process clause of the Fourteenth Amendment more than took the place of the contract clause. But the interpretation which the Supreme Court was to place on the due process clause would not have been possible without Marshall's establishment of the power of judicial review, and the calm audacity with which he had transformed the genius of business enterprise into a set of implied limitations upon state power.

4. THE USES OF NATIONALISM

It is, however, not with the states but on the national judicial-economic front that Marshall's greatest meaning for to-day lies. In a series of decisions beginning with McCulloch v. Maryland [78] in 1819 and Gibbons v. Ogden [79] in 1824 extending through Willson v. Black Bird Creek Marsh Company [80] in 1829, he evolved a broad interpretation of the "necessary and proper" and commerce clauses of the Constitution which was at once tough-minded in its understanding of contemporary economic

[76] Isaacs, John Marshall and Contracts (1921) 7 Va. L. Rev. 413, 421.

[77] In a sense, Marshall's dissent in Ogden v. Saunders was too far ahead of his day. Had he had his way, the contract clause would have become as broad in its anti-regulatory function as the due process clause later became.

[78] 4 Wheat. 316 (U. S. 1819).

[79] 9 Wheat. 1 (U. S. 1824).

[80] 2 Pet. 245 (U. S. 1829).

reality and bold in its vision of the economic future of the nation. This is the nationalistic phase of Marshall's career: it is
also the most brilliant and—if the progressive forces of the Court
win in their present struggle for power with the reactionary
forces—it is likely to prove the most enduring.

I can say this without succumbing uncritically to the elements of sheer rhetoric in Marshall's nationalism. That rhetoric,
like the rhetoric of sanctity of contract, serves to conceal the
shaping forces of Marshall's decisions, and is best cleaved by
the sundering blade of the logic of business interests.

Taken simply as rhetoric, its hollowness is most shockingly
revealed by Marshall's serious negotiations with the New England secession movement on the eve of (and even during) the
War of 1812, his efforts to sabotage the war, his non-too-concealed
willingness in 1812 to stand for the Federalist presidential nomination on a New England program.[81] Nothing in American history is as short-sighted and illiberal as the Federalist party policy
from 1807 to 1815, and Marshall for the most part shared it and
helped shape it. "The record shows," Beveridge admits, "that
John Marshall was as bitterly opposed to the war of 1812 as was
Pickering or Otis or Lowell," [82] to name the Federalist leaders
for whom a split from the rest of the American nation had become an obsession. In the face of a war that was being fought for
the agricultural rather than for the industrial and mercantile
groups, Marshall's principles of nationalism were dangerously
shaken. For Marshall had little of the deeper national consciousness of the common man, based on national expansion and democratic adventure and the promise of American life.[83] His was a
strictly judicial nationalism, on a base of economic realism.

Its guiding logic was the relation of the national power to

[81] 4 *Beveridge*, c. 1, especially 31–35, 47.

[82] *Id.* at 55.

[83] This was finding expression even in the rather crude gropings of a
Henry Clay for a governmentally directed national expansion. For a brilliant
but truncated view of Clay, see 2 Parrington, *Main Currents in American
Thought* (1927) 142–4. See also Bernard Mayo, *Henry Clay* (1937). Although Marshall's nationalism was welcome to Clay and his group, I cannot go with Boudin in his *Government by Judiciary* (1932) vol. 2, c. xii
that Marshall was, with Madison and Clay, one of the leaders of the Young
America movement. Marshall and Clay represented the thought of different
economic and social groups, and their animus was different. It would be
clearer to say that Marshall stood with one foot caught in the old Federalist
party and one reaching toward a new nationalism.

the scope of industrial development. The upswing of a rising capitalism made it necessary that congressional jurisdiction be strengthened as against the power of the states with reference to the two main lines of business expansion of the period—a national banking system and a national transportation system. The first, Marshall accomplished in the famous decision in *McCulloch v. Maryland*. What was involved on the surface was the constitutionality of the Second United States Bank, and the question whether a Maryland state tax on its bank notes was valid. What was involved below the surface was the question whether the government would use every force at its disposal to ensure favorable conditions for the newly emerging banking capitalist class and a free field for its operations.

Marshall made the Maryland bank case the occasion of his most resounding opinion. He had two questions to answer. Did Congress have the power to charter a national bank? Did Maryland have the power to tax it? The first question had been moot for years. It turned on the interpretation of the "necessary and proper" constitutional provision.[84] When, at Alexander Hamilton's instance, the first bank had been chartered in 1791, it was only after a heated discussion of constitutionality—the first general discussion of what the new Constitution meant.[85] When an attempt was made in 1811 to recharter it, there was again a sharp debate on the meaning of the "necessary and proper" clause. When, under stress of monetary chaos and state wildcat banking, a Second United States Bank was created in 1816, it did not lay the ghost of the constitutional problem. The Maryland tax case brought it up again, amidst wide interest.[86]

[84] "The Congress shall have power . . . to make all laws which shall be necessary and proper for carrying into execution the foregoing powers." Art. I, § 8, ¶ 18.

[85] Hamilton's *Opinion as to the Constitutionality of the Bank of the United States* will be found in the Lodge edition of Hamilton's *Writings*, vol. 3, p. 445–93. The Senate debate on the Bank is in 1 *Annals of Congress* (1791) 1940–2012.

[86] The pride of the conservative American bar, William Pinkney, made the principal speech for the Bank—a three-day speech in "a hall full almost to suffocation," before "a crowded audience of ladies and gentlemen" (Story to Stephen White, March 3, 1819, W. Story, editor, p. 325). "I never, in my whole life, heard a greater speech," wrote Story, and while Story was a passionate admirer of Pinkney and everything in his nature yearned in the direction of Pinkney's side of the case, it is true that Pinkney was a great advocate. Foppish, corseted, rouged, impeccably dressed, Pinkney was at his best only when the belles were present and the flower and beauty

The Bank had already begun splitting the opinion of the country—a process which was to come to its climax in the Bank War of Biddle, Jackson, and Taney. Already in the North and East it was the bulwark of the Republic, in the South and West the "great monster." In the three years of its establishment it had first expanded credit and then contracted it—a policy which had not helped its popularity; its branches had been guilty of fraud, speculation, and mismanagement of funds. In those three years eight states had passed laws taxing the branches: and while the *McCulloch* case was being argued a bill was in Congress for repealing the charter. It was imperative that swift action be taken—imperative both for the bank and for the Supreme Court, which was so thoroughly in sympathy with it. A case was "arranged"; how much collusion there was in it is difficult to say, but after the decision the Ohio Legislature declared that "many of the strongest grounds were relinquished or not brought into view" by Maryland counsel.[87] The case was pushed through expeditiously, and three days after Pinkney finished his argument, Marshall had a ten thousand word opinion ready.

The opinion was pretty much a condensation of Pinkney's argument, and yet it was more than that. It was a brilliant essay in the philosophy of government, bold in its logic, uncluttered with learning. There was, it is true, little new in it—little that had not been said in the debates over the "necessary and proper" clause, or that Marshall had himself not said in his first opinion on that clause in 1805.[88] But Marshall showed how old materials gathered from various sources could be welded by a burning passion into a new weapon for new struggles. *McCulloch* v. *Maryland* struck the first resounding blow for a broad construction of the Constitution.

There have been some commentators, and Charles Warren is a good instance,[89] who have deplored the "accident" that the

---

of Washington society had turned out to hear him. See Corwin's description of Pinkney in *John Marshall and the Constitution* (1919) 117, from a sketch by George Ticknor. Not only Story, but Marshall as well and after him Taney, considered Pinkney the greatest lawyer to have appeared before the Court.

[87] 1 Warren, *The Supreme Court in United States History* (revised ed. 1926) 529, n. 1. The quotation is from the Steubenville Herald, but essentially the same opinion was expressed by a committee of the legislature.

[88] United States v. Fisher, 2 Cranch 358 (U. S. 1805).

[89] 1 Warren, *op. cit. supra* n. 87, at 503.

strictly legal struggle over broad or narrow construction should have got tangled up with the excitement over the United Bank. But to take this view is to miss the integral connection between law and economics. The importance of the controversy over broad and narrow construction lay exactly in the uses to which it could be put by the economic interests. The newly emerging industrial capitalism of the time needed the Bank, and the Bank for its very existence needed a broad construction of national power: and Marshall came smashing through with exactly that.[90] He built on the "necessary and proper" clause a doctrine of implied national powers which could be used not only to justify the chartering of a central bank as part of the power to regulate coinage or issue currency, but could also be used to justify a national system of internal improvements. "We must not construe the Constitution," cried Henry Clay in the 1818 Congressional debate on internal improvements, "as one would a bill of indictment." [91] Marshall's decision was like a clarion response to Clay's cry: "Let the end be legitimate, let it be within the scope of the Constitution and all means which are appropriate, which are plainly adapted to that end, which are not prohibited but consist with the letter and spirit of the Constitution, are constitutional." [92]

This was brave doctrine. The Federalist party was dying, unable to survive the sectarianism it had shown during the War of 1812. A new cluster of property-interests was arising, and Henry Clay of Kentucky was a good spokesman for them: a new passion for prosperity was showing itself in the West as in the East. Clay and his group looked to the national government to exert itself to send money circulating through all the channels of trade. Marshall's nationalism was as welcome to them as to Landon Cheves, the President of the Bank, and to the corrupt and interlocking monied interests of New England, New York, and Pennsylvania.

There was, of course, an outcry against the decision.[93] But it

[90] It is worth noting that Webster, of counsel for the Bank, never had any doubt of the outcome even before the argument. 1 Warren, op. cit. supra, at 509.

[91] 31 Annals of Cong. 1165 (1818).

[92] 4 Wheat. 316, 421 (U. S. 1819).

[93] As a result of this decision, and also of Cohens v. Virginia, 6 Wheat. 264 (U. S. 1821) and some of the commerce cases, there was in Congress, in the decade 1821–31, a series of attacks on the Court.

was primarily against the second part of it, rather than the first. For Marshall, after deciding that Congress had power to charter the Bank, waved away Maryland's attempt to tax it with "the power to tax involves the power to destroy." He thus showed himself master of the two-way stretch, interpreting national powers broadly and state power narrowly. Ohio refused to recognize the decision as going beyond the case itself or relevant to her own Bank tax, and for five years carried on a guerilla warfare against Court and Bank.[94] Spencer Roane, Chief Judge of the Virginia Court of Appeals and Marshall's *bête noire*, attacked the decision in a series of letters in the *Richmond Enquirer*,[95] which so nettled Marshall that he published in the *Philadelphia Union* under a fictitious name a lengthy defense of the decision. Jefferson, writing to Roane from Monticello, must have looked back to the days when the "necessary and proper" clause had been used by the courts in upholding the Alien and Sedition laws, and when he had himself spoken with a bitter vision of the national powers to which this "filiation of necessities" might lead. He wrote now: "After twenty years . . . we find the judiciary on every occasion, still driving us into consolidation. In denying the right they usurp of exclusively explaining the Constitution, I go further than you do." [96] And Madison, far more amenable than Jefferson and Roane to the drift of events—Madison who had said in 1811 that regardless of what we might have thought originally of the constitutionality of the Bank it had been settled by twenty years of acquiescence, now wrote: "It was anticipated I believe by few if any of the framers of the Constitution, that a rule of construction would be introduced as broad as pliant as what has occurred." [97]

In taking this position, it does not follow that the Virginia dynasty was (as Warren has suggested)[98] either blaming Marshall

[94] This was settled in Osborn v. Bank of U. S., 9 Wheat. 738 (U. S. 1824). See E. L. Bogart, *Taxation of the Second Bank of the United States by Ohio* (1912) 17 *Am. Hist. Rev.* 312–3 and 1 Warren, *The Supreme Court in United States History* (revised ed. 1926) 528–38.

[95] Dodd, *Chief Justice Marshall and Virginia, 1813–1821* (1907) 12 *Am. Hist. Rev.* 776, 780–1. Roane wrote the articles under several *noms de plumes*.

[96] Letter to Roane, Sept. 6, 1819, 10 *Writings* (Ford ed. 1892) 140.

[97] Letter to Roane, Sept. 3, 1819. 8 Madison's *Writings*, edited by G. Hunt (1900) 450.

[98] 1 Warren, *The Supreme Court in United States History* (revised ed. 1926) 514, 518, 542.

for not declaring the Bank unconstitutional or implying that the Court had the exclusive power to pass on its constitutionality. Their reasoning was as follows: the Bank is unconstitutional, whoever does the interpreting; Congress has chosen to charter it, but that is Congress's affair; certainly the Court does not have the exclusive power of interpreting the Constitution; in any case, Maryland's power to tax the Bank is a part of its sovereignty as a state.

Two years later the question of state sovereignty was raised in even sharper form when two lottery vendors, the Cohen brothers, had sold in Virginia tickets for a lottery authorized by Congress in the District of Columbia. They were convicted under a Virginia anti-lottery law and appealed to the Supreme Court.[99] The only question the Virginia counsel were willing to argue was that of jurisdiction: could an appeal be to the Supreme Court from a criminal case in a state court, even where a federal question was involved? Marshall held that it did; and then, by a tactic somewhat similar to that of *Marbury* v. *Madison*, held that Congress had not intended to authorize the sale of the lottery tickets in Virginia. Thus Marshall was again willing to cede the smaller if he could gain the larger.

One result of these decisions was a renewal of the popular hostility to the Court.[100] Jefferson, who after the 1819 term had called the judges a "subtle corps of sappers and miners constantly working underground to undermine the foundations of our confederated fabric," now wrote bitterly: "the battle of Bunker Hill was not fought to set up a Pope." [101] Virginia, Ohio, and Kentucky were in full revolt; there was talk of a movement in Congress to repeal Section XXV of the Judiciary Act of 1789, which granted appellate jurisdiction to the Supreme Court over state courts and on which the Cohens' decision rested. This failed. But for the next ten years the Democrats in Congress did not cease to attack the exercise of the judicial power.

That they were unable to do anything about it was due to several causes. First, it was not clear what would take the place of the Court in the function of finality of Constitutional interpre-

[99] Cohens v. Virginia, 6 Wheat. 264 (U. S. 1821).

[100] Roane and Marshall had another passage at arms; and after Roane had attacked the decision, Marshall had the satisfaction of exerting pressure to keep the attack from being reprinted in the American Law Journal.

[101] Jefferson to Ruggles, May 3, 1822, quoted in 1 Warren, *The Supreme Court in United States History* (revised ed. 1926) 564, n. 3.

tation. Secondly, the judicial nationalism of Marshall was mixed up with too many issues that were already splitting the country —the money power as represented by the Bank of the United States; the slave power as involved in the Congressional attempt through the Missouri Compromise (1820) pending when Mc-Culloch v. Maryland was being argued and discussed to regulate slavery in the territories; and government interventionism through subsidies, which meant a good deal to the Western states. These were the controlling issues—these and the constant upswing of capitalist development and national expansion. It was Marshall's good fortune to float his nationalist judicial doctrines on this tide, when the whole tempo of economic development was in his favor, and when an attack on the Court would immediately founder on the rocks of these issues.

Marshall's handling of the commerce clause cases [102] best stamps the Golden Age of the Court's history. Article I, section 8 clause 3 of the Constitution gives Congress power "to regulate commerce with foreign nations, and among the several states." That this has become probably the most hotly contested clause in the Constitution is not at all strange, for "to regulate commerce among the several states" is a clause that reaches directly into both the nature of our economic system and the nature of our federal system. Scarcely a word of that clause but has given rise to a mountain of learned and fine-spun discussion. What does "regulate" mean: does it involve only aid, or may it mean to restrain or prohibit? What does "commerce" mean: does it mean merely transportation, or does it include the essentials of the economic process? What does "among" mean: does it mean that the power stops at the states' boundaries, or does the power extend beyond those boundaries into the state itself? Casuistries like this do not grow up of their own accord. In Marshall's and Taney's day they were part of the battle of the capitalist and industrialist versus the agrarian and slavery interests: later in the days of Fuller, White, and Day and in our times they were part of the struggle between a planless and a regulated capitalism.

Marshall hammered out his commerce clause doctrine in

[102] For discussion of the commerce clause in general, see Frankfurter's excellent little book, The Commerce Clause under Marshall, Taney and Waite (1937); Corwin, Commerce Power versus States Rights (1936); Hamilton and Adair, The Power to Govern (1937) especially 42–59, 145–183; and R. L. Stern, That Commerce which Concerns More States Than One (1934) 47 Harv. L. Rev. 335.

three principal cases—shrewdly, carefully, pragmatically. When the case of *Gibbons* v. *Ogden* [103] came up for settlement in 1824, the commerce clause was practically untrodden ground.[104] What was chiefly available, as Walton Hamilton has pointed out, was a body of verbal and business usage clustering around the word "commerce." Marshall made ample use of this. But above all else he was aiming at the sure establishment of national supremacy, and he chose his own methods.

Gibbons v. *Ogden* involved a steamboat monopoly granted by the Republican Legislature of New York to Robert Livingston, a powerful member of the Republican machine, and Robert Fulton, the inventor of the steamboat. An attempt was being made by an independent steamboat company to break up this monopoly, and it had behind it the hearty concurrence of other states and of popular opinion as a whole. Only the extreme states' rights men of Virginia and other southern states were jealous of what Marshall might do, not out of concern for navigation but because of the possible effect of his doctrine on attempts by states to set up fugitive slave laws. Marshall had to move with discretion. He listened to a brilliant array of counsel pour their eloquence out to a more than usually crowded court-room. Webster had sat up all night to prepare his argument against the monopoly. He afterward looked back with pride on the effect he had on the Chief Justice: "I think I never experienced more intellectual pleasure than in arguing that novel question to a great man who could appreciate it, and take it in; and he did take it in, as a baby takes in its mother's milk." [105]

But Webster was claiming too much. Justice Johnson, in a concurring opinion, did hold to Webster's view that when Congress was given the power to regulate commerce, it had the exclusive power whether it exercised it or not, and any state act of regulation was void. According to this view the fact that the independent steamboat company had a federal license to navigate under the federal Coasting License Act of 1793 was not

[103] 9 Wheat. 1 (U. S. 1824).

[104] See *Hamilton and Adair, op. cit. supra* note 101, at 174 *et seq.* for discussion of Jefferson's memorandum on commerce when he was Secretary of State, and Hamilton's *Report on Manufactures.*

[105] This appears in Peter Harvey's *Reminiscences and Anecdotes of Daniel Webster* (1877) 142. Webster also said, "The opinion of the Court as rendered by the Chief Justice was little else than a recital of my argument."

essential to the case. Marshall's opinion, in the words of Mr. Justice Frankfurter, "was either unconsciously or calculatedly confused." [106] In his actual decision he rests on the Federal Act as supreme over a conflicting state act; but the main part of his opinion is an essay on the commerce power as exclusively federal. No doubt he was testing states' rights opinion; he was fearful of saying too openly that state authority would henceforth be limited by the commerce clause, whether or not the federal government had acted legislatively.

What has remained, however, is not Marshall's decision but his essay; not his caution, but his daring. He had created the doctrine of the "dormant" power of the commerce clause—a doctrine that was to make of the clause a powerful engine for narrowing the scope of state power and increasing the scope of federal power.

This decision, however, and that of *Brown v. Maryland* [107] and *Willson v. Black Bird Creek Marsh Company* [108] which rounded it out, differed from the decisions limiting state powers which I have discussed in the previous section. For Marshall was not concerned here primarily with limiting state authority; he was concerned with increasing federal authority. And it is significant, therefore, that while his states' rights decisions dwell on judicial supremacy, these nationalist decisions do not. It is true that these cases were actually building up the Court's power, and that through them the Court, as well as Congress, became the arbiter of vast questions of national policy. But there is a difference of emphasis. So anxious was Marshall to uphold the congressional power to rule exclusively in its domain, as against the state power, that *Gibbons v. Ogden* contains what is, at least by implication, one of the most forceful arguments against judicial review of congressional legislation that we have in the literature.

First Marshall had defined the three crucial terms of the clause. Commerce, he said, "undoubtedly is traffic, but it is something more, it is intercourse." [109] "The word 'among' means intermingled with . . . commerce among the states cannot stop at the external boundary line of each State, but may be intro-

---

[106] *Frankfurter, op. cit. supra note* 101, at 17.
[107] 12 Wheat. 419 (U. S. 1827).
[108] 2 Pet. 245 (U. S. 1829).
[109] 9 Wheat. 189 (U. S. 1824).

duced into the interior . . . comprehensive as the word 'among' is, it may very properly be restricted to that commerce which concerns more States than one." [110] And the power to "regulate" is "to prescribe the rule by which commerce is to be governed." [111] After these definitions, Marshall is anxious to make it clear that the states cannot set up their own ideas of the wisdom of the congressional exercise of this power. That is absolute: the only restraint upon it (within the Constitution) is the self-restraint of Congress: "The wisdom and the discretion of Congress, their identity with the people, and the influence which their constituents possess at elections, are . . . the sole restraints on which they have relied to secure them from its abuse. They are the restraints on which the people must often rely solely, in all representative governments." [112] Thus Marshall, in defending congressional power over commerce, was adopting a position of national legislative supremacy which could even be used against judicial supremacy.

I am convinced that Marshall did this because the legislative power he feared was not that of Congress, but of the states. And the irony of his position is that the doctrine of vested rights (later applied to due process) and the doctrine of judicial supremacy, which he had developed in the state-power cases, combined eventually to whittle down his concept of national supremacy in the domain of the commerce power and the "necessary and proper" clause, and defeat it.[113]

5. WITH THE STREAM

We must not construe Marshall's nationalistic decisions in terms too noble and high-flown. The actual circumstances of the commerce cases which came before his Court were such that Congress was using the clause to aid and not restrain business enterprise. The two main lines of business expansion of the day were a national banking system and a national transportation system. To allow the states, always suspicious of business enterprise, to interfere with either would have been, Marshall saw,

[110] *Id.* at 194.
[111] *Id.* at 196.
[112] *Id.* at 197.
[113] See T. R. Powell, "Commerce, Pensions and Codes" (1935) 49 *Harv. L. Rev.* 1–43. See also my "John Marshall's Long Shadow" (1935) 84 *New Republic* 148.

fatal for the unimpeded development of business. To remove such obstructions, to ensure favorable conditions for business, was in the early stages of industrial capitalism the prime function of a central government. Here Congress and the Court were not yet at war with each other: it was not necessary to emphasize the Court's role of constitutional guardian as against Congress.

Marshall had here the advantage of working with the stream of history.[114] He had vision enough to see that political power had to be coterminous with the scale of economic activity. He saw it dimly and confusedly, and it was all tangled in his mind with a hatred of states' rights and of the common man, and with a protective obsession about the rights of property. But his chief historical meaning for us lies none the less in this dim insight of his.

The position of his opponents, the Virginia dynasty—Jefferson, John Taylor, Spencer Roane, Madison, and Monroe—embodied an archaic economic vision, whatever the merits of their political views. Jefferson at 82, writing in 1825, a year before his death, was bitter not only about the judicial power but the whole centralizing tendency in the national government. "Take together the decisions of the Federal Court, the doctrines of the President and the misconstructions of the Constitutional Compact acted on by the Legislature of the Federal branch, and it is but too evident that the three ruling branches of that department are in combination to strip their colleagues, the State authorities, of the powers reserved by them. . . . Under the power to regulate commerce, they assume indefinitely that also over agriculture and manufactures, and call it regulation to take the earnings of one of these branches of industry—and that, too, the most depressed—and put them into the pockets of the other— the most flourishing of all." [115] With this one must take Monroe's veto of the Cumberland Road Act of 1822. With it one must take also John Taylor's *Construction Construed and Con-*

114 Corwin remarks, and rightly, in his *Court Over Constitution* (1938) 100, that "throughout the whole latter half of his Chief-Justiceship Marshall was consciously waging an uphill fight against States Rights, or—in his own phrase—against the 'confederization of the Union.' " I agree with this in terms of constitutional and political doctrine. That accounts for the jeremiads in Marshall's letters. What he was not aware of was that in terms of economic tendency the victory was already his.

115 Letter to William B. Giles, Dec. 26, 1825, quoted in 1 Warren, *The Supreme Court in United States History* (revised ed. 1926) 620–1.

stitution Vindicated,[116] his *Tyranny Unmasked*,[117] and his *New View of the Constitution*.[118]

Taylor was the political theorist of the Jefferson school, as Roane was its constitutional theorist. Together these men were setting their faces against the future. However able (and Taylor was probably with Calhoun, the ablest anti-capitalist theorist in America until the generation of Henry Demarest Lloyd, Daniel De Leon, and Thorstein Veblen), they were dreamers. They dreamt the Physiocratic dream of a society that was even then beyond recall—a republic of small farmers. They failed to see that technology was settling that question for them. They were partly blinded by their fears for the slavery interest, and made the mistake of identifying the capitalist interest inevitably with the national power. Partly, also, they were caught by the dead hand of their own preoccupation with states' rights theory in the past. They failed to see that the issue was now not between states' rights and the national power, but between the types of national control of business that would be developed. If, instead of following a policy of states' rights obstructionism, they had come out frankly for national legislative control of the new economic forces in the interests of the agrarian as well as the industrial groups, Marshall's much vaunted nationalism would have changed its tune.

For what it amounted to was aid and tolerance for business enterprise, both on a national scale. As between a policy of states' rights obstructionism and a policy of federal jurisdiction, it was obviously the latter that was part of the victorious campaign of history.

[116] 1820, written after the *annus mirabilis* of the Court in 1819.

[117] 1822, written after *Cohens v. Virginia*.

[118] 1823. On Taylor, Beard has done a brilliant piece of work in his *Economic Origins of Jeffersonian Democracy* (1915) 197–209, 322 *et seq.* 2 Parrington, *Main Currents in American Thought* (1930) 14–19 follows him.

3. Chief Justice Taney: Prophet of Reform and Reaction

ROBERT J. HARRIS

EDITORIAL NOTE. The first term of the Supreme Court under the chief justiceship of Roger B. Taney confirmed the worst fears of panicky, morose conservatives: a Jacobin localist had taken the place of the great Marshall. As one Democratic newspaper put it concisely, "The vested rights class cry out bloody murder." Two years later, after Taney handed down an opinion for the Court repudiating a circuit court decision which was a death sentence to all interstate business conducted by corporations, a Whig newspaper exultantly editorialized, "The Supreme Court is yet sound; and much as we cherish Whig victories, yet we cherish this Conservative victory much more: it is the triumph of the Constitution and the Union again." Another Whig paper thought that Taney's opinion was as far from Locofocoism "as Alexander Hamilton himself could have desired." A few years later, Senator Henry Clay sought out Chief Justice Taney to explain that while no man had more fiercely opposed his appointment, Clay had become satisfied that no one else could have been selected better able to "wear the ermine which Chief Justice Marshall honored"—and the two men, former enemies, shook hands as tears trickled down their cheeks. A difference in emphasis, men learned, was not necessarily a difference in kind.

In the following essay on the Court under Taney, Robert J. Harris sees him, somewhat paradoxically, as the prophet of both reform and reaction. The essay, as its title might indicate, is remarkably balanced; it is also a dispassionate, comprehensive survey of the second period in the Court's history. Among its excellences is an appreciation of the infrequently understood fact that the Taney Court, though a spokesman for judicial self-restraint, considerably expanded its own jurisdiction and strengthened the national judicial power.

Many writers stumble on slavery or Jacksonianism when discussing Taney; for Harris it is the latter. His evidence scarcely supports his point that, "As a judicial spokesman of Jacksonian reform, Taney laid the foundations of the police power and the welfare state." Taney, to be sure, had a broader vision of community rights and tolerance for majority rule than did Marshall, but one could be well to the left of Marshall and still remain essentially conservative. Like Jackson himself, Taney had no part of much that is called Jacksonian democracy. He had a dim understanding of the police power, none of the welfare state. He promiscuously identified the police power as "nothing more or less than the powers of government inherent in every sovereignty to the extent of its dominions," which distinguishes it not at all from other powers, such as taxation or eminent domain. The Charles River Bridge opinion was more than the assault of the police power on vested rights; it was a conscious promotion and protection of the "millions . . . which have been invested in railroads and canals."

It misleads to say, as Harris does, "The outstanding contribution of Chief Justice Taney and the Court over which he presided was the emancipation of state power from the shackles forged for it by the Marshall Court in defense of vested interests of property and contract." The shackles were not broken, not even weakened. Taney accepted and strengthened every one of the Marshall Court's novel contract clause doctrines. Even the general doctrine in the Charles River Bridge Case, to the effect that the Court will refuse to infer from corporate franchises special privileges not expressly granted, derived from an opinion by Marshall; it was he, not Taney, who ruled that a grant of tax exemption could not be inferred. Harris makes that doctrine sound like Taney's. He misleads, too, in his discussion of the West River Bridge Case, making it seem to be an authority for the proposition that any property can be controlled in the public interest. All the Court did in that case, following quite conservative state courts, was rule that the sovereign power of eminent domain cannot be contracted away, that is, that any property might be taken by the state for a public use at just compensation, claims from the contract clause notwithstanding. Benjamin F. Wright Jr., in his study, The Contract Clause of the Constitution, which Harris does not cite, points to "the simple fact that the contract clause was a more secure and broader base for the defense of property rights in 1864 than it had been in 1835." During Taney's service the clause "was applied much more frequently and to a wider variety of subject matter."

Carl B. Swisher, Taney's biographer, explains Taney's invalidation of debtors' relief legislation on contract clause grounds, by pointing out that those cases involved the defense of landed property, rather than corporate charters. But the contract clause cases, as a group, as well as other cases involving corporations, proved unquestionably that it made no difference whether the property rights under legislative assault were in real estate or corporations. As Harris notes in connection with his discussion of the Bank of Augusta Case, corporations were the beneficiaries of several important decisions. The Bank of Augusta Case, which Harris construes as "in keeping with the theme of state sovereignty," met with outraged state protests—the reception given to many Taney Court decisions—to the effect that state sovereignty had been prostrated.

One may also question whether Harris does not place too much weight on Taney's allegedly truculent, competitive federalism and his concept of dual federalism, especially as a limitation of Congress's commerce powers. Taney rarely exalted state power at the expense of national power. His refusal to permit Marshall's dogmatic doctrine of dormant or unused Congressional power serve as a bar on state action is good constitutional law today. His doctrines of concurrent commerce powers and selective exclusiveness permitted the states to regulate commerce, even interstate commerce, in the absence of national regulation, in the absence of an actual or operative conflict between state law and national, or in the absence of a need for a uniform national rule on the subject to be regulated. These views today characterize the concept of cooperative, not competitive, federalism.

These criticisms of Harris's essay derive in part from my subjective weighting. Yet his interpretations surely represent a substantial body of scholarly opinion. On balance the essay merits high respect, not only when it is sound and illuminating, which it is for the most part, but when it exasperates, even when it stumbles.

CHIEF JUSTICE TANEY:
PROPHET OF REFORM AND REACTION

GENERAL THEORIES OF THE CONSTITUTION

Roger Brooke Taney's judicial career began and ended in controversy.[1] His appointment as Chief Justice in 1836 came not long after his nomination to be Secretary of the Treasury had been rejected and his nomination to be an Associate Justice of the Supreme Court had been indefinitely postponed because of his role as a central figure in the great controversy between the Jackson administration and the Bank of the United States.[2] These successive nominations of Taney to high position evoked a flood of partisan invective against him in an age which was hardly characterized by restraint. In the course of time, however, Taney was able to win for himself a strong position in the esteem of his fellow citizens, but he lost this position as a result of his opinion in the unfortunate Dred Scott case.[3] After this decision he was denounced with every opprobrious epithet which malignant righteousness could contrive.[4] The fluctuations in Taney's public reputation continued even after his death, but a century after the decision of the Dred Scott case his position in American constitutional history was secure.

Taney's standing as a Chief Justice is second only to that of Marshall, and this standing is due to a number of factors. First, Taney served for a very long time as Chief Justice, twenty-eight years, longer than any other save Marshall. Second, Taney's

[1] The best biography of Chief Justice Taney is Swisher, Roger B. Taney (1935). A useful account of Taney's judicial opinions and political and constitutional theories is found in Smith, Roger B. Taney: Jackson Jurist (1936).

[2] 2 Warren, The Supreme Court in United States History 285 (1924).

[3] Dred Scott v. Sandford, 60 U. S. (19 How.) 393 (1857).

[4] 3 Warren, op. cit. supra note 2, at 25. After Taney's death Charles Sumner declared: "The name of Taney is to be hooted down the pages of history. . . . He administered justice at last wickedly, and degraded the judiciary of the country, and degraded the age." Swisher, Roger B. Taney 581–82 (1935). Sumner was opposing a bill to provide for placing a bust of Taney in the Court room. It was finally placed there after the death of Chief Justice Chase when Congress authorized an appropriation for the busts of the two Chief Justices.

immediate successors as Chief Justice, Chase, Waite, and Fuller, were at best mediocre, both as presiding officers of the Court and as jurists or statesmen. Subsequent successors, with the possible exception of Chief Justice Hughes, because of brevity of tenure or lack of talents, or both, have not made any permanent imprint upon the Court as an institution because of their office as Chief Justice; although two of them, White and Stone, must be reckoned with, but largely in their capacity as Associate Justices. Third, during the twenty-eight years he was Chief Justice, Taney was the dominant figure of a Court which included such personalities as Joseph Story whose views became eccentric with the reconstruction of the Court, John McLean whose obsequiousness to presidential ambition led him to turn Whig and then Republican, James Moore Wayne, the Georgia nationalist, and John Catron, the Tennessee Democrat, to mention only some of the more outstanding of Taney's associates. Finally, as the chief of a comparatively homogeneous Court, despite fairly frequent dissents and separate concurrences, Taney had a clear-cut theory of government and the role of the Court in it which he was able to an impressive degree to imprint upon the Constitution and the Union in important contributions, some of which have proved comparatively permanent.

To a great extent Taney's constitutional views had been formed prior to his becoming Chief Justice at the age of fifty-nine. Though a Federalist originally, he was inclined toward agrarianism as befitted a member of the landed gentry of Maryland. His ideal of the good society was that he had known in Maryland which was founded upon an agricultural economy nurtured by slavery and supplemented by light industry and exchange. His ideal form of government was that which he regarded as existing under the constitution of 1789, a confederation or union of sovereign states bound together by a written constitution which was binding upon the states regardless of its nature as a compact. The general government he regarded as one of limited and express powers. The important units of government were those of the states which had not only the right but the duty to govern men and things within their dominion in such a way as to advance the welfare of all. He was skeptical of all concentrations of power and especially of economic power. These views, to be sure, were something of a paradox for even an agrarian Federalist who accepted neither the constitutional nationalism of Hamilton, Marshall, and Webster nor the particularism of the men of the Hartford Convention. Accordingly, as his party died of inanition, Taney found a congenial political home in the Jacksonian Democracy.

As attorney General and Secretary of the Treasury in Jackson's cabinet Taney had opportunities on a number of occasions to give official expression to his views on the Constitution, national and state power, and the relationship of government to the economic order. Although he personally deprecated the institution of slavery, he accepted it as a necessary fact of social existence, and contended in opinions rendered while Attorney General that slavery and the status of slaves were matters exclusively within the powers of the states, even transcending the treaty power. In this respect, indeed, he stated his views on the social and legal status of Negroes in a manner almost parallel to those enunciated in the *Dred Scott* case twenty-five years later.[5] As architect of Jackson's policy on the Bank of the United States Taney was articulate in his condemnation of the Bank's great powers over creditors, other banks, and government itself, powers "with which no corporation can be safely trusted in a republican government." [6] And in a letter to the President, designed to encourage a veto of the bill to renew the Bank's charter, he contended that "the continued existence of that powerful and corrupting monopoly will be fatal to the liberties of the people." [7] In other ways he demonstrated an antipathy to bank currency closely similar to those of that states rights agrarian and Jeffersonian publicist, John Taylor of Caroline.

The age of Jackson and of his coadjutors and successors was an age both of reform and reaction. On the side of reform a great variety of state legislation looked to the regulation of business corporations, banks, insurance companies, issues of stock, the amelioration of labor, the emancipation of women, the prohibition of intoxicants, and the further democratization of government through the extension of the suffrage and the popular election of state executive and judicial officials. However, the ominous rumblings of the slavery controversy cast a long and deepening shadow over the land, particularly after the Nat Turner slave insurrection in 1831, and a pall of reaction descended upon many of the slave states in the form of legislation repressive of slaves, free Negroes, and whites. These in turn were accompanied

5 *Swisher, Roger B. Taney* 150–55 (1935).
6 *Id.* at 166.
7 *Id.* at 228.

by fugitive slave laws, personal liberty laws in the North, and the rising tide of abolitionism, all of which tended to create an atmosphere of unreason and to tear asunder not only the party of Jackson and Taney but the Union as well. In the meantime, in one way or another, many of the issues pertaining to reforms and slavery were to come to the Supreme Court of the United States for adjudication on constitutional questions, and it fell to the lot of Taney to play a paradoxical role as the spokesman for the Jacksonian Democracy on the issues of reform and the voice of reaction on the questions arising out of slavery. Regardless of the apparent inconsistency of these roles Taney was able to bring to the resolution of perplexing questions a consistent body of constitutional theory.

First of all Taney and his Court, though not overtly reversing Chief Justice Marshall's conception of implied federal powers and liberal constitutional interpretation, were inclined to take a more literal view of the Constitution and national powers than that prevailing during the tenure of the great Chief Justice. In the *Dred Scott* case [8] Chief Justice Taney declared that changes in public opinion regarding the unfortunate status of Negroes should not induce the Court to give the Constitution a more liberal construction in their favor than they were intended to bear when the instrument was adopted. The way to change the Constitution is through amendment and until altered "it must be construed now as it was understood at the time of its adoption." Then he went on to say of the Constitution: "It is not only the same in words, but the same in meaning, and delegates the same powers to the government, and reserves and secures the same rights and privileges to the citizen; and as long as it continues to exist in its present form, it speaks not only in the same words, but with the same meaning and intent with which it spoke when it came from the hands of its framers, and was voted on and adopted by the people of the United States." [9]

Any other rule of interpretation, he contended, would abrogate the judicial character of the Court and render it a mere reflex of public opinion and popular passion. However, the question arises, how are the intent and meaning of the framers to be determined? Taney's answer is that they are to be determined by recourse to the language of the Declaration of Independence

[8] *Dred Scott v. Sandford*, 60 U.S. (19 How.) 393 (1857).
[9] *Id.* at 426.

and the Articles of Confederation, the plain words of the Constitution, state and congressional legislation, preceding, contemporaneous with, and following the adoption of the Constitution, and uniform action of the executive department. All this, of course, is a considerable departure from Marshall's sentiment that the Constitution was "intended to endure for ages to come, and, consequently, to be adapted to the various crises of human affairs." [10]

Equally remote from Marshall's conception of the Constitution as the product of the whole people of the United States, is Taney's view of it as the work of thirteen sovereign states. This view rests upon the historical fiction enunciated in *Martin* v. *Lessee of Waddell* [11] that when the Revolution succeeded "the people of each State became themselves sovereign" and succeeded to all the rights, privileges, and powers of the British Crown. Nor did they cease to be sovereign upon the ratification of the Constitution. With the exception of the powers surrendered by the Constitution "the people of the several states are absolutely and unconditionally sovereign within their respective territories" with full power to tax persons and things within their respective territories.[12] These statements, to be sure, are little more than obiter dicta hardly necessary to the points actually decided, but they do manifest an overriding solicitude for states rights even though they more nearly resemble the Madisonian conception of divided sovereignty than Calhoun's league of sovereign states.

Taney's conception of dual sovereignty and dual governments operating within the same territory permeated his constitutional theory generally and his ideas on federalism in particular. In Taney's outlook federalism was hardly harmonious in that it involved frequently recurring conflicts between angry and rival sovereignties mitigated by the benign influence of adjudication by a judicial system that was the creature of neither sovereignty and hence above the strife and conflict of jealous governments in their competition for power. As the arbiter between the Nation

[10] *McCulloch* v. *Maryland*, 17 U.S. (4 Wheat.) 316, 415 (1819).

[11] 41 U.S. (16 Pet.) 366, 410 (1842). The dicta in this case and Pollard's Lessee v. Hagen, 44 U.S. (3 How.) 212 (1845), were heavily relied upon by California, Louisiana, and Texas in the cases involving the ownership and control of oil in the *Tidelands Oil* cases. United States v. California, 332 U.S. 19 (1947); United States v. Louisiana, 339 U.S. 699 (1950); United States v. Texas, 339 U.S. 707 (1950).

[12] *Ohio Life Ins. and Trust Co.* v. *Debolt*, 57 U.S. (16 How.) 416 (1854).

and the states it was equally the duty of the Court to maintain national supremacy in its proper place and to protect the states in turn from federal encroachment upon their powers which by their own force limited federal powers and national supremacy in this *bellum omnium contra omnes* between sovereignties.

COURTS AND JUDICIAL POWER

Chief Justice Taney's conception of judicial power and the role of the courts flowed naturally from his doctrine of a truculently competitive federalism. Unlike Marshall who looked upon the federal judiciary and the Supreme Court in particular as an organ for maintaining national supremacy, expanding national power, and restraining state authority, especially when it adversely affected the vested interests of property, Taney regarded the Supreme Court as an impartial umpire between the rival sovereignties of state and nation which existed outside and beyond the national government. This conception of the role of the Court is well articulated in the great case of *Ableman* v. *Booth* [13] which, despite its nationalistic overtones, is strictly in the tradition of dual federalism. Here he sustained for a unanimous Court the power of the Supreme Court of the United States to review proceedings of state courts and held that a state court has no authority to release on habeas corpus proceedings a prisoner held in federal custody or to assume final authority to pass upon the validity of an act of Congress in language that is reminiscent in part of the opinions of Story and Marshall respectively in *Martin* v. *Hunter's Lessee* [14] and *Cohens* v. *Virginia*.[15] Though sovereign within its limits, Wisconsin's sovereignty, he declared, is limited by the Constitution of the United States. "And the powers of the general government, and of the state, although both exist and are exercised within the same territorial limits, are yet separate and distinct sovereignties, acting separately and independent of each other within their respective spheres." [16]

The main purpose of the Constitution, he declared, was "to secure union and harmony at home," and to do this it was necessary that many rights of state sovereignty be ceded to the Union, and that in its sphere of action "it should be strong enough to execute its own laws by its own tribunals, without interruption

---

[13] 62 U.S. (21 How.) 506 (1859).
[14] 14 U.S. (1 Wheat.) 304 (1816).
[15] 19 U.S. (6 Wheat.) 264 (1821).
[16] *Ableman* v. *Booth*, 62 U.S. (21 How.) 506, 516 (1859).

from a state or from state authorities." The supremacy conferred upon the national government "was clothed with judicial power, equally paramount in authority to carry it into execution" and afford a uniformity of judicial decisions upon cases arising under the Constitution, laws and treaties of the United States.[17] Had Taney stopped here he would have been following the reasoning of Marshall and Story rather closely, but he went on to assert that the judicial power was indispensable not merely to national supremacy "but also to guard the states from any encroachment upon their reserved rights by the general government." Because internal tranquility between the nation and the states was regarded as impossible without "such an arbiter" as the Supreme Court every precaution was taken to fit it for its high duty. Accordingly, he asserted:

> It was not left to Congress to create it by law; for the states could hardly be expected to confide in the impartiality of a tribunal created exclusively by the general government without any participation on their part. . . . This tribunal, therefore, was erected, and the powers of which we have spoken conferred upon it, not by the Federal government, but by the people of the states, who formed and adopted the government. . . . And in order to secure its independence, and enable it faithfully and firmly to perform its duty, it engrafted it upon the Constitution itself, and declared that this court should have appellate power in all cases arising under the Constitution and laws of the United States. So long, therefore, as this constitution shall endure, this tribunal must exist with it, deciding in the peaceful forms of judicial proceeding the angry and irritating controversies between sovereignties, which in other countries have been determined by the arbitrament of force.[18]

The net effect of the Taney Court's theories of federalism and the conception of the Court as an arbiter between clashing sovereignties was to increase the judicial power and especially that of the Supreme Court, for it meant that in addition to enforcing national supremacy the Court would police the no-man's land between the nation and the states and apply the Tenth Amendment inflated beyond its historical significance to alleged federal encroachments upon states rights. In other ways, too, Chief Justice Taney and his Court contributed to the expansion of federal judicial power. This is notably true of *Propeller*

[17] *Id.* at 517.
[18] *Id.* at 521. See Tarble's Case, 80 U.S. (13 Wall.) 397 (1872), for a similar attempt by the Wisconsin courts to challenge federal power.

Genesee Chief v. *Fitzhugh* [19] in which Taney rendered one of his better opinions. Here in a bold and creative stroke the Court rejected the restrictive English rule of admiralty jurisdiction in favor of one more suited to the geography of the United States, technological developments in transportation and the growing commerce on inland waters. In so doing the Court reversed its ruling announced by Marshall in the case of *The Thomas Jefferson* [20] where admiralty jurisdiction was confined to the high seas and upon rivers as far as the ebb and flow of the tide extended in conformity with the English rule, and upheld an Act of Congress of 1845 which extended the admiralty jurisdiction of the federal courts to the inland navigable waters of the United States beyond the ebb and flow of the tide. In justifying this result Chief Justice Taney pointed to the differences between English and American geography which rendered the principle of the ebb and flow of the tide adequate for England and the original thirteen states but inapplicable to the United States as it had grown territorially with its vast stretches of rivers and lakes comparable to inland seas as a result of the invention of the steamboat which overcame the resistance to upward passage of unchanging currents. Moreover, admiralty jurisdiction was found necessary both to the safety and convenience of commerce and the administration of laws of war. Finally, as a concession to the states, in an opinion which significantly expanded national legislative and judicial powers, Chief Justice Taney found the new rule necessary to the preservation of the principle of state equality, for without a change in the rule the newer inland states would be denied the benefits of admiralty jurisdiction enjoyed by the coastal states. The opinion and reasoning of the Chief Justice in the *Genesee Chief* represent the judicial process at its best in the fusion of legal history and principles with the raw materials of national needs, environmental factors, and subsequent political developments in national and commercial expansion in a manner that was both creative and conservative, bold and yet traditional. [21]

[19] 53 U.S. (12 How.) 443 (1852).
[20] 23 U.S. (10 Wheat.) 428 (1825).
[21] The result in the case of the *Genesee Chief* was anticipated in part in Waring v. Clark, 46 U.S. (5 How.) 441 (1847), where the Court qualified the rule in *The Thomas Jefferson* by holding that the admiralty jurisdiction of the federal courts was not limited by English rules of admiralty. This case extended admiralty jurisdiction to a boat collision on the Mississippi

Two other cases expanding the federal judicial power during the Taney period are worthy of notice. In *Swift v. Tyson* [22] Justice Story, for a majority of the Court and with Taney's silent concurrence, rendered an opinion which held that in commercial matters in diversity of citizenship cases the federal courts were not bound by state court decisions, but rather by the general principles of jurisprudence. This holding, which was designed to produce a uniformity of decisions on matters of a commercial nature, resulted in even greater diversity and confusion and represented a considerable increase in federal judicial power because in the absence of congressional legislation it meant that the federal courts would formulate the rule of decision in cases of a commercial nature loosely and broadly construed. [23] Later Chief Justice Taney opposed the extension of the formula in *Swift v. Tyson*. [24] Taney was ill during most of the 1844 term and did not participate in the hearing and decision of *Louisville, C. & C. R.R. v. Letson*. [25] The case is important both as an extension of federal jurisdiction and as illustrative of the ability of the Taney Court to accommodate itself to the exigencies of corporations. An earlier case [26] had ruled that the citizenship of a corporation for purposes of diversity jurisdiction followed that of the individual shareholders. This rule combined with that of another case [27] to the effect that in diversity proceedings all the persons on one side of the suit had to be citizens of different states from all persons on the other side was making it progressively more difficult for corporations to docket cases in the federal courts at a time when corporations were becoming more impor-

---

River ninety-five miles above New Orleans. Taney's intense interest in federal admiralty jurisdiction is reflected by his dissent in Taylor v. Carryl, 61 U.S. (20 How.) 583, 600 (1858), where he argued that the principle of judicial comity should not be extended to a conflict between a federal court sitting in admiralty and a state court on the ground that the admiralty power was superior. In respect to admiralty jurisdiction, Taney was a pronounced nationalist and was as solicitous for admiralty jurisdiction in the United States as Lord Stowell was in England.

[22] 41 U.S. (16 Pet.) 1 (1842). For an excellent account of the consequences of *Swift v. Tyson*, see Wendell, *Relations Between Federal and State Courts* 113 (1949).

[23] *Ibid.* See also *The Constitution of the United States Annotated* 604–605 (Corwin ed. 1953).

[24] Lane v. Vick, 44 U.S. (3 How.) 464 (1845).

[25] 43 U.S. (2 How.) 497 (1844).

[26] Bank of United States v. Deveaux, 9 U.S. (5 Cranch) 61 (1809).

[27] Strawbridge v. Curtiss, 7 U.S. (3 Cranch) 267 (1806).

tant as economic units in the national economy and the dispersal
of stock owners on an interstate basis was becoming more general. The *Letson* case reversed the rule governing the citizenship
of corporations and established the principle that the citizenship
of a corporation for diversity purposes is to be determined by
the state of incorporation and thereby opened the federal courts
to corporate refugees from hostile state courts.

Not all of the decisions of the Taney Court had the effect
of expanding judicial power. By expanding the "political question"
concept Chief Justice Taney indeed prepared the way for remov-
ing many issues from judicial determination and for placing
some clauses of the Constitution beyond the power of the court
to read. In doing this he created, so to speak, a kind of judicial
index librorum prohibitorum. The first great expansion of the
political question concept came in the leading case of *Luther* v.
Borden [28] where the Chief Justice delivered the opinions of the
Court holding that the question of the lawful government in
Rhode Island and the corollary issue of what is a republican form
of government as a consequence of Dorr's Rebellion were political
questions for Congress and the President, and not for the courts
to determine. Chief Justice Taney referred to the difficulties of
courts in obtaining testimony upon which to decide such issues,
the possibility of conflict with the President, and the ensuing
anarchy which would result. On such issues, the courts, he concluded, were therefore bound to take notice of the decisions of
the political branches of government and to follow them. In two
other cases in which Taney spoke for the Court the concept of
political question was extended to the recognition of foreign
governments [29] and the effect of written declarations annexed to
a treaty at the time of ratification.[30] Similarly, in his dissent in
Rhode Island v. *Massachusetts* [31] he took a restrictive view of the
Supreme Court's original jurisdiction and contended that a
boundary dispute between two states which involved sovereignty
and jurisdiction as distinguished from property was a political
question.

By a vigorous and technical construction of the term "cases

[28] 48 U.S. (7 How.) 1 (1849).
[29] *Kennett* v. *Chambers,* 55 U.S. (14 How.) 38 (1852).
[30] Doe ex dem. *Clark* v. *Braden,* 57 U.S. (16 How.) 635 (1854).
[31] 37 U.S. (12 Pet.) 657, 752 (1838). See also his dissent in the last
installment of Rhode Island v. Massachusetts, 45 U.S. (4 How.) 591, 639
(1846).

and controversies" Chief Justice Taney contributed not only to a contraction of the federal judicial power but also to a prolonged confusion concerning the types of proceedings the lower federal courts could hear and the Supreme Court could review. Building upon the foundations laid in *Hayburn's Case* [32] which held that the federal courts cannot perform non-judicial functions and another principle to the effect that they cannot render advisory opinions, Chief Justice Taney as spokesman for the Court in *United States v. Ferreira* [33] went farther to hold that the duty imposed by an act of Congress upon a territorial court to examine and adjudicate claims of Spanish subjects against the United States and to report its decisions and evidence thereon to the Secretary of the Treasury who was to pay the claims if satisfied that they were just and within the terms of the treaty with Spain was non-judicial and hence beyond the power of the Supreme Court to review upon appeal. Although he regarded the duty imposed upon the Court and the Secretary as judicial in nature, it was not judicial "in the sense in which judicial power is granted by the Constitution to the courts of the United States." Had the Chief Justice stopped here, he would have done no more than confirm the existing law, but he went on to declaim that "the duties to be performed are entirely alien to the legitimate functions of a judge or courts of justice" and to imply that an award of execution is an essential element of the federal judicial power.

In Taney's last judicial utterance, *Gordon v. United States*,[34] this implication was expressed with dogmatic finality. The case involved the act creating the Court of Claims which provided for appeals to the Supreme Court after which final judgments in favor of claimants were to be referred to the Secretary of the Treasury for payment out of any general appropriation made by Congress for the payment of private claims. Because the act made execution of the judgment of the Court of Claims and of the Supreme Court dependent upon future action of the Secretary and Congress, Taney regarded it as nothing more than a certificate of opinion to the Secretary and in no sense a judicial judgment. Congress was accordingly without authority to require the Court to take appeals from an auditor and to express an

[32] 2 U.S. (2 Dall.) 409 (1792).

[33] 54 U.S. (13 How.) 40 (1852).

[34] The case as finally decided in 1865 after Taney's death is reported in 69 U.S. (2 Wall.) 561 (1864). Taney's opinion was published as an appendix in 117 U.S. 697 (1886).

opinion upon a case in which its judicial power could not be exercised, in which its judgments would not be final and conclusive upon the parties, and in which processes of execution could not be awarded to carry judgments into effect. "The award of execution," he concluded, "is a part and an essential part of every judgment passed by a court exercising judicial powers. It is no judgment in the legal sense of the term without it." [35] This confusion of finality of judgment and an award of execution was incorporated into many subsequent Supreme Court decisions,[36] and until 1927 consequential relief was regarded as an essential element of judicial power so as to render declaratory proceedings in state courts unreviewable by the Supreme Court and to withdraw significant types of proceedings entirely from the jurisdiction of the federal courts. In *Fidelity Nat'l Bank v. Swope*[37] the Court finally took the position that an award of execution "is not an indispensable adjunct to the exercise of the judicial function" and thereby cleared a constitutional path for the Declaratory Judgment Act of 1934. Chief Justice Taney's Puritanical conception of the judicial function also led him to excoriate a feigned controversy designed to elicit a Supreme Court opinion in *Lord v. Veazie*.[38]

STATE POWER AND THE CONTRACT CLAUSE

The outstanding contribution of Chief Justice Taney and the Court over which he presided was the emancipation of state power from the shackles forged for it by the Marshall Court in defense of vested interests of property and contract. This emancipation was begun during the first term of court over which Taney presided in his great opinion in *Charles River Bridge v. Warren Bridge*.[39] Here the Court held that authorization of the construction of a bridge across the Charles River which ultimately was to become a free bridge while the charter of a toll bridge nearby had many years to run was no impairment of the

[35] Gordon v. United States, 117 U.S. 697, 702 (1886).

[36] See, e.g., In re Sanborn, 148 U.S. 222 (1893); Frasch v. Moore, 211 U.S. 1 (1908); Muskrat v. United States, 219 U.S. 346 (1911); Postum Cereal Co. v. California Fig Nut Co., 272 U.S. 693 (1927).

[37] 274 U.S. 123, 132 (1927).

[38] 59 U.S. (18 How.) 25 (1850). Despite his tendency to exalt judicial power Taney lent his concurrence to the decision in Cary v. Curtis, 44 U.S. (3 How.) 236 (1845), which upheld a broad power of Congress to regulate the jurisdiction of the federal courts.

[39] 36 U.S. (11 Pet.) 420 (1837).

obligations of a contract in reasoning which lashed at monopoly and special privilege. With a degree of contempt appropriate to a member of the landed gentry toward trade he quoted approvingly an English case [40] to the effect that in "a bargain between a company of adventurers and the public . . . any ambiguity in the terms of the contract, must operate against the adventurers, and in favor of the public," and the adventurers can claim nothing that is not clearly given.[41] In other words franchises, grants, and charters will be strictly construed and special privileges will not be deemed to be conferred by implication. This is so because "the object and end of all government is to promote the happiness and prosperity of the community by which it is established, and it can never be assumed that the government intended to diminish its power of accomplishing the end for which it was was created." [42] He then pointed to the United States as a country which was "free, active, and enterprising, and continually advancing in numbers and wealth" so that new channels of transportation and communication were necessary. Progress in communication and transportation should not be obstructed by legal rules vesting exclusive privileges in existing facilities. Otherwise we should be "thrown back to the improvements of the last century" and obliged to stand still until the claims of turnpike companies are satisfied and they are ready to permit the states "to avail themselves of the lights of modern science and to partake of the benefit of those improvements which are now adding to the wealth and prosperity, and the convenience and comfort, of every other part of the civilized world." [43]

This faith of Chief Justice Taney in reform and material progress was paralleled in *West River Bridge Co. v. Dix* [44] where Justice Daniel in the opinion of the Court in which Taney silently concurred declared that "the tenure of property is derived mediately or immediately from the sovereign power of the political body" and there is "nothing peculiar to a franchise which can class it higher, or render it more sacred than other property." All property, he continued, is held subject to "the

[40] *Stourbridge Canal Co. v. Wheeley*, 2 Barn. & Adol. 792, 109 Eng. Rep. 1336 (K. B. 1831).

[41] *Charles River Bridge v. Warren Bridge*, 36 U.S. (11 Pet.) 420, 544 (1837).

[42] *Id.* at 547.

[43] *Id.* at 554.

[44] 47 U.S. (6 How.) 507, 534 (1848).

paramount power and duty of the State to promote and protect the public good." The principles of the *Charles River Bridge* case were subsequently applied by Taney to hold that a state's taxing power was unaffected by the consolidation of two corporations because one of them enjoyed the privilege of tax exemption [45] and to refuse to extend privileges of tax exemption conferred upon banks to insurance companies.[46] In this latter ruling Taney made his customary obeisances to state sovereignty, took the position that no legislature could deprive its successors of the taxing power, asserted that since the company's charter contained no grant of a tax exemption it could not be implied, and declared that every contract in a charter presupposes that some consideration is given by the corporation that the community may benefit.

Sweeping as these assertions are of state power unrestricted by the contracts clause, they did not by any means destroy the utility of that clause as a protection to contractual rights. In *Bronson v. Kinzie*,[47] for example, Chief Justice Taney as spokesman for the Court, invalidated as applied to previous contracts an Illinois statute giving mortgagors the right to redeem property within twelve months from its sale by repaying the purchase money with ten per cent interest. Moreover, the opinion was written in terms which would have won for the most part the applause of John Marshall. To be sure the statute involved contracts between private persons, but Taney concurred in the result in the *State Bank of Ohio* case [48] where the Court invalidated an Ohio tax on banks because it was different from a semi-annual tax of six per cent on the net profits of banks in lieu of all other taxes as provided by the general banking act. Because the bank had been chartered under the earlier statute the tax provisions were regarded as a contract. Finally, Taney recognized the state court reversals of earlier decisions in exceptional situations could impair the obligations of contract as effectively as a statute.[49]

The tenor of other decisions of the Taney Court affecting corporations demonstrate that the Chief Justice and his brethren were far from being aggressively hostile toward corporations.

45 *Philadelphia, W. ℵ B. R.R. v. Maryland*, 51 U.S. (10 How.) 376 (1850).
46 *Ohio Life Ins. Co. v. Debolt*, 57 U.S. (16 How.) 416 (1854).
47 42 U.S. (1 How.) 311 (1843).
48 *State Bank of Ohio v. Knoop*, 57 U.S. (16 How.) 369 (1854).
49 *Ohio Life Ins. Co. v. Debolt*, 57 U.S. (16 How.) 416 (1854).

Among these decisions are those defining citizenship for purposes of diversity jurisdiction,[50] attempting to create a general commercial law for the whole country,[51] and extending the admiralty jurisdiction of the federal courts to all of the navigable waters of the United States,[52] all of which are discussed elsewhere in this essay. One of the more significant cases revealing the alertness of Taney to the needs of the business community is his opinion in *Bank of Augusta v. Earle*.[53] Although Taney and a majority of the Court refused to accord to corporations the privileges and immunities of interstate citizenship and admitted on the other hand that the laws of a state creating a corporation could have no extraterritorial operation, with the result that a corporation could "have no legal existence out of the boundaries of the sovereignty where it is created," they went on to hold that a corporation chartered in one state could engage in business in another in the absence of clear and express prohibitions to the contrary. This conclusion was based upon the assumption that the comity of nations bound the sovereign states of the Union under the Constitution to a greater degree than it could be presumed to bind foreign nations. The decision, to be sure, left the states free to ban foreign corporations at their discretion and in this respect was in keeping with the theme of state sovereignty so often propounded by the Taney Court.

State Power and Interstate Commerce

One of the most persistent and troublesome questions which confronted the Court from 1824 until 1851 was whether the power of Congress to regulate interstate commerce was exclusive of state power; and, if not, to what extent the states could regulate such commerce. The issue was avoided by the Marshall Court in *Gibbons v. Ogden* [54] where the New York statute creating a steamboat monopoly was invalidated as being in conflict with an act of Congress rather than being void per se under the commerce clause over the protest of Justice Johnson who argued that the power of Congress to regulate commerce was exclusive. In *Gibbons v. Ogden*, too, Marshall referred to the "immense mass" of state legislative power to enact police legislation. The

[50] *Louisville, C. & C. R.R. v. Letson*, 43 U.S. (2 How.) 497 (1844).
[51] *Swift v. Tyson*, 41 U.S. (16 Pet.) 1 (1842).
[52] *Propeller Genesee Chief v. Fitzhugh*, 53 U.S. (12 How.) 443 (1852).
[53] 37 U.S. (12 Pet.) 519, 588 (1839).
[54] 22 U.S. (9 Wheat.) 1 (1824).

question was avoided again by the Marshall Court in *Willson* v. *Blackbird Creek and Marsh Co.*[55] by the holding that Delaware could authorize the construction of a dam across a small navigable creek in the absence of an act of Congress designed to control navigation over small navigable streams. By the time Chief Justice Taney ascended the Court, the conflict between the power of Congress to regulate interstate commerce and the police power of the states had been complicated by the lengthening shadows cast by the controversy over slavery, and it is no exaggeration to say that the outlook of the Taney Court in handling commerce cases was consciously or unconsciously conditioned by considerations of the possible impact of its decisions upon slavery even in those cases in which slavery was not involved.

The first case to reach the Taney Court invoking the commerce clause and the police power was *Mayor of New York* v. *Miln*[56] where the Court, with Taney's silent concurrence, sustained a New York statute regulating ships coming into New York City in a manner designed to discourage the immigration of paupers on the ground that the statute was an internal police regulation and that persons were not a subject of commerce. Justice Barbour, who spoke for the Court, went on to invoke what he called the "undeniable and unlimited jurisdiction [of a state] over all persons and things within its territorial limits" unless restrained by the Constitution and to assert that "all those powers which relate merely to municipal legislation or . . . internal police, are not thus surrendered or restrained. . . ."[57] In other words, there is an area of state power which the commerce power cannot control and into which it cannot intrude. Ten years later the Court was again confronted with the issue in the *License Cases*[58] where the Court sustained statutes of Massachusetts, New Hampshire, and Rhode Island providing for the regulation of the sale of intoxicating liquors under license. Although the Court had no difficulty in agreeing upon the result, the judges could not agree upon the reasons for it and there were six separate opinions. Taney's opinion expressly assumed the existence of an internal traffic within each state which is separate from and independent of interstate commerce, and hence within the power of the state to regulate at its discretion and beyond the authority of Congress to control. Although a state may "pre-

[55] 27 U.S. (2 Pet.) 245 (1829).
[56] 36 U.S. (11 Pet.) 102 (1837).
[57] *Id.* at 139.
[58] 46 U.S. (5 How.) 504 (1847).

vent the introduction of disease, pestilence, or pauperism from abroad," these are not articles of commerce. Spirits and distilled liquors are articles of commerce, and since Congress authorizes their importation, no state can prohibit their introduction. However, he argued, the statutes in question did not purport to prevent the importation of liquors except insofar as the New Hampshire statute operated upon an import from another state while still in the hands of the importer for sale and thereby subject to federal control. Even so "the mere grant of power to the federal government cannot . . . be construed to be an absolute prohibition to the exercise of any power over the same subject by the States." Hence, a state may "for the safety or convenience of trade or for the protection of the health of its citizens, make regulations of commerce for its own ports and harbors, and for its territory; and such regulations are valid unless they come in conflict with a law of Congress." [59] In other words, the states have a concurrent power to regulate commerce and may exercise it not only in the absence of federal regulation, but also in conformity with existing federal regulation. If a state regulation of commerce conflicts with an act of Congress, then such regulation must yield to the supremacy clause in Taney's view.

The inability of the justices of the Supreme Court to agree upon a solution to the problem presented by the conflict between state power and the commerce clause presented itself even more dramatically in the *Passenger Cases* [60] where the Court by a vote of five to four invalidated statutes of New York and Massachusetts levying taxes upon immigrant aliens coming into their ports. Of the two statutes that of Massachusetts was the more stringent in that lunatics, idiots, paupers, and maimed, aged, and infirm persons could land only under bond as security against their becoming public charges. The New York statute also taxed at a lower rate American citizens from other states landing in the state from vessels employed in the coastal trade. Justice McLean argued that the commerce power of Congress was exclusive and should be reaffirmed. Justices Wayne, Catron, McKinley, and Grier in separate opinions thought such reaffirmation unnecessary. In dissent Taney was joined by Justice Nelson, and Justices Daniel and Woodbury dissented in separate opinions.

Taney's dissent in the *Passenger Cases* represents an extreme assertion of state authority at the expense of national power and national supremacy. As regards aliens he contended that "the

[59] *Id.* at 579.
[60] 48 U.S. (7 How.) 283 (1849).

several States have a right to remove from among their people, and prevent from entering the State, any person, or class or description of persons, whom it may deem dangerous or injurious to the interests and welfare of its citizens; and that the State has the exclusive right to determine, in its sound discretion, whether the danger does or does not exist, free from the control of the general government." [61] The power of Congress to regulate interstate commerce did not in his view prevent the states from regulating it within their own territorial limits unless in conflict with an act of Congress. Taney pointed to the selection of immigrants by ship owners or masters, in many cases foreigners, and their possible disposition to bring in the worst and most dangerous elements of the population. He invoked the specter of a "mass of pauperism and vice" flooding a state with "tenants from their almshouses or workhouses, or felons from their jails" if Congress had the power attributed to it by the Court. Although Congress in his opinion could regulate the transportation of passengers in foreign vessels, it could not compel a state to receive or retain persons who were regarded as dangerous to its peace or the health of its citizens, or a burden upon its industrious citizens. In any event, passengers were not imports and could be taxed. Despite these grandiose assertions of state power, Taney thought the New York tax on American citizens unconstitutional, and he even made a concession to nationalism. "For all the great purposes for which the federal government was formed," he declared, "we are one people, with one common country. We are all citizens of the United States; and, as members of the same community, must have the right to pass and repass through every part of it without interruption, as freely as in our own States." [62] This right he based upon the general rights of citizens of other states as members of the Union, a firmer ground than the Court has on occasion taken.[63]

[61] *Id.* at 467.

[62] *Id.* at 492. In his opinion for the Court in *Almy v. California,* 65 U.S. (24 How.) 169 (1861), Chief Justice Taney pronounced invalid a California tax on bills of lading for shipment of gold and silver outside the state. The tax was regarded as a tax on exports and was held to be indistinguishable from the tax on imports in *Brown v. Maryland,* 25 U.S. (12 Wheat.) 419 (1827).

[63] Reference is made to the bizarre opinion of Justice Byrnes in *Edwards v. California,* 314 U.S. 160 (1941), where the right of an American citizen to enter a state is rested upon the commerce clause rather than upon the privileges and immunities of interstate or United States citizenship.

The question of the exclusive nature of congressional power over interstate commerce was partially resolved in *Cooley v. Board of Port Wardens* [64] where Justice Curtis devised a formula which was approved by a majority of the Court including Taney. Under Curtis' formula emphasis was shifted from the nature of the power exercised to the nature of the subject matter regulated so that matters requiring uniform national regulation were subject to the exclusive power of Congress to regulate commerce and those not requiring it were subject to state regulation in the absence of congressional action. To be sure, the Taney court could not always agree upon those matters requiring uniform and those subject to diverse regulation as manifested by the decision in *Pennsylvania v. Wheeling and Belmont Bridge Co.*[65] A majority of the Court held invalid a Virginia statute which authorized the construction of a bridge across the Ohio River. The bridge obstructed navigation to the harassment of Pennsylvania which had expended large sums of money in canals and railroads and which saw its investments jeopardized. Chief Justice Taney and Justice Daniel dissented in separate opinions. The Chief Justice reiterated his customary theme that in the absence of congressional regulation of the subject matter Virginia's authorization of the bridge was a valid exercise of state power. Moreover, if the authorization were an evil it could easily be corrected by Congress. The failure of Congress to act did not in his belief warrant the judicial power to "step in and supply what the legislative authority has omitted to perform." [66]

From Taney's doctrines concerning the commerce power a number of propositions are explicit or implicit. First of all, there is the principle, for a time followed by the Court, that the existence of the states as political units possessed of reserved powers is a limit upon the power of Congress to regulate interstate commerce. Second, there is the assumption that there is a

[64] 53 U.S. (12 How.) 299 (1852).

[65] 54 U.S. (13 How.) 518 (1852).

[66] *Id.* at 581. Approximately two months later Congress enacted a statute which set aside the decision in this case by declaring the bridge in question to be no obstruction to navigation. The validity of this statute was challenged in *Pennsylvania v. Wheeling and Belmont Bridge Co.*, 59 U.S. (18 How.) 421 (1856). The Court upheld the act as a valid regulation of commerce, and Taney was with the majority. Justice McLean protested that Congress had no power to annul a judgment of the Court. Justices Grier and Wayne agreed with him on this issue, but concurred in the result reached.

judicially definable line between what is interstate or foreign commerce and what is purely internal commerce as distinct and separate entities. This assumption in turn envisages commerce in terms of movement which has a beginning and an end, before and after which the states, and the states alone, may regulate.[67] Finally, even in the restrictive area of national power the states have concurrent powers to regulate interstate and foreign commerce in the absence of any conflict with an act of Congress. In other words the commerce clause of its own force does not preclude state action. Such theorems, it is unnecessary to state, not only exalted state power at the expense of national authority, but some of them rested upon a narrow and technical conception of commerce inconsistent with the grand purposes of the commerce clause and totally at variance with the realities of the economic order in Taney's own age.

Taney's emphasis upon state power with the result either of weakening constitutional limitations or of minimizing national power is shown in other opinions in which he spoke for the Court, concurred, or dissented. During the first term he presided over the Court he joined the majority to sustain the power of Kentucky to authorize a state chartered bank to issue notes despite the prohibition in the Constitution against the emission of bills of credit by the states on the technical ground that the notes were not issued upon the credit of the state.[68] The effect of the decision was obviously to vest in the states a power to authorize a bank to do something they could not do themselves. In dissent Justice Story invoked the memory and views of Marshall in vain. In a brief concurring opinion in Groves v. Slaughter [69] Taney averred that the power over slavery and the introduction of slaves into their territory resided exclusively with the states and their action upon this subject could not be controlled either by virtue of the commerce power or any power conferred by the Constitution. Taney's tendency to look upon the grant of federal power as no prohibition of action by the states and to regard the union of states as possessing an international character is illustrated by his concurring opinion in Cook v. Moffat [70] where

[67] For a good treatment of the tenth amendment as a limit to the commerce power, see Corwin, The Commerce Power Versus States Rights (1936).

[68] Briscoe v. Bank of Kentucky, 36 U.S. (11 Pet.) 257 (1837).

[69] 40 U.S. (15 Pet.) 449, 508 (1841).

[70] 46 U.S. (5 How.) 295, 309, 311 (1847).

he reiterated the rule contended for earlier by Justice Johnson,[71] to the effect that the power of Congress to enact uniform bankruptcy laws is not exclusive. He then proceeded to declare that bankruptcy laws of the states have no force beyond their boundaries other than the respect and comity which the established usages of civilized nations extend to the bankrupt laws of another. How far such comity should be extended in his opinion was exclusively a matter for each state to determine for itself in the absence of any authorization by the Constitution to the federal courts to control them in this particular. Moreover, federal courts when administering state law were bound to follow the bankruptcy laws of the state in which they were sitting. A similar solicitude for state power is shown in *Mager v. Grima*,[72] where a unanimous Court speaking by the Chief Justice sustained a Louisiana tax on legacies when the legatee was not a citizen of the United States or domiciled within the state. The tax in question, he reasoned, was nothing more than an exercise of the power possessed by every state and sovereignty to regulate the manner and terms of inheritance. Because every state or nation could refuse to permit aliens to inherit property within its limits Louisiana could subject inheritance by aliens to specified conditions. Seven years later this decision was followed in *Prevost v. Greeneaux* [73] where the same tax was sustained on the ground that a subsequent treaty of 1853 with France accorded French nationals the right to take or own property in the United States if the laws of the states permitted it. Of greater significance than the ruling is Taney's comment that a subsequent treaty could not divest the state of rights of property under a tax law even if it conveyed such an intention. In other words the power of the states to regulate the holding or taking of property limits the treaty power and the power of Congress to provide minimum standards of justice for the treatment of aliens.

NATIONAL POWER

Despite its preoccupation with preserving state power in any conflict with federal authority there are cases in which the Taney Court sustained national supremacy. In many of these, to be sure, federal power was sustained in a parsimonious manner in qualified language so that the Court's enthusiasm for national power

[71] *Ogden v. Saunders*, 25 U.S. (12 Wheat.) 213, 271 (1827).
[72] 49 U.S. (8 How.) 490 (1850).
[73] 60 U.S. (19 How.) 1 (1857).

was hardly infectious. Even in *Ableman v. Booth* [74] federal judicial supremacy was asserted in terms of dual sovereignty. In a few cases, however, Taney was unqualifiedly on the side of federal power and national supremacy. In *Holmes v. Jennison*,[75] for example, the Court was evenly divided on the question of whether the Governor of Vermont could surrender a fugitive charged with murder to Canadian authorities. Joined by the nationalists, Story, McLean, and Wayne, Taney asserted that the power exercised by Vermont was a part of the foreign relations of the United States and particularly of the treaty power. The grant of power to the national government to conduct foreign relations and to make treaties when combined with the prohibition against the states' entering into any agreement or compact with a foreign power effectively rendered the national treaty power exclusive. Accordingly, any delivery of a fugitive to a foreign state would constitute an agreement or compact under the doctrine that the constitution has regard to substance and not form. He concluded by pointing to the confusion and disorder which would flow from state rendition of fugitives to foreign authorities and to the lack of any advantage that would accrue to the states. Similarly, Taney gave his tacit assent to Justice Wayne's opinion for a unanimous Court that a Pennsylvania county could not levy a tax upon the office of a captain of a federal revenue cutter on grounds of national supremacy.[76]

The relatively unimportant question of whether Tampico became a part of the United States within the meaning of the customs laws as a result of its conquest and occupation during the Mexican War arose in *Fleming v. Page*.[77] This afforded Chief Justice Taney an opportunity to discuss the nature of the war power and the powers of the President as commander-in-chief of the armed forces. The "genius and character of our institutions are peaceful," he said, "and the power of Congress to declare war was not conferred upon Congress for the purposes of aggression or aggrandizement," but to enable the general government to enforce its own rights or those of its citizens by arms. Accordingly a war declared by Congress "can never be presumed to be waged for the purpose of conquest or acquisition of territory." Although the United States may extend its boundaries by con-

---

[74] 62 U.S. (21 How.) 506 (1859).
[75] 39 U.S. (14 Pet.) 540 (1840).
[76] *Dobbins v. Erie County*, 41 U.S. (16 Pet.) 434 (1842).
[77] 50 U.S. (9 How.) 603 (1850).

quest, it can do so only by the exercise of the treaty power or legislative authority. The President cannot annex territory as commander-in-chief, because his powers in this respect are purely military and relate only to the direction and employment of the armed forces in such a way as he may deem most effectual to harass and conquer the enemy.[78] This restrictive conception of the war and his respect for private property converged in *Mitchell v. Harmony* [79] to lead Taney and a majority of the Court to limit the powers of military commanders to seize private property by holding that an army officer cannot plead in his defense in a civil suit the illegal order of a superior. Although admitting the power of the military to seize private property to keep it from falling into the hands of the enemy or to take it for public use with full compensation, in all cases "the danger must be immediate and impending; or the necessity urgent for the public service, such as will not admit of delay," and is not justified just "to insure the success of a distant and hazardous expedition." It is the duty of the Court to determine the circumstances in which private property may be taken by a military officer in time of war, and the law does not permit it "to be taken to insure the success of any enterprise against a public enemy which the commanding officer may deem it advisable to undertake."

In *Jecker v. Montgomery*,[80] a third case arising out of the Mexican War, Chief Justice Taney spoke for the Court which unanimously held that neither the President nor any military officer could establish a prize court in a conquered country and authorize it to adjudicate the claims of the United States or of private persons in prize cases or to administer the law of nations. The decision was based upon the principle that every court of the United States must derive its jurisdiction and power from the Constitution or laws of the United States under the clause in Article III which vests the judicial power of the United States in one Supreme Court and such inferior courts as Congress may ordain and establish. Accordingly, a tribunal created in Monterey by a naval commander and sanctioned by the President was held to be no more than an agent of the military power and in no sense a court of the United States with authority to adjudicate prize cases.

With such conceptions of the war power and the authority

[78] *Id.* at 614.
[79] 54 U.S. (13 How.) 115, 134 (1852).
[80] 54 U.S. (13 How.) 498 (1852).

of the President as commander-in-chief, it was inevitable that
Taney would privately question the assumption of war powers
by President Lincoln during the Civil War and that he would
officially challenge the exercise of presidential power when the
issue was properly presented in a case. On April 27, 1861, as a
consequence of disorders in Maryland Lincoln ordered General
Scott to suspend the writ of habeas corpus if in his judgment the
public safety required it. Soon afterwards an active secessionist,
John Merryman, was arrested upon military orders and confined
to Fort McHenry. A petition for his release in habeas corpus
proceedings was presented to Taney who issued the writ direct-
ing General Cadwalader to bring Merryman before him for a
hearing. Cadwalader refused to do this until so ordered by the
President, whereupon Taney directed that an attachment be
issued against him, but then the military authorities refused to
permit the marshal to enter the fort in order to serve the writ.
Taney then wrote his opinion in Ex parte Merryman [81] where he
contended that only Congress could suspend the writ of habeas
corpus and strongly denounced the President's action on the
ground that the civil administration of justice in Maryland was
unobstructed save for the intervention of the military who in
the circumstances could not lawfully supersede the civil authorities. The principle that only Congress can suspend the issue of
the writ of habeas corpus and then only in those areas where
the civil courts are not open and functioning was accepted by
the Court soon after the Civil War ended when guided by the
afterthought that springs from the wisdom of hindsight a majority
of the justices celebrated the ritual that the Constitution obtains
in war as well as peace, once the war is ended.[82] In other ways
Taney expressed his opposition to what he regarded as an arbitrary
military despotism and looked forward to a peaceful separation
of North and South as "far better than the union of all the
present states under a military government, and a reign of terror
preceded too by a civil war with all its horrors, and which end as
it may will prove ruinous to the victors as well as the van-
quished." [83]

[81] 17 Fed. Cas. 144, No. 9487 (C.C.D. Md. 1861).
[82] Ex parte Milligan, 71 U.S. (4 Wall.) 2 (1866); Duncan v. Kahana-
moku, 327 U.S. 304 (1946).
[83] Swisher, Roger B. Taney 554 (1935) (Letter to Franklin Pierce,
June 12, 1861). Interestingly enough is Taney's tacit concurrence with
Justice Grier's opinion in the Prize Cases, 67 U.S. (2 Black) 635 (1863),

Late in his career the Chief Justice wrote the opinion for the Court in *Kentucky* v. *Dennison* [84] which is representative of his views on national power as mitigated by the federal principle. The case involved the refusal of the Governor of Ohio to surrender a fugitive from Kentucky under the extradition clause of the Constitution as implemented by an Act of Congress of 1793. The language of the Constitution and the statute is as imperative as the force of words can be, but Chief Justice Taney held that the duty of a governor upon whom a demand is made for the rendition of a fugitive from justice, though mandatory, is a moral and not a legal obligation and hence unenforceable either judicially or legislatively. The reasoning of the opinion is interesting. It begins with a historical account of extradition proceedings in the American colonies, under the Articles of Confederation and the Constitution of 1789. In this account Taney lays down as historical truth the propositions that the thirteen colonies became separate and independent sovereignties by virtue of the Declaration of Independence and that the states preserved their sovereignty under the Articles of Confederation and the Constitution. Moreover, the extradition clause in Article IV is regarded as a compact among these independent sovereignties and the Act of Congress of 1793 as providing no means for compelling a state to perform the moral duty of surrendering fugitives from justice upon the requisition of other states. Nor does the Constitution arm the federal government with this power. "Indeed, such a power would place every state under the control and dominion of the general government, even in the administration of its internal concerns and reserved rights. And we think it clear that the Federal government, under the Constitution, has no power to impose on a state officer, as such, any duty, and compel him to perform it; for if it possessed this power, it might overload the officer with duties which would fill up all his time, and disable him from performing his obligations to the state, and might impose on him duties of a character incompatible with the rank and dignity to which he was elevated by the state." [85]

All this seems to be a circuitous way of saying that the gov-

---

which sustained the President's power to meet force with force in the Civil War and to institute a blockade of Confederate ports in the absence of a declaration of war by Congress. Taney did dissent to the Court's decision concerning one of the vessels condemned as prize of war.

[84] 65 U.S. (24 How.) 66 (1861).

[85] *Id.* at 107.

ernor of a state cannot refuse to surrender a fugitive from justice
in extradition proceedings, but if he does, nothing can be done
about it. Such a line of reasoning not only runs counter to the
"necessary and proper" and "supremacy" clauses of the Constitution, but in rendering the extradition clause totally impotent,
it ran counter to one of Taney's own cherished canons of constitutional interpretation. This doctrine was that in expounding
the Constitution "every word must have its due force and appropriate meaning; for it is evident that no word was unnecessarily
used or needlessly added." [86] The opinion, however, did conform
to his conception of dual sovereignties operating through the mal-
feasance of circumstance in only one geographical area.

SLAVERY

Disasters of the magnitude of the Dred Scott case are neither
born of immaculate conception nor produced through spontaneous generation. Indeed, as regards the Dred Scott opinion, events
and Supreme Court decisions in some ways seemed to have been
marching in step to an inexorable tragic dénouement. In the
disposition of constitutional issues arising from slavery Chief
Justice Taney and his Court brought to bear doctrines expounded
in decisions having no direct relation to the "peculiar institution,"
although references to slavery in some of these opinions [87] lend
partial support to the conclusion that the Court devised such
contrivances as dual federalism for the purpose of handling slavery
cases presented to it. In any event the doctrine of state sovereignty which the Taney Court had used so effectively to permit
the states to embark upon social and economic reforms was
equally potent as an instrument for the protection of slavery and
the advancement of reaction.

In Groves v. Slaughter [88] the opinion of the Court by Justice
Thompson held that a provision of the Mississippi constitution
prohibiting the importation of slaves as merchandise after 1833
was not self-executing and that in the absence of implementing
legislation contracts to bring slaves into Mississippi for sale were
valid. However, the anti-slavery McLean, ever eager to decide
issues arising out of slavery on a broader basis than the case
necessitated, wrote a concurring opinion in which he pointed

[86] Holmes v. Jennison, 39 U.S. (14 Pet.) 540, 570 (1840).
[87] Notably, Taney's opinion in the Passenger Cases, 48 U.S. (7 How.)
282, 464, 474 (1849).
[88] 40 U.S. (15 Pet.) 449 (1841).

to the exclusion of slaves from the operation of the commerce clause by the compromise concerning the slave trade and concluded that the power of slavery being local in character belonged to the states. Such a power was necessary to them in order to protect themselves against "the avarice and intrusion of the slave dealer" and to guard its citizens "against the inconveniences and dangers of a slave population." The right to exercise this power he placed "higher and deeper" than the Constitution and rested it upon the law of self-preservation.[89] This provoked Taney into writing a brief concurrence in which he asserted that the power over slavery was exclusively vested in the states and that slavery could not be controlled by Congress under the commerce clause or any other provision of the Constitution.

One of the more troublesome issues arising out of the slavery controversy was the question of national and state power over the capture and return of fugitive slaves. In *Prigg* v. *Pennsylvania* [90] the Court invalidated a Pennsylvania statute relating to fugitive slaves, and by implication all other statutes thereon, because the power of Congress to enforce the provisions of the Constitution providing for the surrender of escaped slaves was held to be exclusive and by its own force to prohibit state action on the subject. In his opinion for the Court Justice Story also intimated that it might be unconstitutional to impose upon the states the obligation to enforce the duties of the federal government. The nationalistic opinion of Story evoked protests from a strong minority of the Court who concurred in the result. Taney objected in particular to those portions of the opinion holding the power of Congress over fugitive slaves to be exclusive and implying that state officials were absolved from any duty to protect an owner's right to fugitive slaves. Justices Thompson, Baldwin, and Daniel also took exception to the opinion. Justice Wayne concurred altogether with Story, and Justice McLean differed on only one point, that concerning the lack of any obligation of the states to enforce the fugitive slave law. Justices Catron and McKinley tacitly concurred in Story's opinion. The plethora of opinions in the *Prigg* case and the divergent reasoning expounded in them provoked the acidulous John Quincy Adams with usual exaggeration to characterize the opinions as "everyone of them dissenting from all the rest, and everyone coming to the same

[89] *Id.* at 508.
[90] 41 U.S. (16 Pet.) 539 (1842).

conclusion, the transcendent omnipotence of slavery in these United States, riveted by a clause in the Constitution." [91]

One fact that the Prigg decision did indicate was that the Court was sharply and almost hopelessly divided over the issues arising out of the slavery controversy whenever it went beyond the bare necessities of the case to decide questions on a broader basis. The case could readily have been settled upon the basis, which Story himself discussed, that the Fugitive Slave Act superseded all state legislation on the subject; and had that been done the Court undoubtedly would have been less divided despite the nationalistic tendencies of McLean and Wayne to hold the powers of Congress generally exclusive and hence prohibitory of state action. Whether considerations of this nature influenced the Court is a matter of rank speculation, but eight years later the Court achieved a remarkable unity in a slavery decision with only two brief concurring opinions. The case was Strader v. Graham,[92] involving the status of slaves who occasionally were carried by their masters into Ohio temporarily and then returned to Kentucky. Speaking for the Court, Chief Justice Taney pointed to the "undoubted right" of every state "to determine the status, or domestic and social condition of the persons residing within its territory," except insofar as state power may be limited by the Constitution. He found nothing in the Constitution to control the law of Kentucky upon this subject, and concluded that the status of the Negroes depended altogether upon the laws of Kentucky after their return to the state. The Strader decision by virtue of its confinement to the narrow issues presented in the case pointed to a moral, but the justices either did not comprehend; or if they comprehended they did not heed, with tragic consequences to the country and the Court.

In most relevant respects the Dred Scott case resembled Strader v. Graham. Like the slave musicians who had been taken to Ohio the previously anonymous Dred Scott had also been taken by his master from a slave state, Missouri, into free territory, first to Illinois for approximately two years and then to Fort Snelling in the Territory of Upper Louisiana for approximately two more years after which his master returned to Missouri with Scott and his family. Ultimately the Scotts were sold to Sanford who was close to the abolitionist movement and consented to the bring-

---

[91] Quoted in 2 Warren, op. cit. supra note 2, at 359.
[92] Strader v. Graham, 51 U.S. (10 How.) 82, 93 (1851).

ing of friendly proceedings in the state courts to determine Scott's status. The Supreme Court of Missouri ruled that Scott was still a slave under the laws of the state. Scott then brought a suit in the United States Circuit Court in Missouri which decided his case in the same way. The only differences between Dred Scott's case and *Strader v. Graham* were: first, that Scott had been removed to free territory for a longer period of time than the minstrel slaves, and once into a territory of the United States in which slavery had been prohibited by the Missouri Compromise; and, second, that he had brought suit subsequently in a federal circuit court and thereby raised the issue of his citizenship. Neither of these differences was sufficient to warrant a departure from the manner used in disposing of the *Strader* case, but after a second hearing the Court decided to determine the broader issue of Scott's citizenship and the constitutionality of the Missouri Compromise.

The reasons for the Court's singular action in deciding the merits of the *Dred Scott* case over which it had no jurisdiction are well known, are outside the domain of constitutional law, and need no detailed recapitulation. Suffice it to say that as the slavery controversy grew in bitterness and intensity, it increased the hazards to the political life expectancy of statesmen in and out of Congress. Accordingly an effective majority in Congress supported by ambitious politicians outside was more than eager to shift the settlement of the slavery dispute and the responsibility for it to the Supreme Court under a policy of congressional non-intervention which was incorporated into law by the Great Compromise of 1850 [93] and the Kansas-Nebraska Act of 1854.[94] A few years later that uneasy and inept politician, James Buchanan, as President-elect of the United States was corresponding with two justices of the Supreme Court in an effort to induce Justice Grier to join with other judges to settle the slavery issue and take it out of politics.[95] Moreover, Justice McLean whose

[93] 9 *Stat.* 446, 453 (1850).

[94] 10 *Stat.* 277 (1854). The various proposals in Congress to leave to the Court the settlement of the issue of slavery in the territories is well told in Mendelson, *Dred Scott's Case—Reconsidered*, 38 *Minn. L. Rev.* 16 (1953). See also 2 *Warren, op. cit. supra* note 2, at 481–98; McLaughlin, *A Constitutional History of the United States* 513–14, 520–22, 525–26, 540–50 (1935).

[95] Catron wrote a letter to Buchanan suggesting that he "drop Grier a line" concerning the necessity of settling the agitation over slavery. Buchanan apparently did so, and Grier wrote to Buchanan a detailed account of how

flaming presidential aspirations were never snuffed by lack of
air in the judicial sanctuary made it known that he and Justice
Curtis would discuss the merits of the case in dissents, and
thereby in a sense provoked the other judges to answer them.
It is most probable, too, that Taney and his brethren actually
believed they could settle a political question within the framework of judicial procedure. Finally, the action was perhaps but a
logical culmination to what had been an overweening solicitude
for property in the form of slaves even to the evisceration of
national power. But whatever the reasons, the majority of the
Court abandoned its original plan to dispose of the case on
narrow issues and what was to have been Justice Nelson's opinion for the Court based on *Strader* v. *Graham* became only one
in a series of six concurring opinions following that of Chief
Justice Taney's opinion for the Court.

In reaching the conclusion that Dred Scott was still a slave,
despite his nomadic wanderings as the servant of an army officer,
Chief Justice Taney laid down three propositions any one of which
was more important than the status of Dred Scott. The first was
that the Negro was not a citizen of the United States or of any
state and could not become a citizen under the Constitution. In
the second place, Taney ruled that Congress had no power to
regulate slavery in the territories under a very narrow interpretation of congressional authority over territories generally. Finally,
he dragged in the due process clause of the fifth amendment by
the scruff of the neck to assert without further support that an
act of Congress which deprived a person of his liberty or property
because he came or brought his property into a territory of the
United States "could hardly be dignified with the name of due
process of law." [96] Aside from noting that this was the first time
that an official opinion of the Supreme Court of the United
States expressly held the due process clause to be a limitation
upon legislative power no other comment is necessary. The first
two propositions are worthy of analysis because of the labyrinthine
reasoning underlying them.

To support his conclusion that a Negro was not and could

---

the judges were to treat the case and showed it to Wayne and Taney. These
letters are reproduced in 3 Warren, *op. cit. supra* note 2, 16–19. In his inaugural address on March 4, 1857, Buchanan, who already knew what the
Court's decision would be, pronounced the issue of slavery in the territories
"a judicial question."

[96] 60 U.S. (19 How.) at 450.

not be a citizen of a state or of the United States Taney emphasized citizenship in terms of those persons who were citizens at
the time of the adoption of the Constitution. This led him to
make the frequently distorted and misunderstood assertion that
at the time of the adoption of the Constitution Negroes were
considered "as a subordinate and inferior class of beings, who
had been subjugated by the dominant race, and whether emancipated or not, yet remained subject to their authority, and had
no rights or privileges but such as those who held the power
and the government might choose to grant them." [97] Taney then
invoked English law, colonial legislation, and early state statutes
to argue that the Negro was not a citizen of the United States
or of any state at the time of the adoption of the Constitution.
Much of the legislation cited bore little or no relevance to citizenship including as it did prohibitions against miscegenation, requirements for the registration of free Negroes, prohibitions
against the education of Negroes, and exclusion of Negroes from
the militia and the suffrage. He also appealed to the texts of the
Declaration of Independence, the Articles of Confederation, and
the Constitution. The spurious nature of these arguments was not
neglected by the dissenters. Justice Curtis' dissent is particularly
relevant: first, for its emphasis upon the rule prior to the Fourteenth Amendment that state citizenship was primary and national citizenship secondary so that native born citizens of a state
were also citizens of the United States; and, second, for his
citation of laws showing that Negroes were citizens of five states[98]
and therefore citizens of the United States at the time of the
adoption of the Constitution.

Having determined that Dred Scott was not a citizen and the
federal courts had no jurisdiction of the suit under that clause of
the constitution extending the judicial power to suits between
citizens of different states, Taney might have concluded his opinion; but he and a majority of the Court were men with a mission.
Hence, they were dangerous, as men with a mission sometimes are
when they miscalculate the consequences of their acts. And lawyers and judges, of all people, insist most upon the principle
that a man intends the consequences of his acts. Accordingly,
Taney proceeded with even more spurious reasoning to decide

[97] *Id.* at 404–05.

[98] *Id. at* 572–89. The states were Massachusetts, New Hampshire, New
Jersey, New York, and North Carolina.

the delicate issue of the power of Congress to regulate slavery in the territories, an issue which most judicious and ambitious politicians had avoided out of temerity, prudence, or both.

To substantiate the conclusion that Congress has no general power of legislation in territories of the United States Taney construed most narrowly the power of Congress "to dispose of and make all needful Rules and Regulations respecting the Territory or other Property belonging to the United States." This power, Taney argued, had no connection with the general powers of legislation delegated to the Federal Government, but was associated with a specified power over movable property. Moreover, he argued that the term "rules and regulations" was employed in contrast to general powers of legislation and therefore conferred no power upon Congress to prevent a citizen from taking his property into a territory of the United States. From this argument Taney proceeded to declare that Congress had no constitutional power to acquire and maintain colonies to be ruled at its own pleasure and no authority to enlarge its territorial limits in any way except by the admission of new states. Hence citizens of the United States who migrate to a territory of the United States could not be treated as colonists. Whatever territory the federal government annexes "it acquires for the benefit of the people of the several States who created it. It is their trustee, acting for them, and charged with the duty of promoting the interests of the whole people of the Union in the exercise of the powers specifically granted." [99] The power to acquire territory, Taney grudgingly conceded, carried with it the power to establish a government for it, and with respect to the form of government he conceded to Congress a broad discretion. However, when territory is acquired "the Federal government enters into possession in the character impressed upon it . . . with its powers over the citizen strictly defined, and limited by the Constitution" [100] in terms of express prohibitions, delegated powers, and the character of the Union as a federation "of States, sovereign

[99] 60 U.S. (19 How.) at 450. The argument that territory can be acquired only for the purpose of forming one or more states was perhaps not wholly consistent with the aspirations of pro-slavery imperialists to acquire territory that would have required long tutelage to become a state if indeed it ever would have; but after all there was little consistency in the constitutional arguments of either side in the agitation over slavery.

[100] *Id.* at 449.

and independent within their own limits . . . and bound together by a general government, possessing certain enumerated and restricted powers." [101]

In the process of his argument Taney quoted but misconstrued Marshall's opinion in *American Ins. Co. v. Canter* [102] where it was made clear that whatever the source from which Congress derives the power to govern territories it is unquestionable. However, as regards federal authority Marshall and Taney had their own different definitions of the power to govern; and with respect to territory Taney used his cherished concept of dual sovereignty to limit federal power to acquire it and to govern it afterwards. In any event he limited the war and treaty powers as sources of power to acquire territory by what Justice Holmes once called the "invisible radiation from the general terms of the 10th amendment" [103] and emasculated the power of Congress to govern territories which in the last analysis is as broad within a territory as that of a legislature is within a state. In so doing he ignored Marshall's admonition against construing the Constitution as though it were a deed or a contract and repudiated some of his own conceptions of governmental power and the adaptation of the Constitution to the growth of the country and technological developments. The consequences to the Court over which he presided were disastrous. To protect slavery, Taney performed an act of judicial immolation from which the Court did not recover until approximately a quarter of a century later when it aligned itself with the rising industrial oligarchy as the guardian of the kind of property Taney would have liked least.

CONCLUSION

Two major themes characterize Taney's constitutional opinions. One has to do with the power and duty of government, primarily the state governments, actively to legislate for the health, happiness, and welfare of all the people. The other is the theme of dual sovereignty with emphasis upon a limitation of national power. The first theme has such corollaries as beliefs in progress, in the adaptation of law to new conditions, in the limitations of the judicial power to decide issues of social policy, and hence in the competence and power of the legislature. The

[101] *Id.* at 447–448.
[102] 26 U.S. (1 Pet.) 511, 542 (1828).
[103] *Missouri v. Holland,* 252 U.S. 416, 434 (1920).

second theme with its emphasis on a precise line of demarcation between national and state power subject to judicial determination under an unchanging Constitution has as its corollaries conceptions of inactive government at the national level, of a static and conceptualistic jurisprudence, of the omnicompetence of the federal judiciary, and of a Congress of narrowly contracted powers. The first theme was and in a real sense continues to be a prophecy of reform; the second for a long time was a prophecy of reaction as regards judicial interpretation and continues to be such in a political context.

As a judicial spokesman of Jacksonian reform Taney laid the foundations of the police power and the welfare state. As a spokesman of reaction he contributed to the erection of a superstructure of constitutional limitations which long after his death was to obstruct Congress in its efforts to regulate the national economy characterized by clusters of concentrated economic power greater than that ever possessed by the United States Bank,[104] and to hamper national attempts to mitigate the conditions of labor.[105] Moreover, by infusing the due process clause with a substantive content as a limit upon congressional power he contributed in part to the conversion of due process into an instrument for the judicial veto of state legislation enacted in pursuance of the police power.[106] To be sure Taney could hardly have anticipated the consequences of his doctrines, and if he had he would hardly have approved of some of the uses to which they were put. After all, Taney, in emphasizing states rights, did believe in the active exercise of state powers and in this respect was intellectually remote from those antagonists of governmental power who later used the tenth amendment to constrict national power and, simultaneously, the fourteenth to restrict state power

[104] The more notable dual federalism cases limiting congressional power to regulate the economy under the commerce and taxing powers are: Carter v. Carter Coal Co., 298 U.S. 238 (1936); United States v. Butler, 297 U.S. 1 (1936); Schechter Poultry Corp. v. United States, 295 U.S. 495 (1935); United States v. E. C. Knight Co., 156 U.S. 1 (1895).

[105] Carter v. Carter Coal Co., 298 U.S. 238 (1936); Schechter Poultry Corp. v. United States, 295 U.S. 495 (1935); Bailey v. Drexel Furniture Co., 259 U.S. 20 (1922); Hammer v. Dagenhart, 247 U.S. 251 (1918).

[106] Lochner v. New York, 198 U.S. 45 (1905); Coppage v. Kansas, 236 U.S. 1 (1915); Charles Wolff Packing Co. v. Court of Industrial Relations, 262 U.S. 522 (1923), and the line of cases following it; Smyth v. Ames, 169 U.S. 466 (1898), and its progeny of cases, among others.

over the same subject matter. His basic error in this respect was his confidence in the capacity of the state governments to control large segments of economic power which like the Bank challenged the authority of all government, national and state. In relying upon state power for executing most of the great tasks of government Taney lacked the tough realism which was characteristic of his thought on the Bank and corporate charters.

To say that Taney was a prophet of reform and reaction is to speak in terms of paradox; but Taney's life and career were in many respects a paradox, both personally and officially. As a Catholic educated at a Presbyterian college, he imbibed the tenets of each religious faith, and his political beliefs reflected the influence of each. However, in his belief in material progress, his lack of sympathy, except in an abstract way, for paupers, slaves and other submerged persons, he was closer to the man from Geneva and the Puritan than to the Catholic ethic. Similarly, his lack of concern for the natural law was not Catholic. Emphasis upon the positive law led in turn to a neglect of natural rights and personal liberty. Taney's only concern for personal liberty is reflected in his opinions on Lincoln's conduct of the Civil War by the exercise of what he regarded as despotic military powers and his fear of the Bank as a threat to the liberty of the people in a political context. Moreover, liberty like the right of property, and other rights, was founded on the positive law. Physically Taney combined extremely frail health with excessive longevity, and physical frailty contributed to an asceticism in his private life and his judicial utterances. As a descendant of an indentured servant he did not care to have many more like his ancestor enter the country. As a man of a reticent and retiring nature he lived much of his long life in the spotlight of public controversy which he did not relish, but from which he did not shrink.

As a jurist he made significant innovations in constitutional law without destroying its continuity and he supplemented Marshall's work in such a way that much of constitutional law ever since has been based upon the respective foundations laid by these two Chief Justices, sometimes the foundations of Marshall, sometimes those of Taney, and sometimes those of each in combination. Although it would be oversimplification and even exaggeration to say that constitutional interpretation after 1937 has been nothing more than a blend of Marshall's and Taney's views on national power and social legislation respectively, it is true that since 1937 the Court has generally followed Marshall in its conceptions of national power and Taney when he spoke as the prophet of reform. Marshall and Taney were great Chief Justices in their separate ways, but each lived long enough to corroborate at least partially Justice Holmes' harsh dictum that "all society rests on the death of men." [107]

[107] 1 *Holmes-Laski Letters* 431 (Howe ed. 1953).

4. The Path of Due Process of Law

WALTON H. HAMILTON

EDITORIAL NOTE. Walton H. Hamilton's superb essay on "The Path of Due Process of Law" combines wit, grace, and trenchancy with a philosophic touch that makes constitutional history an exciting excursion into the history of ideas. His subject is a major event in the theology of constitutional jurisprudence: the miraculous transubstantiation of process into substance and human rights into vested rights. Such was the result of surgery by judicial metaphysicians operating on the recently adopted Fourteenth Amendment. The accomplishment was revolutionary; its development, evolutionary. It was also bizarre, haphazard, and unplanned.

In Hamilton's account the Lochner decision of 1905, striking down a New York statute that fixed a ten-hour working day for bakery employees, climaxed the evolution. That decision, he rightly says, was "an apostolic letter to the many legislatures in the land, appointing limits to their police power and laying a ban upon social legislation." The Lochner case certainly brought to full flower the liberty of contract doctrine, drawn from the substantive interpretation of the due process clause. But substantive due process had "first won in a clean-cut combat with the police power" in 1898, not 1905, when the Court, in Smyth v. Ames, held unconstitutional state-fixed railroad rates which did not permit what the company—and the Court—thought to be a "fair" profit. Rate fixing by economic formulas not approved by the Court was denounced as a deprivation of property in violation of due process of law.

The Smyth, case which plunged the Court into the economic thicket of utility regulation, deserves to be remembered, along

129

with the Lochner case, as having placed the Court on the threshold of a new era of judicial power. By filtering through the Fourteenth Amendment the entire range of social and economic legislation passed by the states, the Court became a superlegislature controlling the direction of American public policy. The famous comment by Justice Holmes, that the Fourteenth Amendment had not enacted Herbert Spencer's Social Statics was, in effect, a monumental mistatement of the facts. Constitutional law, permeated with the principles of classical economics and social Darwinism, became sword and shield for entrepreneurial liberty. "The capitalist," as Brooks Adams wrote, had good reason to regard the Constitution "as a convenient method of obtaining his way against a majority." Armed with its substantive interpretation of due process, which made the Fourteenth Amendment a bundle of property rights, the Court exercised judicial review with reckless abandon. From Smyth v. Ames through the constitutional crisis of 1936, there were 401 decisions invalidating state legislation, of which 212 were in cases involving the Fourteenth Amendment. In the entire history of the Court before 1898 there had been only 171 cases, involving all parts of the Constitution, in which state legislation had been judicially vetoed.

Hamilton narrates that part of the story by which the Court forged the substantive doctrines which enabled it to place the sign of the almighty dollar on the Fourteenth Amendment. But it is a story of several dimensions. Hamilton does not relate the part which made the amendment the graveyard of Negro hopes, nor the part which made it a withered wasteland for the historic procedural rights which due process once exclusively connoted. The Court found in the amendment no bar against compulsory racial segregation and no authority for Congressional protection of civil rights. The Slaughterhouse case, whose seminal contributions to property rights are so luminously discussed by Hamilton, was also the point of departure for a line of opinions that left the freedman to the tender mercies of their former white masters. The Court ruled that although the amendment protected the privileges and immunities of United States citizenship, the great bulk of fundamental civil rights derived from state citizenship; they were therefore beyond the powers of federal protection.

As for the procedural rights of the criminally accused, the Court's interpretation of due process in its once orthodox sense was mean and shriveling. In a 1900 case the Court capped the trend of decision by suggesting, contrary to history, "Trial by jury has never been affirmed to be a necessary requisite of due process of law." In 1915 the latitudinarian substantive interpretation of due process concluded, in one case, in the voiding of a state prohibition of yellow-dog contracts, while in another case an application of the procedural interpretation forced Holmes, dissenting, to protest, "Mob law does not become due process of law by securing the assent of a terrorized jury." The Court could see in the Fourteenth Amendment's clauses only constitutional limitations on the power of government to touch business enterprise. The regulation of employment agencies, minimum wage legislation, price fixing, a ban on the labor blacklist, and many other reforms were deemed violative of due process. In one case the Court, endorsing the claim of a street-car company to a return of 7.44% on the value of its property, ruled that municipally fixed rates yielding 6.26% were "confiscatory" and thus a denial of due process.

Hamilton traces only the genesis of substantive due process, not its apocalypse. He covers only 1873–1905, a single degeneration. But it is a tale filled with fascination and awe, mighty in its implications, devastating in its fulfillment. Not the least part of the tale is the way a whole clause of the Constitution, intended to protect the privileges and immunities of United States citizenship, virtually "disappeared," as Hamilton says, from constitutional law, a victim of judicial interpretation. Yet he muses whether just one more vote in the Slaughterhouse case would have made any difference in the long run. Had Bradley's views rather than Miller's prevailed, what was accomplished under the due process clause might have been accomplished under the privileges and immunities clause. The change might simply have been one of form and style rather than content, so compelling were the pressures of business enterprise on society and the law.

THE PATH OF DUE PROCESS OF LAW

I

In the law the judgment of yesterday is the precedent of today. The words are set down in the reports, and there they abide for all time to be drawn upon now and then as "the opinion of the court" demands. The meaning is rooted in the case and the occasion, the exchange of views in executive session, the idiom of the day, the temper of the times, the preferences of the judges. Its specific reference and concrete meaning are inseparable from the record which called it into being; and along with these, it gradually recedes into the mists of legal history. As in a continuous process judgment follows judgment into precedent, a doctrine is fashioned. Its raw material is a common sense which comes from without the law; its lines take on content from the prevailing opinion to which it is exposed; it is hammered into shape through a conflict of interests within a formidable procedure of litigation by unlike-minded jurists. As a product of a protracted intellectual process it is a part of all that it has met. It is rare that a legal rule which rides high is the rule "originally laid down" in "the leading case"; and a doctrine on the make, like its human kin, usually exhibits scant respect for its humble beginnings.

In an era of constitutional law that flickers to a close no doctrine has enjoyed greater prestige than "due process." It has come to be the symbol habitually invoked by private right, the barrier that guards the frontiers of business against the interference of the state, a sanction by which the judiciary reviews the work of the legislature. It has woven itself into the folkways of an industrial culture and called into being an august corpus of the law. Yet into an eminence that already shows signs of decay it has emerged out of an estate of little repute. The account of its coming-up in the world is among the most dramatic of stories. It bristles with color and conflict, with surprise and paradox. A novelist who made ideas his characters would not—for fear of provoking disbelief—have dared to allow his imagination to contrive such a series of events. Yet beneath the curious rhetoric of case and coincidence, of confused citation and vagrant judgment, the logic of events was always in command of a doctrine headed for parts unknown.

It all began quietly enough. The phrase "due process of law" is of ancient lineage. For a long time it had been an authoritative term for the established ways of justice. An injunction that "no person" shall "be deprived of life, liberty or property without due process of law" had for decades reposed quietly within the Fifth Amendment. It served a necessary purpose in forestalling arbitrary imprisonments, in preventing seizures of possessions, in compelling resort to ordinary procedures, and in forbidding public officials to act without legal warrant. But in all the years that stretched away from the early days of the Constitution to the close of the Civil War it was not an invitation to those who found acts of Congress distasteful to appeal to the judiciary for relief. Save for an *obiter dictum* here and there—as by Mr. Chief Justice Taney in the Dred Scott case [1]—the records of the United States Supreme Court are singularly unconcerned over what later became so mighty a matter. A like provision adorned with procedural concern the constitution of many a state. As the Civil War approached, a New York court declared that due process had to do with the substance of legislation; [2] and in litigious cause or congressional speech state acts which denied to freed men of color the full privileges of citizenship were challenged as against due process of law. But such a demand for a substantive reading was casual and lacked authority. If there was a higher law in whose name legislation might be struck down by a court, it was elsewhere in the Constitution or in the great unchartered domain of natural rights. In reputable opinion due process of law was firmly fixed within the ancient domain of procedure.

It was the Civil War which disturbed the verbal calm. The course of events made the emancipation of the slaves a military and political necessity. The ways of thought again became receptive to the philosophy of Mr. Jefferson and to the self-evident truths of the Declaration of Independence. The rights "to life, liberty and the pursuit of happiness"—already inalienable within an order of nature—were written into the constitutions of several of the conquered southern states. An injunction in perpetuity against slavery and involuntary servitude were made a part of the supreme law of the land, and a correlative amendment undertook to safeguard the rights of the newly enfranchised blacks. It began with the novel declaration that "all persons born or naturalized in the United States and subject to the jurisdiction thereof, are citizens of the United States and of the state wherein they reside." Then, in words whose revolutionary character could be appreciated only by men of the age who had been steeped in an older political philosophy, it was provided that "no State shall make or enforce any law which shall abridge the privileges or immunities of citizens of the United States; nor shall any State deprive any person of life, liberty, or property without due process of law; nor deny to any person within its jurisdiction the

[1] *Dred Scott* v. *Sanford*, 19 Howard 393 (1856).
[2] *Wynchamer* v. *People*, 13 N.Y. 378 (1856).

equal protection of the laws." A number of other provisions, all
relating to matters growing out of the late rebellion, were followed by a final section which granted, not to the courts but
"to the Congress," "power to enforce, by appropriate legislation,
the provisions of this article." A little later the Constitution
was made further to stipulate that "the right of citzens of the
United States to vote shall not be denied or abridged by the
United States or by any state on account of race, color, or previous condition of servitude." In occasion, ideology, and intent
the Fourteenth Amendment seems clearly of a piece with the
Thirteenth and the Fifteenth.

Yet high authority would dismiss context as irrelevance and
would have construction accept "the plain and obvious meaning
of the words." The bother is that the language is general and
abstract. The clauses are filled with verbal symbols quite receptive to a content strong enough to possess them; not one single
concretion is to be found to suggest interpretation or to point
direction. The language is exposed to the greatest of all historical
fallacies, which is to confuse event with intent and to read the
exposition of a later age back into the pristine statement. The
men who framed and ratified the amendment had only the dim-
mest knowledge of events to come; they had to explore its constitutional possibilities without benefit of the labors of jurists
recently seated or not yet upon the bench; they had to set down
general words in terms of the problems then current. For them
the clauses lived with the breath of their own age. It is only by
historical reconstruction that the contemporary meaning of the
Fourteenth Amendment is to be rediscovered. An understanding
requires an appreciation of the crisis, the intellectual heritage,
and the expediencies out of which it emerged. It demands even
more an oblivion to the gloss of a later day which lies thick upon
the text.[3] It is easy enough from the vantage point of what
came of it all to look back over our shoulders and to give order
and purpose to the course of judicial events. But in 1868—and

[3] An understanding of the Constitution in the making rests upon a
genetic account of its doctrines. Yet the paraphernalia of learning is set
against such an inquiry. Few bodies of material are as adequately indexed
as the law reports; but the headings are abstract concepts, verbal symbols,
and legalisms. Records are not reported, and dates and occasions are swept
away as of no account. Entries are set down as if the law were universal and
unchanging; and holdings from a miscellany of times and jurisdictions are
brought together to spell out a doctrine. The ghost of theology is still at
large, and inconsistencies are leveled beneath the skills of the system-builder.

decreasingly in the years to come—the immediate past was more insistent than the distant future. The folk of the time had to meet events head on.

II

If words are in want of definition, the proper appeal is to the law. And it was hardly half a decade after the amendment had been adopted before the meaning of its high-sounding phrases became the concern of the United States Supreme Court. Due process made its judicial entree with the fanfare of trumpets and in the livery of a strange master. The men who had taken part in the late rebellion had been disenfranchised; the reconstruction program of the black Republican Congress was in full swing; and in the states which had made up the Confederacy the legislatures had fallen into the hands of freed men of color and carpetbaggers. A flood of reckless legislation ensued; some marked by social vision, some savoring strongly of privilege and corruption, all anathema to the white aristocracy which before the war had been in the saddle. The Old South had lost in war and at the polls. But someone within its defeated ranks had the vague idea that an appeal to the courts might yet save the situation. Whose it was is lost to history. But an adage was current, "Leave it to God and Mr. Campbell"—and presently Hon. John Archibald Campbell [4] was putting his ex-judicial mind to a difficult problem.

Who chose the particular statute which in single combat was to stand for hundreds of its kind has escaped the record. But whether choice fell to an unknown, to Mr. Campbell, or to a group, a more strategic selection could not have been made. An act of the legislature of Louisiana had granted to a corporation of seventeen persons for a period of twenty-five years an exclusive franchise in respect to the slaughtering of animals for meat in the parish of New Orleans and the two next adjacent. In giving effect to the act, a citizen had been enjoined from the sale of his land for a rival slaughter-house; a like interdict had been laid upon a

----

[4] John Archibald Campbell was born in 1811 and died in 1889. He became a justice of the United States Supreme Court in 1853 and resigned in 1861, when his state, Alabama, left the Union. Upon his judicial appointment he freed his slaves. In the Dred Scott case he concurred in the judgment of the court in a separate opinion. After the war he resumed the practice of law and frequently argued constitutional cases before the court of which he had once been a member.

boat-load of cattle headed for market by an unorthodox route; butchers who for years had done their deadly work were no longer free to follow their trade; and the local public was forced to have commerce with a monopoly or turn vegetarian. Here were, ready at hand, causes as perfect as if they had been fashioned for the oncoming judicial ordeal.[5] They offered all the raw materials which a popular legal crusade demanded; they gave opportunity to all the symbols by which the emotions are stirred and the judge-within-the-man is moved. American institutions were being flaunted; a monopoly, odious at law and to the people, had been given a legislative blessing; the laborer had been denied his biblical doom and God-given right to work. The enemy was an octopus of a corporation; the cause was the cause of the working-man; the rights at stake were the rights of man. The requisite stuff of persuasion was there; there was need only to chisel it into a compelling legal argument.

The situation clearly invited a challenge of the statute in the name of the higher law. But to Mr. Campbell no ready-made formula was at hand. He had daringly to blaze a new trail; and a number of briefs which are rather successive drafts of the same argument than complementary lines of reasoning attest the arduous progress of his labor.[6] It is impossible for the lawyer of today, with a head full of the things that came later, to appraise the quality of his performance, and even the historian with his art of re-creation can form no certain judgment.[7] In his briefs there is nothing of clean-cut concept, of rule of law chiseled with neatness and precision, of sweep of syllogism to its inevitable therefore. They are clothed in a rhetoric alien to the legal persuasion of today. But history is here—its pages are filled with the conditions of the working classes in America, in England

[5] The suits were consolidated and in the reports appear as the "Slaughter House Cases," 16 Wallace 36 (1873).

[6] Except for edited excerpts in the law reports the briefs have not been published. They are, however, a part of the official record of the case. It seems unnecessary in the pages that follow to tag every reference with a citation to brief and page. The reasons are recited over and over again, and anywhere the reader turns he will chance upon statements of a kind with those quoted here.

[7] The account of the argument in the official report, 16 Wallace 36, is scrappy; the more regimented lines in 21 L. Ed. 394, attest an editorial hand of a later date. A jurist before whom Campbell pleaded regarded it as among the most original and profound of constitutional arguments. A distinguished teacher of the law characterized it to me as "such a brief as a clerk would draw."

and Scotland, in France and Prussia. Learning is here—there is hardly a page not adorned with its apt quotation from some writer on government, jurisprudence, economics, or philosophy. Authority is here—citation of cases are alternated with statements from Turgot and Guizot; Buckle and De Tocqueville; Hallam, Macaulay, and G. C. Lewis; Mr. Jefferson and Adam Smith; John C. Calhoun, Mr. Justice Curtis, and Cooley on *Constitutional Limitations.* A sentence from the *Wealth of Nations* which makes of a man's right to his trade both a liberty and a property was copied from the brief into a dissenting opinion and to this day goes resounding down the law reports. Even the arts have their dialectical due in an occasional line of poetry or a rhymed couplet of a negro minstrel.

The books were at hand—and a skill in their use—to serve the cause of the butchers. The task was to mold a medley of materials into a legal entity. Mr. Campbell had only foresight—not the hindsight of a later generation. His endeavor is marked not with the delicate articulation of the codifier but by the daring of the adventurer and the fumbling of the pioneer. His strategy had the audacity of an ex-member pleading before his old court, of an ex-rebel confronting his victorious enemies. He abandoned the older parts of the Constitution whose well-litigated clauses did not point his way and took his stand upon an article which as yet had drawn forth no judicial utterance. He decided to add another to the many paradoxes with which the history of legal doctrine is strewn. The Fourteenth Amendment was intended to secure the rights of the recently emancipated blacks against their former masters. The ink upon the fresh constitutional entry was hardly dry; yet he proposed to use the self-same article to guard the rights of the southern whites against the political power of the newly liberated Negroes.

In spite of a wandering style that jumps from Illinois to Norway and takes the distance from Scotch thraldom to southern slavery in a stride, the substance of his contention is clear and its focus never lost. His oral argument before the Supreme Court was an exposition of the unity of the Thirteenth and Fourteenth amendments; and the great objective of which they are instruments is the theme of all the briefs. All over the Western world, and almost within a century, a revolution had taken place in the status of the workingman. In France thralls had been eased of their ancient dues; in Prussia serfs had become their own masters; everywhere the feudal ties which had bound vassal to lord had been loosed. Even in the United States of before the war there had been slaves, freed men, and free-born citizens, and "the states might and did make large differences in the positions of men in the social and political system." The Thirteenth Amendment ended not only slavery but involuntary servitude in every degree and form; it made forever unlawful throughout the whole land a servitude for a year, for an hour or even for an occasion. A master could no longer command a servant to dance, to frolic, or to make merry before him.

But the impulse of a mighty revolution was not spent in a single enactment. In the Fourteenth Amendment all ranks were leveled, all marks and perquisites of social status were obliterated. All classes, whatever had been their previous conditions, were made a single people. "The law of citizenship became as broad as the law of freedom"; and every person became the equal of every other person before the legislature and at law. In respect to "conscience, speech, publication, security, occupation, freedom and whatever else is essential to liberty or is proper as an attribute of citizenship," every man became equal to every other man. The amendment—a political as well as a social revolution—"brought the federal government into immediate contact with every person and gave to every citizen a claim upon its protecting power." The natural rights of men, "life, liberty, property, protection, privilege and immunity"—their reiterated beat falls upon page after page—are "the sacred inheritance of the people." The Fourteenth Amendment "was designed to afford a permanent and powerful guarantee to them." They are to be recognized as "the assured estate of the population"; the mandate to the states is not "to abridge or destroy" but "to maintain and preserve them." In respect to these rights, inalienable and indefeasible, the federal government becomes every man's guardian.

With such a philosophic start it was easy to get down to constitutional concretions. Although the reasons are not neatly tooled, the substance of the argument is repeated again and again with cumulative effect. The Fourteenth Amendment created a national citizenship, fitted it out with "privileges and immunities," and placed this heritage from times of old beyond the power of the state government. These privileges and immunities are nothing other than the natural rights of man. Among these rights—quoting Mr. Jefferson and the new constitution of Louisiana—are "life, liberty and the pursuit of happiness." It is—in an argument helped along by Turgot, Adam Smith, and Mr. Campbell's own common sense—impossible for a man to sustain life, to enjoy liberty, and to pursue happiness if denied the chance to work. Man "has a right to labor for himself and not at the will or under the constraint of another." Moreover, a man's right in his own labor is not only a liberty but a property as well. As "a natural right of person" it is a liberty; in "its results or the expectation of results" it is a property—the only property of substance the workingman possesses. It follows that he has a natural right to dispose of his service—note the quiet appearance of a term which later made a mighty sound—by "freedom of contract." An argument so surely upon its way was not to be halted here; and, with strokes so deft that the transition is unobtrusive, Mr. Campbell converts an abstract right to work into the worker's vested interest in his occupation. Every trade must—in an order of nature to which the Constitution has come into accord—be open to all who choose to take its chances; and "no kind of occupation, employment or trade can be imposed upon" the workingman "or prohibited to him so as to avoid election on his part." Here, then, in tangible and specific terms is a constitutional right, a privilege and an immunity of citizenship, a liberty and a property, a claim to the equal protection of the laws, which the national government must under solemn mandate maintain against a state legislature gone astray.

And, having given concretion to his absolutes, with telling strokes the attorney drove the argument home. He had no quarrel with the state in its exercise of the police power; its right to promote by legislation "salubrity, security and order" is not challenged; but the statute on trial is not a health measure. Instead "the recitals of concern for the general welfare," the "delusive and deceitful promises of public good," the "expression of an unusual benevolence for the domestic comfort or the sanitary care of a neglected community" is sheer pretense. The statute emerges from "no proper legislative procedure"; it serves no motive—note the usage of the time—"of the public utility." On the contrary its one characteristic, its sole import, is to create a private corporation and to grant to a favored group of seventeen the exclusive privilege of an ordinary occupation. The ordinance was a return to the age of feudalism; it had created a banality in favor of a single firm; Louisiana had, in defiance of the federal Constitution, become "enthralled ground." There is at issue not one jot or tittle of regulation by the state which

those who are pressing the suits wish to avoid. Instead a monopoly—under the ban of the common law, intolerable in a democracy, forbidden by the Fourteenth Amendment—has been
created at the expense of men who have made "an ancient trade
the business of their lives." The Louisiana statute abridges the
privileges and immunities of citizens of the United States; it
denies to persons life, liberty, and property without due process
of law; it takes from them the equal protection of the laws.
Liberty and property were before there was law. The rights of
man, which belong to the order of nature, are above "the chartered rights" of a corporation. The cause is that of the workingman, of the community, and of the Constitution.

It was a powerful—even if not quite successful—appeal. In
the decision all the justices who spoke for the court or in dissent
addressed themselves to Mr. Campbell's argument. At its judicial debut four out of nine were converted to a novel constitutional doctrine, and the majority of five found it hard going to
contrive a dialectical answer. Chance got in its deft stroke and
shaped the course of constitutional events by a single vote. As
Mr. ex-Justice Campbell, the southerner, argued for national
sovereignty, Mr. Justice Miller, the northerner, denied it.[8] As
the native of Georgia argued that all citizens were one people
in an indivisible union, the unionist from Iowa refused to curb
the authority of the states. As the ex-Confederate asserted that
whites and blacks were equal before the Constitution, the abolitionist on the bench refused to erase the color line. There was,
according to the court, a citizenship of the United States, but
Mr. Justice Miller neglected to remove it from the realm of the
abstract, to define its terms or to endow it with substantive
rights. The Fourteenth was an addendum to the Thirteenth
Amendment; it had been designed to make secure the rights of
the blacks. But white men, though industrious artisans, were
without benefit of its coverage. The legislature had passed the
statute as a health measure, and with the act of a sovereign state
the court would not interfere.[9]

It was, however, only as a judgment to go at that. Mr. Jus-

[8] Samuel Freeman Miller was born in 1816 and died in 1890. At the
age of thirty-one he deserted the vagaries of medical practice for the more
comfortable certainties of Blackstone's Commentaries. The intellectual climate of his native Kentucky was too severe for his abolitionist sentiments, so
he moved over into Iowa. He was lifted from the obscurity of country practice to the highest bench in the land by his fellow-Kentuckian, Abraham
Lincoln, in 1862. He remained on the bench until his death.

[9] "The Slaughter House Cases," 16 Wallace 36 (1873), at p. 57.

tice Field boldly spread upon the record a powerful dissent.[10] The court like lost sheep had gone astray; he with three of his colleagues—especially he—were sound in a just-discovered faith. There was a citizenship of the United States, whose privileges and immunities had by the Constitution been put beyond the reach of the state, and that citizenship knew neither race nor color. The rhetoric was the rhetoric of Field, but the ideas were visible imports from the Campbell briefs. A milder echo of the same argument reappeared as the opinion of Mr. Justice Bradley.[11] In the midst of a paragraph toward the end—as if it were a passing thought—he set it down that a possible mandate with which to curb the power of the legislature might be found in "due process of law." So the cause was lost. The "privileges and immunities of citizenship" lost dominance in constitutional law —and we hear little more of it until its ghost returns after sixty-five years to serve a cause of tax avoidance of the vintage of 1935.[12]

But the loss of a cause is not the loss of a doctrine. Fate, attended by coincidence and paradox, was on the job to pull a trick more audacious than a storyteller would dare to invent. The butchers, still intent upon following the ox to the shambles, had lost their case but not their persistence. The good citizens of the state, with suffrage restored, presently reclaimed the legislature. By statute the monopoly was stripped of its franchise, and the butchers were again free to follow their trade. This time it was the Crescent City Company which refused to accept the voice of the people and girded itself for judicial combat. As the situation demanded, the two combatants exchanged positions, legal weapons, and arguments. The monopoly hurled at the court the Campbell brief done up in fresh verbiage. Since privileges and immunities had failed to prevail, under the thin veil of the refutable doctrine of obligation of contract, the familiar arguments were recited as a denial of liberty and property without due process of law. Counsel for the other side, perhaps a

[10] *Ibid.*, at p. 83. Stephen Johnson Field was born in 1816 and died in 1899. As a war measure a new circuit was created on the Pacific coast "to save California to the Union"; Field was appointed to the Supreme Court in 1863 and served until his retirement in 1897. He was, of all the members, most insistent upon reading substance into due process; and what he often said in dissent eventually came to be "the opinion of the court."

[11] *Ibid.*, at p. 111. Joseph P. Bradley was born in 1813 and died in 1892. He had been an ardent unionist, was appointed to the Supreme Court by Ulysses S. Grant in 1870, and remained a member until his death.

[12] *Colgate v. Harvey*, 296 U.S. 404 (1935).

little shamefacedly, went to Washington with pleas for the
supremacy of the police power, ably buttressed by the judgment
of the United States Supreme Court in the Slaughter-House
cases.

It was with no unity of feeling that the court welcomed the
return of the prodigal case. Mr. Justice Miller and his erstwhile
colleagues must have felt a trifle embarrassed; and their brethren,
Field and Bradley, JJ., could hardly restrain the thought, "O
Lord, Thou hath delivered mine enemy into mine hands." The
cause which in the Slaughter-House cases Mr. Justice Miller had
sustained and the doctrine he had used in its support were now
in collision. He had to desert the cause of reconstruction and
renounce a legislative grant he had pronounced valid—or he had
to recant a neatly woven constitutional argument. In the emergency he did not hesitate; he forsook secular cause and political
concern and valiantly made a stand upon his dialectic. In his
"the opinion of the court" he took many pages to say in substance, "The legislature has given and the legislature has taken
away; blessed be the name of the legislature." [13]

Had Field and Bradley, JJ., been ordinary men, a period
might then have been written to "due process" as it had been
to "privileges and immunities." Had they been content to join
Miller, J., and the majority of the court, or to concur without
opinion, the attempt to fuse substance into the Fourteenth
Amendment might not have survived this return and more
ignominious defeat. The result was to them admirable; but they
could not allow their joy at the discomfort of Mr. Justice Miller
to blind them to the acuteness of their own plight. As the power
of the state was vaulted aloft, they hit upon a telling—even if
outrageous—strategy. As they viewed with an inward dialectical
joy the loss of all its exclusive privileges by the Crescent City
Company, so the call was for a separate concurring opinion. In
this, with superb audacity, they argued, not that the charter
had been rightfully taken away but that it had never been lawfully granted; not that the second act of the Louisiana legislature
was valid but that the first act had all these years been invalid.[14]
Miller, J., had for the court argued the Crescent City case;
Field and Bradley, JJ., in certainty and a dissenting concurrence,

[13] *Butchers' Union Slaughter-House* v. *Crescent City Live-Stock Landing
Co.,* 111 U.S. 746 (1884).

[14] For the concurring opinion of Mr. Justice Field see *ibid.*, at p. 754,
and of Mr. Justice Bradley, *ibid.*, at p. 760. In Mr. Justice Bradley's dissent,
Harlan and Woods, JJ., joined.

reargued and redecided the Slaughter-House cases. The unusual occasion was seized; the peculiar turn of events was capitalized for a little more than it was rightfully worth. And, under the signatures of two eminent jurists, the doctrine of due process was set down in the law reports as an alternative reading to the police power.

After these decisive defeats, the Fourteenth Amendment came quietly into constitutional law. The pomp and circumstance which had attended the previous causes was absent. A municipal ordinance in California had made a pretty verbal display to the effect that laundries carried on in brick buildings were within the law; but, if housed in wooden structures, the authorities must be satisfied that the chance of fire was not a hazard to public safety. In obvious intent and in administration it said that the trade was open to the whites but that orientals were to be subjected to the closest scrutiny before admission to so exclusive a club. Yick Wo, denied the right to work at his chosen trade, essayed judicial combat, had syllogisms broken in his behalf, and came away with a signal victory of the highest court in the land. His right to his trade was as good as that of any other man.[15] The victory was scored, not by a recently emancipated black, not by a southern white whose pride in race did not forbid the use of the Negro's legal protection, but by a yellow man from China. Against the arbitrary act of the state "equal protection of the laws" came into constitutional law where "privileges and immunities" and "due process" had been denied admission. And the new doctrine had been accepted by the court without a single vote in dissent.

The breath of life had been breathed into the Fourteenth Amendment. The right to work at one's chosen occupation had at last become a part of the supreme law of the land. The substance to which "equal protection" gave a verbal home could pass on by contagion into a liberty and a property fortified by "due process." Eighteen years had passed since the amendment was adopted and fourteen since Mr. Campbell had blazed the path for a novel doctrine. But at last, in 1886, even against the action of the state, the rights of man had been accorded the protection of the Constitution.

III

Yet long before this decision another course of events was under way. The Campbell arguments were much too useful to

[15] *Yick Wo v. Hopkins*, 118 U.S. 356 (1886).

be left to butchers, bakers, and laundry workers. At the bar, and at least before the bench, we find them presently clad in the livery of an alien master. In his briefs—with all their concern for the liberties of the workingman—ex-Justice Campbell could not leave the word "property" alone. He made the right to work a property; and somewhat abstractly, on his own and within quotation marks, he declared the idea that property derives from the state to be the most revolutionary of notions; for, "if the state creates, the state can destroy." As with the individual, so with the nation-on-the-make, no clean-cut line was to be drawn; liberty was the liberty to acquire property. To Mr. Justice Field, rounding out his decades on the high judicial bench, liberty and property came to be a single word with a constant shift of accent to the right. In the Crescent City case the familiar dialectic contrived as a plea for liberty appeared in the service of corporate privileges. And long before Yick Wo won his legal tilt against Hopkins and California, attorneys for corporations as plaintiffs in error were presenting in brief and oration a round of exquisite variations on a theme of Campbell.

Although lawyers were admonished for pleading reasons that had been rejected, the recitation went on. In the challenge to the regulation of grain elevators, to the railway legislation of Granger days, to legislative attempts to abate or to subdue the trade in alcoholic beverages, the theme was omnipresent. It was always put forward as a defense of the frontiers of business enterprise against legislative attack. If invariably it fell before the police powers of the state, it acquired momentum and an enhancing repute in the opinions in dissent. As the decade of the eighties moved along, general admissions that legislation must meet the standards of due process were wrung from the court while it was still loath to apply the doctrine in the instant case. It was, however, not until the nineties that the personnel of the bench became radical enough to give effect to novel doctrine. Then, by judicial surgery, the Interstate Commerce Act was stripped of its sting and the Sherman Anti-trust Act limited to an innocuous domain. Although the first real program of national regulation was rendered impotent rather than declared invalid, and the Fourteenth Amendment was not called into service, a judicial opinion had come to prevail in which a due process, fitted out with substance, might by the court be thrown as a buttress about corporate interest.

The first decisive commitments came—if not off stage—at

least in the realm of dicta. In arguing a case of tax avoidance
for a railway company, Mr. Roscoe Conkling attempted to use
a humble confession to advance the cause of his client. He hinted
that the Fourteenth Amendment was the result of a conspiracy
between politicians and industrialists; and admitted that, in congressional committee, the word "person" had been chosen instead
of "citizen" to extend the protection of the due process clause
to the corporation. His prestige at the bar was at its height; he
had refused the high office then held by Mr. Chief Justice Waite
and the hardly less honored seat then occupied by Mr. Justice
Blatchford. He quoted at some length from the minutes of the
congressional committee; and, although the record had not been
published and he did not produce it, his remarks made quite an
impression. It left no decisive imprint in the reports; for, although the court found it easy to listen to elaborate constitutional argument, it found it difficult to resolve the issue. As the
months passed without result, a motion to dismiss was allowed
on the ground that the question had become moot, and the
issue was left in abeyance.[16] It was long afterward that the
minutes of the committee were made available, and it was discovered that Conkling had taken excerpts from their context,
tempered entries to his cause, and reshaped quotations to serve
his argumentative purpose.

But decades before historical research was to reveal a deliberate indulgence in historical error his confidential knowledge
had had its effect.[17] Four years later, in 1886, an attorney for
the same railroad, in another case of tax avoidance, proposed to
argue the same issue. He was stopped by Mr. Chief Justice
Waite, who announced that the court was prepared to admit,
without argument, that a corporation was a person within the
intendment of the equal protection clause.[18] Again a case, elab-
orately argued on constitutional grounds, was disposed of with-

[16] San Mateo County v. Southern Pacific R.R., 116 U.S. 138. The case
was argued December 19, 20, 21, 1882; as the passage of time brought no
decision, a motion to dismiss was eventually made on December 17, 1885,
and allowed four days later. It is of note that the official record is so barren
of the issue in controversy that there is no mention of Conkling's name,
and only the attorneys appearing on the motion to dismiss are listed.

[17] Howard Jay Graham, "The Conspiracy Theory of the Fourteenth
Amendment," Yale Law Journal, XLVII (1938), 371.

[18] Santa Clara County v. Southern Pacific R.R. Co., 118 U.S. 394
(1886) at p. 396. The point had been voluminously argued in briefs submitted by counsel.

out recourse to constitutional doctrine; and the elevation of the corporation to the protective eminence of a person remained a dictum. But the dictum was set down in the reports; and, oblivious to its lack of authority, it began presently to assert its claim as a holding.

The eighties gave way to the more receptive attitude of the nineties. Courts must await their causes; and from the play of minds upon issues which are potential the law takes its course. A simple case from Minnesota concerned with the regulation of railroad rates touched off a conflict of values and quickened the germs of doctrine into life. A state commission, acting in pursuance of statute, had fixed rates for milk moving within the boundaries of the commonwealth. No notice had been given, no hearing held, no opportunity accorded for the presentation of evidence. A railroad company, denied an opportunity to present witnesses, regarded the act of the commission as "unjust, unreasonable and confiscatory" and appealed to the judiciary. To minds steeped in the requisites of common law process such behavior was most irregular, and the majority of the court chose to find a procedural issue.[19] The act deprived "the Company of its right to a judicial investigation, by due process of law, under the forms and with the machinery provided by the wisdom of successive ages for the investigation judicially of the truth of a matter in controversy." It "substitutes as an absolute finality the action of the Railroad Commission" which "cannot be regarded as clothed with judicial function or possessing the machinery of a court of justice." As a result—with an easy transition from procedure to substance—if "without a judicial investigation" the company "is deprived of the power of charging reasonable rates," it is "deprived of the lawful use of its property and thus, in substance and effect of the property itself." Thus the ancient right of access to the court, with little bother of what is a proper cause of action, is used to proclaim a judicial overlordship over what had up to the moment been set down as the province of the legislature.

The self-assumed task of the court did not go unchallenged. The presence of opinions other than that "of the court" indicates a still unformed state of mind. As Mr. Justice Blatchford, for five members of the court, stated the issue, its answer is rea-

19 *Chicago Milwaukee and St. Paul Ry. Co.* v. *Minnesota*, 134 U.S. 118 (1890). The opinion of the court was delivered by Mr. Justice Blatchford; but the line of argument bears the craftsmanship of Mr. Justice Brewer.

sonable enough. But in the impact of the law upon the state of facts there were other ways of putting the question. In a concurring opinion, Mr. Justice Miller writes down a series of propositions which are a primer of the division of labor between legislature and judiciary in respect to public regulation.[20] There is "an ultimate remedy . . . especially in the courts of the United States" against "a tariff of rates" set down "arbitrarily and without regard to justice . . . so unreasonable as practically to destroy the value of property," whether established by legislation or commission. This "is a denial of due process of law in a proceeding which takes the property of the Company." And, going beyond the decision which ordered the cause remanded "for further proceedings not inconsistent with the opinions of this court," he declared that, "if this"—that is his own—"be a just construction of the statute of Minnesota, it is for that reason void." Eighteen hundred and ninety is a far cry from 1873, and in the intervening years Mr. Justice Miller had drifted far across the line which he himself drew.

It is likewise curious to discover Mr. Justice Bradley in dissent just as due process comes into its own. But, in putting the question before the court in his own way, he remains true to— even if not quite consistent with—his ancient faith. His attack is substantive, not procedural.[21] The regulation of railroad rates is a legislative and not a judicial prerogative; it involves "considerations of policy as well as of remuneration." "The state might build its own railroads if it saw fit," for it has a "duty" to provide "means of intercommunication between one part of its territory and another." This duty is devolved upon the legislature, and if "it commissions private parties, whether corporations or individuals, to the performance, it is its prerogative to fix the fares and freights" for "such transportation." The chartered rights of carriers are not above the state. The court has confused the issue and treated the present case "as if the constitutional prohibition was that no state shall take private property for public use without just compensation—and as if it were our duty to judge of that compensation." The act was not struck down; but chartered rights were moving into the succession; and the brew of nullity, in the name of due process, was in the pot. Campbell was dead; Bradley stood fast; Miller came

[20] *Ibid.*, at p. 459.
[21] *Ibid.*, at p. 461. In his dissent Gray and Lamar, JJ., concurred.

over; and Field, eternally right, marched with the marching doctrine.

Another six years passed. A number of significant causes came and went stamped with the attitude of the changing bench. But not until 1897—and then only through a reaching-out toward issues that need not have been raised—did an opportunity come for a better fitting of due process to the current temper of the court. A Louisiana statute had prescribed a regulation of insurance companies within the state; the officials had attempted to bring under its penal provisions a firm which had contracted for marine insurance upon shipments of cotton with a New York company. It seems to have been admitted by all concerned that the contracts had been made in New York and that in the instant case the only matter of local concern was the notices sent of shipments upon which the insurance was to take effect. It was easy enough for the court to waive so incidental a part of the transaction out from under the act. That done, the decision of the case demanded no more than the simple comment that an act of Louisiana had no application to a matter beyond the jurisdiction of the state. It might even have been declared null and void as an interference with commerce among the several states. But so obvious a disposition was not for the new blood within the court. Mr. Justice Peckham, a fresh recruit, had the zeal of the reformer and a faith in the enlightened opinion of his own day untroubled by doubt. The holding depends upon the way the question is put; and he chose—with the consent of his brethren—to view the act as a "real" interference with "the liberty of the defendants to place insurance on property of their own" where they pleased. Thus the issue became larger, more general, and more significant than the unresolved query in the litigation. As thus stated no question of the right of the court to review the matter was raised by any of the nine justices. That hurdle had been gotten over by a succession of rhetorical yieldings in a number of important cases—helped along by the high vault in the Minnesota milk rate case. As formulated by the spokesman for the court, business privilege was squarely opposed to state regulation with "due process of law" as the arbiter.[22]

It is idle to argue that he went out of his way to do it; for, to the individualistic mind of Mr. Justice Peckham, his was the only way. It was a superb opportunity to bring the orthodoxy

[22] *Allgeyer v. Louisiana*, 165 U.S. 578 (1897).

of classical economics into the higher law, and he was not going to allow it to pass. In a rhetoric which is strongly familiar, the dissent of yesterday becomes the opinion of the court. He quotes Mr. Justice Bradley in the Crescent City case as if he had been the spokesman for the court; and the familiar arguments, even the illustrations of the Campbell brief, are repeated. The "inalienable rights" of the Declaration of Independence; the pursuit of happiness; the right of the butcher, the baker, and the candlestick-maker are all there. As Peckham quotes Bradley, who paraphrases Campbell—thus piling a superfluous Ossa upon a Pelion of dicta—"I hold that the liberty of pursuit—the right to follow any of the ordinary callings of life—is one of the privileges of a citizen of the United States." Although the path of his argument is beset with questions, his faith in the efficacy of free contract to take care of all the affairs of business rises above all bother over relevance. The privileges and immunities of citizenship may be outmoded, but there is a constitutional successor. A nimble sentence may be made to travel a long doctrinal way; its hurried words may overcome formidable obstacles where the argument at a leisurely pace would break down. Thus, "it is true that these remarks are made in regard to questions of monopoly, but they well describe the rights which are covered by the word 'liberty,' as contained in the Fourteenth Amendment." The "privilege" quoted is that of "pursuing an ordinary calling or trade"; but—without setting down a period or evoking a therefore—smoothly he glides along through "the acquiring, holding, and selling" of "property" to "the right to make all proper contracts in relation thereto." Thus, in the name of due process of law, freedom of contract is thrown up as a fence about the domain of business enterprise against the incursions of the state. And no one on the high bench said to the contrary.

In the Allgeyer case "the police power" remained in the background. The cause had little concern with human rights; a trio of judicial bows acknowledged an abstract authority to regulate; and judicial silence prevented a conflict between an upstart due process and the more venerable doctrine. Again the next year a head-on collision was avoided when—with Brewer and Peckham, JJ., in dissent—a statute of Utah establishing an eight-hour day in smelters and underground mines won the imprimatur of the court; [23] and it was only in 1905 that due process

[23] *Holden v. Hardy*, 169 U.S. 366 (1898).

first won in a clean-cut combat with the police power. A statute
of New York had limited the hours of employees in bakeshops
to ten in any one day or sixty in any one week; and, because of
his lack of workaday respect for the act, the People of New
York were at odds with a certain Mr. Lochner. The judgment
of the Supreme Court—one of the habitual five to four variety
—was again delivered by the learned jurist and sound economist,
Mr. Justice Peckham.[24] He had only to elaborate his former
argument, now fortified by the official citation of *Allgeyer* v.
Louisiana. Freedom of contract, in respect to trade or employment, was an aspect of the liberty and property which a state
might not abridge without due process of law. The challenge of
the police power was met by a formidable parade of personal
and common-sense opinion that the hours of bakers had little
or no relation to the public health.

Again the distinguished jurist made the question before the
court far broader than the issue which the case presented. If
such an act were allowed to stand, "a printer, a tinsmith, a
locksmith, a carpenter, a cabinet maker, a dry goods clerk, a
bank's, a lawyer's, or a physician's clerk"—in inelegant verbal
parade—would "all come under the power of the legislature."
In fact "no trade, no occupation, no mode of earning one's living, could escape this all pervading power." Since "there is no
contention that bakers as a class are not equal in intelligence
and capacity to men in other trades" or are "not able to assert
their rights and care for themselves," the real question is the
general use of "the protecting arm of the state" to interfere with
"the independence of judgment and of action" among men of
every occupation. "Statutes of the nature of that under review
limiting the hours in which grown and intelligent men may
labor to earn their living, are meddlesome interference with the
rights of the individual." And, since such "interference on the
part of the legislatures of the several states with the ordinary
trades and occupations of the people" seemed "to be on the increase," it was time to call a halt. The opinion of the court was
intended to be an apostolic letter to the many legislatures in the
land appointing limits to their police power and laying a ban
upon social legislation.

So it might have become but for the dissent. Mr. Justice
Harlan objected that the question of the relation of hours to

[24] *Lochner* v. *New York*, 198 U.S. 45 (1905).

health was one of fact; that as reasonable men members of the
legislature were entitled to their opinion; and that "there are
few, if any, questions in political economy about which entire
certainty may be predicated." With him White and Day, JJ.,
concurred. A youngster of sixty-four, newly come to the court,
seized his chance and scribbled the most famous dissent in all
legal history. Mr. Justice Holmes insisted that "general propositions do not decide concrete cases." He accused the court of
interpolating economic doctrine, insisted that "a constitution is
not intended to embody a particular economic theory, whether
of paternalism and the organic relation of the citizen to the
state or of laissez faire"; and protested against freezing the law
into "Mr. Herbert Spencer's *Social Statics*." It is common for
latter-day liberals to set this down as the first blast of the trumpet
in behalf of a social oversight of human rights; but the historian
is more likely to view it as a lance worthily broken in behalf
of an ancient cause now in retreat. But the four dissenters saw
as clearly as the five, who, by the virtue of being one more,
were the court, that the challenged act might be "the first installment of a general regulation of the hours of work"; and
they wished to keep the way open. It was probably too late for
Harlan, J., or even for Holmes, J., to argue that in such matters
the legislature was the sole and exclusive judge and that the
court had no rightful power of review; at least such an argument
was not attempted. The all but equal vote led to an even balance
of doctrines. Neither the police power nor due process was to
be preferred; in an even-handed formula liberty and property are
to be set against public policy; as case follows case these concepts are to be filled with the values of life, a balance is to be
struck and a judgment rendered. An engaging number of rules
for the game of review have come and gone; the decisions of
the court have with the circumstances, its personnel, and the
temper of the times swung now toward one side, now toward
the other. But the balance of values recorded in *Lochner* v.
People of New York has endured as the judicial formula for the
ultimate judgment upon legislation designed to promote the
public interest.

Thus a collusion of occasions and persons, causes and ideas,
shaped the course of doctrinal events. It was quite untouched
by conspiracy, unless it be of the gods or of that Providence
which is said to preside over American institutions. A constitutional doctrine contrived to protect the natural rights of men

against corporate monopoly was little by little commuted into a formula for safeguarding the domain of business against the regulatory power of the state. The chartered privileges of the corporation became rights which could be pleaded in equity and at law against the government which created them. In a litigious procedure in which private right was balanced against the general good the ultimate word was given to the judiciary. A last ironic note attends the closing story; the words of the doctrine of due process remain true to their democratic origin; it is only the substance which has come to serve a strange master. But such an antithesis language and content is "of the nature of things." For in respect to the public control of business, the Constitution of the United States dates, not from 1787, nor from 1868, but from 1905.

IV

All of this has to do with the rhetoric of the coming of due process. The account has as its narrow concern a sequence of judicial events; it is drawn from the official records of a single court; in all its detail it can be supported by the sanctions of exact documentation. But the larger story of the making of the doctrine lies elsewhere; in the development of industrialism, in the changing state of opinion, in the assembly of ideas from far and near into a principle of law, in urges within an economic order that could not be judicially denied. A part of that history has been written; distinguished scholars have garnered from legal literature the germs of the doctrine and have shown how the catholic concept of due process offered a home to notions of natural rights. But if the raw material has been exhibited and the verbal history of the doctrine written, the impulses within the social order—in particular, economic interest and legal persuasion—have not been accorded their part in the drama. Here off stage are the forces which gave life to abstractions. The records of the court reflect only in a series of passing shadows their tumultuous vitality. And the history of due process is far more than the judicial record it has left.

A shift from rhetoric to logic, from recorded doctrine to compelling impulse, is an engaging hazard. It is an inquiry into a series of "if's," many of which escaped actuality by the narrowest of margins. If in the Slaughter-House cases the Campbell argument had commanded just one vote more, what difference would it have made? We would doubtless by now possess an august corpus on the privileges and immunities of citizenship, and the entries under due process would be correspondingly thin. But would the hypothetical domain be a great and humane code concerned with the rights of man? Or would the corporation, which became a person, just as easily have passed into the protected position of a citizen of the United States? And, in such an event, would the only change be that all that is now written down as liberty and property would be entered as the privileges of citizenship?

Or was the logic of the commitment inevitable—and the specific legal doctrine by which business enterprise sought immunity from regulation a mere rhetorical device? Due process was fashioned from the most respectable ideological stuff of the later nineteenth century. The ideas out of which it was shaped were in full accord with the dominant thought of the age. They were an aspect of common sense, a standard of economic orthodoxy, a test of straight thinking and sound opinion. In the domain of thought their general attitude was omnipresent. In philosophy it was individualism; in government, laissez faire; in economics, the natural law of supply and demand; in law, the freedom of contract. The system of thought had possessed every other discipline; it had in many a domain reshaped the law to its teachings. A respect for the obligations of contract had been set down in the Constitution in 1787; the "ancient maxim," *caveat emptor*, had become dominant in the law of sales by the forties; an individual responsibility for industrial accidents was definitely established in torts shortly after the middle of the century. An impact that had been irresistible elsewhere should surely have won its way into constitutional law. Its coming seemed inevitable; the constitutional concept which it made its domicile was a mere matter of doctrinal accident. Words on parchment could not be adamant before so powerful a thrust; privileges and immunities, due process, equal protection, were all available; and, had there been no Fourteenth Amendment, "the obligations" might have been made to encompass "the freedom" of contract; or, as a last resort, a vague natural right as a higher law might have been found to permeate the whole Constitution.

The wonder is not that laissez faire made its entrance but that it found so insecure a lodgment within the Constitution. Ex-Justice Campbell had a superb case, his strategy was adroit, he suited his arguments to a state of mind which it took a civil war to produce—yet he could not quite command a majority of the court. It was nearly twenty years before, even as a dictum, the protection of the Fourteenth Amendment was accorded to a corporation, and it was nearly twenty more before the first instalment in a program of social legislation was struck down by the court. Even when it was at last accorded constitutional standing, its victories were often obtained by the narrow margin of five to four. Its triumph did not come until half a decade after the turn of the century, when it had ceased to be common sense, when legislators were forsaking its precepts, and when in philosophy, economics, and government it was on the way out. Even then its victory was inconclusive; it could never claim the faith of the full bench; and it had to share its sovereignty with the antithetical doctrine of the police power.

Freedom of contract took up its abode within "due process of law" too late for easy and secure lodgment. Its legal insecurity may rest upon personnel; a change of a justice here and there would have affected mightily the course of judicial events. It seems strange that so many jurists stood steadfast against the seductions of laissez faire; history, political science, and economics can boast no such record. Or it may be due to the older and established doctrine that the state might intervene with regulation to promote public safety, public health, public morals, and public welfare—against which the cause of the independence of the business system could achieve only a partial success. Or does the whole story, in irony, paradox, and compromise, derive from the innate conservatism of the law—a rock of ages which even the untamed strength of laissez faire could move but could not blast?

5. Economic Due Process and the Supreme Court: An Exhumation and Reburial

ROBERT G. McCLOSKEY

EDITORIAL NOTE. *Like the corpse of John Randolph's mackerel, shining and stinking in the moonlight, economic due process of law is dead. In 1937 the Court held unconstitutional a state act construed to take private property for a private, rather than a public, purpose; since then there has not been one single case in which state economic legislation has been held unconstitutional as a violation of the Fourteenth Amendment's due process clause. In 1963, in the case of Ferguson v. Skyupa, the Court declared that under our constitutional system, "it is up to legislatures, not courts, to decide on the wisdom and utility of legislation." There was a time, observed Justice Black, speaking for all but Justice Harlan, when the due process clause had been used to strike down laws which "were thought unreasonable, that is, unwise or incompatible with some particular economic or social philosophy." But the Court had long since returned to "the original constitutional proposition" that courts should not substitute their social and economic beliefs for the judgment of legislatures. The Court did not doubt that an argument might always be constructed to show the social utility of some conduct proscribed by a state, "but such arguments are properly addressed to the legislature, not to us." The Court declared that it refused to sit as a "superlegislature to weigh the wisdom of legislation" and refused, also, to rehabilitate the doctrine of economic due process. "Whether the legislature," remarked Black, "takes for its textbook Adam Smith, Herbert Spencer, Lord Keynes, or some other is no concern of ours."*

155

The Court had by no means abandoned judicial review. During the same term as the Ferguson case, it held unconstitutional: the Georgia County unit system for voting in primary elections; state requirements that public schools begin with daily readings from the Bible; state denial of counsel to an indigent defendant in a criminal prosecution; a local school-transfer plan that was predicated on racial grounds; an act of Congress divesting an American of his citizenship for remaining abroad in wartime to escape military service; a state use-tax that discriminated against interstate commerce; the use of local trespass laws to punish sit-ins and other public demonstrations where state law or official action required owners of private property to follow a policy of racial segregation; a state act aimed at the N.A.A.C.P., precluding the solicitation and management of legal business; and the practices of a state commission intimating prosecution for noncompliance with recommendations for the removal from sale of objectionable literature. From this representative sampling of cases there emerges a clear constitutional policy in favor of First Amendment freedoms, the principle of equal protection, due process in its various procedural connotations, and the free or unburdened flow of commerce.

With respect to Fourteenth Amendment cases involving due process of law, Walton H. Hamilton's double entendre, that "liberty and property came to be a single word with a constant shift of accent to the right," is no longer descriptive. The abandonment of economic due process was accompanied by the revival and expansion of procedural due process as well as by a new substantive due process which shifted the accent leftwards to the word "liberty." The Court invested that word with the content of the First Amendment freedoms in much the same manner as in former years it had clothed the word "property" with the content of vested rights doctrines. In short, most of the guarantees of the Bill of Rights are now protected by the Fourteenth Amendment against state abridgment.

The following essay by Robert G. McCloskey modestly, though misleadingly, purports to trace the decline and virtual demise of economic due process. McCloskey does far more. In a constitutional universe dominated by civil libertarianism and government management of the economy, he has the courage to champion a lost cause—that of economic due process, the good sense to do so with restraint, and the wisdom to do it in a manner that makes economic liberty kindred to civil liberty, that is, part of the bundle of personal rights instrumental to the development of free citizens in an open society. McCloskey also finds a large gap or inconsistency in the rationale underlying our constitutional structure, the result, he says, of a judicial policy which asserts supervision over certain personal rights and rejects it over economic ones. He then asks a series of hard, penetrating questions that will shake the confidence and test the premises of anyone who takes for granted the "rightness" of things as they are.

McCloskey, on the other hand, does not rack up all the points. He takes for granted what he should have proved, that economic or substantive due process, rather than, say, the equal protection clause, is the remedy to the problem that he poses concerning vital but vulnerable economic rights. He takes for granted that economic due process can have any constitutional validity; the wonder is that it ever had any, not that it no longer has. It was always a judicially contrived, oxymoronic concept that distorted history, logic, and plain meaning. Thus, even if economic rights possessed all the worth ascribed by McCloskey, their defense by economic due process might still be unsupportable. Indeed, the fact that freedom of occupation is as important to most men as freedom to speak, is no argument that the remedy for abridgment is necessarily to be found in the Constitution. The Constitution is not a corrective for the legislative ills that afflict modern America. Statutes may be futile, fatuous, or foolish without being unconstitutional. The Constitution's protections are limited. Although McCloskey gives the impression that the right to be a lady bartender is as important as the right of a religious minority to worship freely, the problem is not that others may have a different scheme of values; the problem, rather, is that the Constitution quite explicitly protects religious liberty, but radiates from the vague contours of due process no visible protection to bartenders—nor to riverboat pilots, occulists, nor any other occupation.

The remedy for McCloskey's valiant plea for "some freedom of occupation and economic choice" may properly belong with the state courts, not the Supreme Court, and with state constitutional law, not federal. A state act not violative of the federal constitution may conflict with the state constitution. In Olsen v. Nebraska, discussed by McCloskey, the very statute sustained by the Supreme Court against an economic due process claim was subsequently voided by the state supreme court; since no federal question was involved, the decision was not reviewable. That the Fourteenth Amendment poses no bar to certain legislation does not, in other words, mean that the economic rights imperilled are necessarily deprived of the support of law. The amendment is simply indifferent to the economic policies of the states.

McCloskey tends to use attractive language, such as "economic rights" and "liberty of economic choice," to describe the subject which he champions. Since he is not advocating laissez-faire or the "rights" which were victorious in Adkins, or Smyth v. Ames, or Lochner, it is not always clear just what his cause is, other than "the right to work"—a concept needing far more clarification than it receives in the following essay. Several of the "right to work" cases which McCloskey discusses would be described by others as civil liberty cases—the very sort of civil liberty which he argues should have no preference in comparison to economic liberties.

McCloskey is grieved that the Court should exalt or elevate civil liberties, especially First Amendment freedoms, at the expense, he unconvincingly says, of economic liberties. He seems to think that all rights are equal, that to protect some and not others degrades or neglects the latter. Yet the most sophisticated judges, not the current absolutists, but Holmes, Hughes, Cardozo, and Frankfurter, graded rights. And who would contend that the Second and Seventh Amendments protect liberties as fundamental as the First or Fourth? In any case it should be remembered that it is the Constitution itself, not the Supreme Court, which lays down the distinctions which McCloskey queries. Justice Jackson's opinion in the Second Flag Salute case, contains a response which many find satisfactory:

> In weighing arguments of the parties it is important to distinguish between the due process clause of the Fourteenth Amendment as an instrument for transmitting the principles of the First Amendment and those cases in which it is applied for its own sake. The test of legislation which collides with the Fourteenth Amendment because it also collides with the principles of the First, is much more definite than the test when only the Fourteenth is involved. Much of the vagueness of the due process clause disappears when the specific prohibitions of the First become its standard. The right of a State to regulate, for example, a public utility may well include, so far as the due process test is concerned, power to impose all of the restrictions which a legislature may have a

'rational basis' for adopting. But freedoms of speech and of press, of assembly, and of worship may not be infringed on such slender grounds. They are susceptible of restriction only to prevent grave and immediate danger to interests which the State may lawfully protect. It is important to note that while it is the Fourteenth Amendment which bears directly upon the State it is the more specific limiting principles of the First Amendment that finally govern . . .

The First Amendment's prohibitions are not only explicit; they are categorical. The protection accorded to procedural rights by the Fourth, Fifth, and Sixth Amendments is equally explicit; not so in the case of McCloskey's economic rights. Yet the word "property" is in the Fourteenth Amendment's due process clause where it ranks in no way below "liberty." In the opinions of the Supreme Court, liberty is now "writ large." McCloskey wants its spaciousness to encompass economic as well as other freedoms. If it can mean, under certain circumstances, no law respecting an establishment of religion, why, under other circumstances, can it not mean occupational freedom? And, finally, with the demise of economic due process, one might ask, in support of McCloskey's position, whether contemporary constitutional law does not give to the "property" of the due process clause a meaning as empty or niggardly as has been accorded the privileges and immunities clause.

It is true that the Constitution no more embodies a set of economic beliefs or arrangements than it does a theology; but property or economic rights, from the time of the framers to the present, have merited respect and consideration. One can, that is, endorse McCloskey's general argument without accepting many of its specifics. To reject it altogether, or, for that matter, any part of it, requires the capacity to tangle with a first-class mind that is subtle, questing, and provocative.

ECONOMIC DUE PROCESS
AND THE SUPREME COURT:
AN EXHUMATION AND REBURIAL

I. The Problem

American political life has often been marked by a tendency to adopt policies today and to think about them in some remote tomorrow, if at all. This national habit of mind is presumably rooted in our famous pragmatic temperament. Much can be—and has been—said for it. But the attribute, like most attributes, has the defects of its merits. If Jack builds a house without thinking the plan through in advance, he may then justly congratulate himself that he is at least sheltered from the elements while his more deliberative neighbor still shivers. But he should not be surprised if it turns out that the corners are a little awry or that the second bedroom impinges on what he hoped would be an ample living room. He must accommodate himself to the fact that the ad hoc decisions of the past may set unforeseen limits on his way of life in the future.

These general reflections about American propensities and their consequences are also applicable to the modern history of America's peculiar institution, the Supreme Court of the United States. Since about 1937, the Court has been rebuilding its constitutional dwelling place, knocking down a wall here, constructing a new corridor there, in response to a bewildering succession of conflicting impulses. If these impulses are united by some commonly shared understanding about the form and extent of the ultimate structure, the Justices have been remarkably taciturn about revealing it. Vast new areas of constitutional supervision have been opened in such decisions as *Palko* v. *Connecticut*,[1] *Burstyn* v. *Wilson*,[2] and *Brown* v. *Board of Education*,[3] to name only three among many. Other regions, once significant, have been closed off to judicial intervention: the fields of the national commerce power and of economic due process are the standard examples.[4] Still others have been temporarily opened, then more or less firmly shut again—or vice versa. One thinks of picketing as free speech,[5] on the one hand, and the flag-salute issue, on the other.[6] Each of these developments has been accompanied by one or more Court opinions offering a particularized justification: it would be nice to have that extra livnig room; or, no house

1 302 U.S. 319 (1937).

2 343 U.S. 495 (1952).

3 347 U.S. 483 (1954).

4 See Stern, *The Problems of Yesteryear—Commerce and Due Process*, 4 Vand. L. Rev. 446 (1951).

5 See Cox, *Strikes, Picketing and the Constitution*, 4 Vand. L. Rev. 574 (1951).

6 Minersville School Dist. v. Gobitis, 310 U.S. 586 (1940); West Virginia Bd. of Educ. v. Barnette, 319 U.S. 624 (1943); see Manwaring, *Render Unto Caesar* (1962); Kurland, *Religion and the Law* 41–47 (1962).

really needs a separate dining room these days. But little attempt has been made to reckon with their effect on each other or on the over-all structure that was taking shape.

The purpose of this paper is to trace one such development in the disorderly constitutional flux of the past twenty-five years: the decline and virtual demise of "economic due process." Such a survey might seem to be mere bootless antiquarianism. But the story of the senescence of this once-robust doctrine may provide us with hints about several live questions that concern students of the Supreme Court. What is the character of the process which the Court goes through when it reaches a radical turning point in its doctrinal history? Why does this process take the form it does? More specifically, why did the Court abandon the cause of economic rights, and why so completely? Can the abandonment be fully justified in the light of any consistent view of the rights themselves or of the Court's role in our political system? If not, is it either likely or desirable that the law should retrace its steps in this field, or has the possibility of a second guess been foreclosed by the general drift of judicial history?

II. THE DEMISE OF A DOCTRINE: THE METHOD

The judicial reaction against economic due process after 1937 is unique in the history of the Supreme Court. There have been gradual shifts from negativism to permissiveness, as in the anti-trust field during the decades after *E. C. Knight;* [7] there have been abrupt departures from salient negative doctrines as in *Nebbia* [8] or in *Graves v. New York.* [9] But it is hard to think of another instance when the Court so thoroughly and quickly de-molished a constitutional doctrine of such far-reaching signifi-cance. The concomitant destruction of "dual federalism" in the commerce field is doubtless the closest analogue. But there the negative standard had rested in fact on a comparatively scanty handful of precedents, and the Court in *United States v. Darby* [10] could draw on a line of contrary pronouncements beginning with Marshall. On the other hand, the judicial power to strike down an economic statute on the ground that it was "arbitrary, capri-cious, or unreasonable" had been frequently exercised and seemed to stand on a solid base. Most of the Court's critics and some of

---

[7] United States v. E. C. Knight Co., 156 U.S. 1 (1895).
[8] Nebbia v. New York, 291 U.S. 502 (1934).
[9] Graves v. New York ex rel. O'Keefe, 306 U.S. 466 (1939).
[10] 312 U.S. 100 (1941).

its friends might have hoped in the early 1930's that the "rational basis" standard would be applied more leniently. But only a singularly prescient observer could have dreamed that the Court would soon abandon the concept altogether.

Yet that is what happened. There is no need to retell the familiar story in detail,[11] but a few high points are worth repeating. *West Coast Hotel* v. *Parrish*[12] is commonly and rightly thought of as the watershed case. We know that it was because of what occurred thereafter. But the actual words of Chief Justice Hughes in that case did not suggest very plainly that the whole doctrine of substantive due process was scheduled for destruction. He spoke of the wage regulation as "reasonable," citing a 1911 decision,[13] and he even invoked in defense of the present law the distinction made in 1908 between men and women as parties to a labor contract.[14] It was still possible to believe, then, that the Court was merely overruling *Adkins*, but maintaining its power to strike down other economic legislation that might fail the reasonableness test. *Senn* v. *Tile Layers Protective Union*,[15] a little later in the Term, suggested that the range of allowable legislative judgment was growing but not that it was unlimited. In *United States* v. *Carolene Products*,[16] a year later, Justice Stone for the majority went a little further, declaring that regulatory legislation is valid unless the facts "preclude the assumption that it rests upon some rational basis." But he still assumed "for present purposes" that an economic statute could be attacked by disproving the facts that were supposed to provide the law with its rational base, and his approval of the law seemed to rest in part on his judicial knowledge that there were facts to support a legislative ukase against "filled milk." But by 1941, in *Olsen* v. *Nebraska*,[17] the Court was ready to

---

11 See Stern, *supra* note 4; Rodes, *Due Process and Social Legislation in the Supreme Court—a Post Mortem*, 33 Notre Dame Law. 5 (1957); Hetherington, *State Economic Regulation and Substantive Due Process of Law*, 53 Nw. U. L. Rev. 13, 226 (1958); Wood, *Due Process of Law 1932–1949* (1951).

12 300 U.S. 379 (1937), overruling Adkins v. Children's Hospital, 261 U.S. 525 (1923).

13 Chicago, B. & Q. R.R. v. McGuire, 219 U.S. 549 (1911), cited 300 U.S. at 392.

14 Muller v. Oregon, 208 U.S. 412 (1908), cited 300 U.S. at 394.

15 301 U.S. 468 (1937).

16 304 U.S. 144, 152 (1938). (Emphasis added.)

17 313 U.S. 236.

take another long stride away from the pre-1937 doctrine. The subject matter of this case evoked fond memories of those bygone days, for it concerned regulation of employment-agency rates, and such regulation had been roundly condemned by the old Court in *Ribnik* v. *McBride*.[18] But now Mr. Justice Douglas, for a unanimous Court, not only repudiated *Ribnik* and its famous doctrine of "business affected with a public interest," but came close to announcing that the issue of economic regulation was no longer of judicial concern. There is no requirement, he said, that the State make out a case for the needfulness or appropriateness of the law. "Differences of opinion on that score suggest a choice which 'should be left where . . . it was left by the Constitution—to the states and to Congress.' " [19] There was no suggestion here, as there was in *West Coast Hotel* and *Carolene Products*, that the State must point to facts which might reasonably justify the regulation. The presumption of constitutionality was no longer debatable. *Olsen* suggested, as a contemporary comment put it, that there was then "a complete lack of constitutional foundation for the assertion of private right under the due process clause where contractual or proprietary interests are involved." [20]

In case the business community and its legal minions might have missed the point in 1941, the Court made it pellucid in later decisions. Everyone has his favorites among these, but a reference to *Day-Brite Lighting* v. *Missouri* [21] and *Williamson* v. *Lee Optical Co.*[22] should suffice. In the first, the Court, again via Mr. Justice Douglas, declared that it was not the business of the Court to decide whether legislation "offends the public welfare" [23] and that "debatable issues as respects business, economic, and social affairs" were for legislative decision.[24] In the second, the same Justice upheld a law requiring a prescription from an optometrist or ophthalmologist before an optician could even fit old lenses into a new frame. Though the law may exact a "needless, wasteful requirement in many cases," the legislature "might have concluded" that the waste was justified in order to achieve

18 277 U.S. 350 (1928).
19 313 U.S. at 246.
20 40 *Mich. L. Rev.* 743, 745–46 (1942).
21 342 U.S. 421 (1952).
22 348 U.S. 483 (1955).
23 342 U.S. at 423.
24 *Id.* at 425.

the objective of protecting health.[25] When these cases were taken together with a companion series in which the Equal Protection Clause was given a similarly permissive scope,[26] there could be little doubt as to the practical result: no claim o fsubstantive economic rights would now be sustained by the Supreme Court. The judiciary had abdicated the field.

This was the result. But it is of some interest to note how the result had been achieved. Obviously two paths lay open. One was that which seemed to be suggested by Mr. Justice Black's dissent in Connecticut General Life Insurance Co. v. Johnson,[27] i.e., to repudiate in explicit and unmistakable terms the very bases for the Court's jurisdiction over economic questions. Such a course was at least imaginable. The Justices might have reconsidered not only the corporation-as-person doctrine, as Black proposed, but the very idea of substantive due process in the economic field. They might, that is, have held in so many words that economic legislation was no longer subject to judicial review on the question whether it had a "rational basis." This possibility may have been in Stone's mind (though never, one suspects, in his plans) when in Carolene Products he only assumed "for present purposes" that the rational basis test was still relevant; it may partly explain Black's disavowal of that portion of Stone's opinion.[28] Certainly Douglas came close to it in Olsen. A few years later, in the Lincoln Union case,[29] Black came even closer when he implied that the only constitutional limits in the economic field were the specific prohibitions of the Constitution.

The other possibility was to retain the rhetoric of the rational basis standard, but to apply it so tolerantly that no law was ever likely to violate it. This was the course ultimately chosen, one more consonant with Stone's view that such issues were better dealt with "gradually and by intimation."[30] Even Douglas seems to have accepted the rational basis concept for these rhetorical purposes.[31]

---

[25] 348 U.S. at 487.

[26] See, e.g., Railway Express Agency, Inc. v. New York, 336 U.S. 106 (1949); Queenside Hills Realty Co. v. Saxl, 328 U.S. 80 (1946).

[27] 303 U.S. 77, 83 (1938).

[28] 304 U.S. at 155.

[29] Lincoln Federal Labor Union v. Northwestern Iron & Metal Co., 335 U.S. 525 (1949).

[30] Mason, Harlan Fiske Stone: Pillar of the Law 469 (1956); see also Dunham, Mr. Chief Justice Stone, in Dunham & Kurland, Mr. Justice 47 (1956).

[31] See Douglas, We the Judges (1956).

This was perhaps the "judicial" way to bring the result about. It preserved some shreds of the idea of continuity, and that idea, myth or not, is important to the constitutional tradition. It enabled the Justices to feel their way along toward a policy whose contours were probably not yet clear in their own minds. It may have helped to maintain unanimity: it is hard enough to understand how Justice Roberts could have accepted the *Olsen* opinion; it is even harder to envision him concurring in an explicit renunciation of all judicial authority to protect property holders.

So much at least can be said for the approach chosen, leaving aside for the moment the question whether the result itself was desirable. But the matter has another aspect. When policies are established "gradually and by intimation," when the question of their existence is partially obscured by preservation of the old rhetoric, there is always a chance that the destruction of those policies will not be recognized. A flat decision to discard substantive due process root-and-branch would have compelled the Justices to explain themselves, to examine the basis for their abnegation. In the actual event they have never fully done so, at least in public, and this leaves, to say the least, a large gap in the rationale that underlies the structure of modern constitutional law.

The reticence of the Court does, however, provide the non-judicial observer with an opportunity. It leaves him free to speculate about the explanations and justifications that the Justices have neglected to provide. And the speculation at least seems desirable: one of the cardinal doctrines of American constitutional history should not be denied the modest rite of a funeral oration.

III. ACTION AND REACTION

What then was the explanation of this extraordinary shift in judicial values? It must be emphasized that this is not merely the question why the Court took leave of the unyielding negativism represented by such judgments as *Adair v. United States* [32] or *Coppage v. Kansas* [33] or by the anti-New Deal dogmatics of 1934–1936. That question may not be an easy one, for historical questions seldom are, but its mysteries are not unfathomable. An answer would have to begin with the specific enigma of Justice Roberts; after that the road is comparatively clear. His

[32] 208 U.S. 161 (1908).
[33] 236 U.S. 1 (1915).

shift in 1937 created a majority opposed to the extreme version of constitutional laissez faire, and it was to be expected that that majority would be strengthened as new appointments were made in the following years. The shift from *Morehead v. New York ex rel. Tipaldo* [34] to *West Coast Hotel*, startling though it was as a specific event, was not beyond prediction: the basis for it had been well laid in the recent past by both judges and scholars.

The harder question is: Why did the Court move all the way from the inflexible negativism of the old majority to the all-out tolerance of the new? Why did it not establish a halfway house between the extremes, retaining a measure of control over economic legislation but exercising that control with discrimination and self-restraint?

Precisely such a halfway house had frequently been described in judicial opinions of the past, so there is little chance that the post-1937 Justices had overlooked its conceptual existence. Justice Brandeis in *New State Ice Co. v. Liebmann* [35] had admonished the Court against erecting its prejudices into legal principles but had still conceded that "the reasonableness of every regulation is dependent on the relevant facts." [36] Indeed, he conducted an exhaustive examination of those facts in his opinion. Justice Stone had himself carefully adumbrated such a position, saying in *Ribnik* that price regulation is within the States' power when "any combination of circumstances seriously curtails the regulative force of competition, so that buyers or sellers are placed at such a disadvantage in the bargaining struggle that a legislature might reasonably anticipate serious consequences to the community as a whole." [37] To be sure, Justice Holmes had, in *Tyson & Brother v. Banton*,[38] laid down a standard comparable in its permissiveness to the *Olsen* doctrine: [39] "The truth seems to me to be that, subject to compensation when compensation is due, the legislature may forbid or restrict any business when it has a sufficient force of public opinion behind it." This is the de facto policy of the modern Court. But Stone, as has been said, filed a separate dissent in *Tyson*, and even Holmes in other opinions had con-

---

34 298 U.S. 587 (1936).
35 285 U.S. 262, 311 (1932).
36 *Id.* at 301–02.
37 277 U.S. at 360 (dissenting opinion).
38 273 U.S. 418, 445 (1927) (dissenting opinion).
39 *Id.* at 446.

ceded that the supposed rational basis of economic statutes is subject to judicial scrutiny.[40] As a result of such scrutiny, the Court would not strike down an arguably rational law, but it would require some showing by the State that there was a basis for believing it to be rational and would consider evidence to the contrary presented by the affected business. Laws like those involved in the *Lee Optical* case [41] and in *Daniel v. Family Security Life Ins. Co.*[42] might be invalidated, or at any rate more sharply queried.

Assuming then that this standard—this modest residue of the old economic supervision—was consciously and purposefully rejected, what explains the rejection? And, to make the difficulty a little more acute, what accounts for the fact that such survivors of the old Court as Stone and Roberts concurred in the choice, that the *Olsen* opinion was unanimous? A couple of "behavioral" or psychological explanations come to mind as possibilities. They are put forward diffidently, for motive is hard to ascertain with respect to only one man; when a group of nine highly sophisticated individuals is involved, the complexities become awesome.

For one thing, it may be that Stone and Roberts joined in the movement so as to preserve the rhetoric of supervision and thus some faint shadow of doctrinal continuity. Black, as his biographer says, wanted to "reject utterly and completely the doctrine . . . that the due-process clause gives to courts the power to determine the reasonableness of regulations." [43] Considering his well-known enthusiasm for calling a spade a spade,[44] we can well believe that Black would have liked to spell this out in an explicit abdication speech. We cannot tell how many of his brethren would have joined him then. But by the spring of 1941, there were, besides himself, four Roosevelt appointees on the Court, and further appointments were obviously pending. The veterans may have felt that the most they could hope for was the fictional survival of the rational basis test.

A second possible explanation may be more fruitful, since it

[40] See, e.g., Adkins v. Children's Hospital, 261 U.S. 525, 567 (1923) (dissenting opinion).
[41] Note 22 supra.
[42] 336 U.S. 220 (1949). The statute prohibited life insurance companies and their employees from operating undertaking businesses, and undertakers from serving as agents for life insurance companies.
[43] Frank, *Mr. Justice Black: The Man and His Opinions* 111 (1949).
[44] See Mendelson, *Justices Black and Frankfurter: Conflict in the Court* (1961).

relates, not only to the question why the veterans were willing to retreat so far, but also why the newer Justices seemed resolved to do so. It is that extremism had bred extremism in thinking about the role of the Supreme Court. Between 1923 and 1937, a conservative majority had, from time to time, embraced a policy of adamant resistance to economic experiment, and this obstructionist spirit had reached its zenith in the judicial reaction against the New Deal. What the Chief Justice himself had said in the *Railroad Retirement* case [45] was true of the conservative majority in most of the great anti-New Deal decisions. That majority had raised a barrier, not only against particular features of the law, but "against all legislative action of this nature by declaring that the subject matter itself lies beyond the reach" of governmental authority.[46] This intransigence had tended to discredit the whole concept of judicial supervision in the minds of those who felt that government must have reasonable leeway to experiment with the economic order. The result was that the two wings of the Court (and of the country) had almost ceased to communicate with each other. The dissenting opinions of Stone in *United States* v. *Butler* [47] and Sutherland in *West Coast Hotel* [48] are not a dialogue between men who share a common ground but disagree about its implications. The opinions represent wholly different realms of discourse. If the position of the conservatives had been less extreme, there might have been in 1937 the basis for a viable, moderate doctrine of economic supervision. It is almost touching to observe Sutherland, in *Carmichael* v. *Southern Coal & Coke Co.*,[49] after the "revolution" of 1937, urging that the State law could be cured of its constitutional infirmities and that, if it were, the objective of relieving unemployment could be attained despite the Due Process Clause. This language of sweet reason had not been conspicuous in the negative decisions of previous years. Now it came too late. The extreme of the past had generated the extreme of the present. The Court which had claimed the full loaf was winding up without even the half. Such a result is not surprising when dogmatism has been substituted for discussion.

[45] Railroad Retirement Board v. Alton R.R., 295 U.S. 330, 374 (1935) (dissenting opinion).

[46] *Id.* at 375.

[47] 297 U.S. 1, 78 (1936).

[48] 300 U.S. at 401.

[49] 301 U.S. 495, 527 (1937 (dissenting opinion).

Factors like these may help to explain the impulse to discard the old due process doctrine, bag and baggage. Yet one would like to think that a more thoughtful process was going on somewhere below the surface, that the policy of virtual abdication was not merely a reflex against the excesses of the past but a considered and justified decision about the proper scope of judicial review. The written record to support such a supposition is not, alas, very convincing.[50] Scattered remarks in decisions cited above, and in others, assailed the dead horse of "the Allgeyer-Lochner-Adair-Coppage" doctrine,[51] i.e., the Justices argued against "social dogma" and for "increased deference to the legislative judgment" [52] in the economic field. But they did not explain why the abuses of power in those earlier decisions justified abandonment of the power itself, nor why the deference to the legislature should be carried to the point of complete submission. The nearest thing to an explanation is perhaps to be found in Mr. Justice Frankfurter's concurrence in *American Federation of Labor v. American Sash & Door Co.*, where he argued that "the judiciary is prone to misconceive the public good" and that matters of policy, depending as they do on imponderable value issues, are best left to the people and their representatives.[53] This is a coherent and not unconvincing viewpoint, but the trouble with it has always been that it implied similar judicial withdrawal, not only from the economic field, but from other areas that pose questions of policy, such as freedom of expression. Well aware of this difficulty, Frankfurter tried to meet it in this opinion by declaring that matters like press censorship and separation of church and state are different, because "history, through the Constitution, speaks so decisively as to forbid legislative experimentation" with them.[54] Scholarship has since provided reason to doubt that history speaks so plainly after all, even on these subjects,[55]

[50] Freund, *On Understanding the Supreme Court* 11 (1949); Learned Hand said in 1946: "Just why property itself was not a 'personal right' nobody took the time to explain." Hand, *The Spirit of Liberty* 206 (1960). Nobody, so far as I am aware, has yet taken that time.

[51] Lincoln Federal Labor Union v. Northwestern Iron & Metal Co., 335 U.S. 525, 535 (1949).

[52] A. F. of L. v. American Sash & Door Co., 335 U.S. 538, 544 (1949) (concurring opinion).

[53] *Id.* at 556.

[54] *Id.* at 550.

[55] Levy, *Legacy of Suppression* (1960); Brief for Appellees, McCollum v. Board of Educ., 333 U.S. 203 (1948).

and without a strong historical rationale the argument falters badly, for the arguments against judicial intervention in economic affairs become arguments against intervention in the policy sphere generally. Learned Hand of course was ready to accept this implication [56] and Frankfurter himself has come very near to it. But it is certainly not the dominant doctrine of the modern Court, which has fairly consistently held to the "dual standard" enunciated by Stone in the *Carolene Products* case.[57] So we are left with a judicial policy which rejects supervision over economic matters and asserts supervision over "personal rights"; and with a rationale, so far as the written opinions go, that might support withdrawal from both fields but does not adequately justify the discrimination between them.

IV. The Doubtful Distinction between Economic and Civil Rights

Although no such rationale can be detected in the written opinions, however, the possibility of its existence cannot be entirely dismissed. The Supreme Court has sometimes preferred to leave ultimate arguments unexpressed, to let justification for a course of conduct, as well as the course itself, emerge "gradually and by intimation." And this may be the case with the great retreat from economic supervision. Perhaps there is a coherent apologia for that retreat; perhaps this apologia was in the Justices' minds when they shaped the modern constitutional policy. The second "perhaps" can never be transmuted into certainty unless the art of judicial psychoanalysis reaches unforeseen heights. But its plausibility may increase if it appears that there is a rationale which *might* have formed the basis of the policy.

The arguments for demoting economic rights to their modern lowly constitutional status—lowly when compared with "personal rights"—fall into two categories. First, there is a group of arguments based on judgments about the nature and relative importance of the rights concerned. For example, it is sometimes argued that laws limiting freedom of expression impinge on the human personality more grievously than do laws curbing mere economic liberty, and that the Court is therefore justified in protecting the former more zealously than the latter.[58] The individual

---

[56] Hand, The Bill of Rights (1958).

[57] Freund, op. cit. supra note 50.

[58] Hastie, Judicial Method in Due Process Inquiry, in Government under Law 326 (Sutherland ed. 1956). He makes an exception of subsistence.

has, qua individual, "the right to be let alone." [59] The right to free choice in the intellectual and spiritual realm is particularly precious to him. A major difficulty with this formulation is that there is the smell of the lamp about it: it may reflect the tastes of the judges and dons who advance it, rather than the real preferences of the commonality of mortals. Judges and professors are talkers both by profession and avocation. It is not surprising that they would view freedom of expression as primary to the free play of their personalities. But most men would probably feel that an economic right, such as freedom of occupation, was at least as vital to them as the right to speak their minds. Mark Twain would surely have felt constrained in the most fundamental sense, if his youthful aspiration to be a river-boat pilot had been frustrated by a State-ordained system of nepotism.[60] Needless to say, no disparagement of freedom of expression is here intended. But its inarguable importance to the human spirit, on the one hand, does not furnish an adequate ground for downgrading all economic rights, on the other.

So much for a purely individual-centered justification for the disparity between economic rights and other civil liberties. Another suggested rationale looks toward the community rather than the separate individuals within it. Progress, it is said, "is to a considerable extent the displacement of error which once held sway as official truth by beliefs which in turn have yielded to other beliefs." [61] To encourage societal progress, it is important then to protect "those liberties of the individual which history has attested as the indispensable conditions of an open as against a closed society," [62] e.g., freedom of expression.

Presumably this "open society" argument would be relevant no matter how the political system was organized—even a benevolent autocracy must tolerate freedom of expression or risk stagnation. But Alexander Meiklejohn has contended that the point takes on an extra dimension when applied to popular government, to democracy as the West understands that term. In any political system, so the argument runs, the ruler must be fully informed if he is to govern well, and he cannot be fully informed when someone else is deciding what ideas he shall be allowed to

---

[59] Brandeis, J., dissenting, in Olmstead v. United States, 277 U.S. 438, 478 (1928).

[60] Kotch v. Pilot Commissioners, 330 U.S. 552 (1947).

[61] Frankfurter, J., concurring, in Kovacs v. Cooper, 336 U.S. 77 at 95.

[62] Ibid.

hear. In a democracy the people are sovereign, and it follows that they and no one else must decide what and whom they will listen to. And it further follows that the Constitution must protect any freedoms that help the people to acquire "the intelligence, integrity, sensitivity, and generous devotion to the general welfare that, in theory, casting a ballot is assumed to express." [63] In short, the special importance of certain civil rights derives from their special relationship to the process of self-government. Other rights, including the economic, can be abridged when the legislature deems abridgment desirable.

Some such reasoning probably underlies the related point implied by Mr. Justice Stone in the first paragraph of his famous "footnote four" [64] and by Mr. Justice Frankfurter in the concluding words of the first flag-salute opinion [65] (though neither would of course have followed Professor Meiklejohn in the absolutist conclusions he drew). Stone suggested that judicial scrutiny would be especially exacting when legislation restricted "those political processes which can ordinarily be expected to bring about repeal of undesirable legislation," [66] and Frankfurter intimated that the crucial question is whether "all the effective means of inducing political changes are left free from interference." [67] These pronouncements may rest partly on Professor Meiklejohn's point that the governors must be fully informed; but they also seem to involve a separable idea: that a majoritarian system must, in the name of both justice and progress, preserve the right of a present minority to make its views the views of the majority. A businessman's price may be controlled by the mandate of a popularly elected legislature, but, if his right to work politically for repeal of the control law is untrammeled, the fundamentals of a just democratic polity are still maintained and so is the fluidity of the sociopolitical order.

The whole "open society" line of argument in its various forms is convincing enough as a justification for protecting the free trade in ideas. If one feels the need to explain why the free speech guarantees are important, these explanations will do pretty well for a start. But they are rather less satisfactory as the basis

[63] Meiklejohn, The First Amendment Is an Absolute, [1961] Supreme Court Review 245, 255.

[64] United States v. Carolene Products Co., 304 U.S. 144, 152 (1938).

[65] Minersville School Dist. v. Gobitis, 310 U.S. 586, 600 (1940).

[66] 304 U.S. at 152.

[67] 310 U.S. at 600.

for a policy of *not* protecting economic freedom, of regarding it as unimportant in a democratic system. For one thing, it is not entirely clear why liberty of economic choice is less indispensable to the "openness" of a society than freedom of expression. Few historians would deny that the growth of entrepreneurial and occupational freedom helped to promote material progress in England in the eighteenth and nineteenth centuries and in America after the Civil War (although they might of course argue that the price paid for this progress was unconscionably high). It is one thing to argue that economic liberty must be subject to rational control in the "public interest"; it is quite another to say in effect that it is not liberty at all and that the proponent of the "open society" can therefore regard it as irrelevant to progress.

As for the "political process" subthemes of the open-society argument—the Meiklejohn-Stone-Frankfurter rationales just described—they too must be queried insofar as they purport to justify a downgrading of economic rights. In fact, their basic difficulty is that, in exalting the freedoms bearing on the political process, they bypass the question of other freedoms altogether. Meiklejohn's arguments for protecting liberty of expression are cogent, but they do not on their face explain why other, "private," rights should be neglected. A decision to protect Peter does not necessarily involve the decision to abandon Paul. In Meiklejohn's own formulation there is indeed a hint that the political is primary, that a right associated with the governing process somehow, because of that association, matters more than any other. This might be so in some imaginary democratic city-state where the political and the social were identical, but it is more dubious when applied to the United States where the sphere of private value can make high claims of its own. One may agree that it is necessary for popular government to protect the political process. But it does not follow that all concern for rights comes to an end when that protection has been provided. Moreover, there is some evidence that Meiklejohn's categories refuse to stand still, even in his own mind. He is not content to define the governing-process freedoms narrowly. He rightly says that "voting is merely the external expression of a wide and diverse number of activities by means of which citizens attempt to meet the responsibilities of making judgments"; [68] and

[68] Meiklejohn, *supra* note 63.

this enables him to bring literature and the arts within the concept, since they "lead the way toward sensitive and informed appreciation and response to the values out of which the riches of the general welfare are created." [69] We can refuse to swallow whole the dogmas of nineteenth-century rugged individualism and can still believe that some freedom of occupation and economic choice is also instrumental to the development of this self-determining and sensitive citizen-governor.

If Meiklejohn's argument contains the unexamined assumption that the political is primary and almost exclusive, the "Stone-Frankfurter" [70] point described above contains this and an assumption of its own as well: the majoritarian idea in a peculiarly unqualified form. The notion seems to be that the citizen can have nothing really fundamental to complain about in a law if a free majority has enacted it and if he is protected in his right to agitate for its repeal. But this view ascribes a preponderance to the majority will that has certainly not been acknowledged by the American political tradition. In that tradition, it is not assumed that an unjust law becomes just by virtue of majority approval, not even if the victim has the theoretical right to persuade the majority to change its mind. The denial of that right would aggravate the injustice, but the granting of the right does not dispel it. As Justice Jackson said in the flag-salute dialogue,[71] the very purpose of a Bill of Rights was to place certain fundamental rights beyond the reach of majorities.[72] Of course, it may be argued that economic freedom in its various forms can never be so fundamental a right, but that shifts the discussion to a quite different level.

Furthermore this argument overlooks a difficulty partly recognized by Stone himself in the *Carolene Products* footnote [73] and invoked by him in the first flag-salute case, the problem of "discrete and insular minorities," [74] i.e., those who have no realistic chance of influencing the majority to rescind the law that does them harm. Stone was speaking specifically of religious, national,

---

[69] *Id.* at 257.

[70] This term is used only for the purposes of expositional convenience. It does not imply that the particular point referred to represents the full position of either of the two Justices on this question or that their views on the question were identical.

[71] West Virginia Bd. of Educ. v. Barnette, 319 U.S. 624 (1943).

[72] *Id.* at 638.

[73] 304 U.S. at 152, n. 4.

[74] Stone, J., dissenting, 310 U.S. at 606.

or racial minorities, and his suggestion was that prejudice against them might curtail the political processes that would ordinarily be expected to protect their rights. Prejudice against Jehovah's Witnesses for their "queerness" makes repressive governmental action more probable, and precisely because of their queerness they are not likely to be numerous enough or influential enough in any given community so that their weight will be felt in the city council. To speak of their power to defend themselves through political action is to sacrifice their civil rights in the name of an amiable fiction. Yet it is not clear why the thrust of this point should be restricted to ethnic and religious minorities. Perhaps it is true that a prosperous corporation can effectively plead its case at the bar of legislative judgment by resort to publicity and direct lobbying. Economic power may be an adequate surrogate for numerical power; no tears need be shed for helpless General Electric. But the scattered individuals who are denied access to an occupation by State-enforced barriers are about as impotent a minority as can be imagined. The would-be barmaids of Michigan [75] or the would-be plumbers of Illinois [76] have no more chance against the entrenched influence of the established bartenders and master plumbers than the Jehovah's Witnesses had against the prejudices of Minersville School District. In fact the Witnesses may enjoy an advantage, for they are at least cohesive; and other "discrete" minorities, such as racial groups, have occasionally displayed respectable capacities to exert political leverage by virtue of their very discreteness. Not so the isolated economic man who belongs to no identifiable group at all.

V. JUDICIAL CAPACITY IN THE REALM OF
ECONOMIC REGULATION

For one reason or another then, none of these justifications of the Court's modern hands-off policy in the economic field quite stands up. The distinctions they rely on, between economic rights on the one hand and personal rights on the other, tend to blur when we examine them. And, even if it were thought that the distinctions were tenable, the case would remain incomplete. It might, squeezing it hard, justify a difference in the kind and degree of protection afforded economic rights; but it would not warrant a policy of no protection at all.

[75] Goesaert v. Cleary, 335 U.S. 464 (1948).
[76] People v. Brown, 407 Ill. 565 (1951). See *Gellhorn, Individual Freedom and Governmental Restraints* 123–24 (1956).

Although the policy of abdication cannot be justified in terms of an analysis of the nature and relative unimportance of the rights concerned, there is a second line of thought that merits consideration. Perhaps the decision to leave economic rights to the tender mercy of the legislative power is based on the idea that the Supreme Court is peculiarly ill-equipped to deal with this subject. No one would argue that the right enshrined in Article IV, the guarantee of a republican form of government, is unimportant. Yet the Court has refused to protect it, because of well-founded doubts about judicial competence to make effective judgments in this field. It may be that similar doubts underlie the policy of abdication in the area of economic affairs.

At first blush, this argument seems highly persuasive, at least in broad terms. Anyone familiar with the entanglements resulting from Smyth v. Ames [77] will be alive to its merits. Probably no court was really equipped to make the intricate and imponderable economic judgments that the doctrine of that case entailed. And those who remember the Court's crusades against the rise of the welfare state may be dubious about judicial competence on somewhat different grounds. They may feel that economic policy is not only beyond the reach of the Court's expertise, but beyond the reach of its practical power. Whether the nation shall have a minimum-wage law; whether the government shall control prices; whether social security shall be publicly guaranteed—these are questions so "high" [78] and so basic that no court could determine them even if it should. They involve in a word the momentous issue of the welfare state itself, and that issue will be determined by "dominant opinion" with or without judicial approval.

There are, of course, economic subjects so recondite that judicial surveillance of them would be anomalous. The choice between "historical cost" and "replacement cost" as a basis for rate making must be made by the legislature, not because it will always choose well, but because the judiciary lacks the knowledge and expertise for distinguishing good from bad in this area. But this point will carry only as far as its logic will bring it, and there are fields of economic regulation less intricate than the problem of public utility rates. To be sure, even the problems raised in these fields may not be simple. A fair evaluation of Oklahoma's need for its anti-optician law would require the

[77] 169 U.S. 466 (1898).
[78] Finkelstein, *Judicial Self-Limitation*, 37 Harv. L. Rev. 338, 345 (1924).

Court to make judgments about a complex matter. But this can be said about most questions that reach the Supreme Court in any field. Our problem is not to identify the issues that present difficulties and then to discard them as improper subjects for judicial review. That would be to abandon judicial review in most of the fields where it is now exercised. Our problem is to determine whether economic statutes always or usually involve such extraordinary difficulties that a modest judiciary must eschew them, even though that same judiciary does claim the competence to judge other, more difficult, issues.

Is it easier for example for the Court to appraise a law empowering a board of censors to ban an "immoral" movie [79] than a law empowering a real estate licensing board to deny a license unless the applicant is of "good moral character"? [80] The two standards would seem to be equally vague and the possibility of arbitrary administrative action would seem to be as menacing in one situation as in the other. Is it plainly easier to balance New Hampshire's need to get information against Paul Sweezy's right to withhold it,[81] than it is to balance South Carolina's need to stamp out the funeral insurance business against the right of an agent of the Family Security Life Insurance Company to make a living selling such insurance? [82] The "public need" in both cases was all but invisible. Is it easier to see that the State corporate registration law in *N.A.A.C.P. v. Alabama* [83] was being used to facilitate private reprisals against Association members than it is to see that State boards of plumbers, barbers, and morticians sometimes use their publicly granted powers to protect the private financial interests of present guild members to the disadvantage of non-members? [84]

The point is not that the cited cases should necessarily have been decided differently, but rather that the issues they present stand on a common level of difficulty and that judicial scrutiny seems as feasible (or unfeasible) for one issue as for the other. And the further, related, point is that there are kinds and kinds of economic subjects and that it is difficult to fashion a generalization that applies to all. Some subjects may be so inscrutable

---

[79] Kingsley International Pictures Corp. v. Regents, 360 U.S. 684 (1959).
[80] Gellhorn, *op. cit. supra* note 76, at 121.
[81] Sweezy v. New Hampshire, 354 U.S. 234 (1957).
[82] Daniel v. Family Security Life Ins. Co., 336 U.S. 220 (1949).
[83] 357 U.S. 449 (1958).
[84] See Grant, *The Gild Returns to America*, 4 J. Pol. 303 (1942).

that judicial review cannot fruitfully cope with them; but this is not a justification for avoiding other economic subjects which are no more opaque than the "personal rights" issues that are the standard coinage of judicial discourse these days.

This point likewise applies to the suggestion that the Court, as the relatively weak and non-political branch, simply lacks the power to dictate the economic order, however otherwise competent its members may be. No doubt the Court was presumptuous to imagine, before 1937, that it could hold back such waves as the wage-control movement or the demand for social security. The tide of the welfare state was flowing, and no court could have reversed it. But neither does the judiciary have the practical power to halt any major social developments backed by insistent popular demand. And this would be so whether the development involved economic questions or questions of "personal rights." It was the dimension of the issues in the anti-New Deal cases that made them incongruous for judicial decision, not the mere fact that they were economic in character. No such judicial delusions of grandeur would be implied by enforcement of the requirement that an occupational qualification must be rationally based, or by similar modest applications of substantive due process. The awful will of the sovereign people is not likely to be aroused because the Court has told the morticians of Winnemac that they cannot use State power to maintain a monopoly—or at least no more than it is aroused by other constitutional decisions that issue almost weekly during each Term. In short, while doubts about judicial expertise and power may warrant withdrawal from some economic questions, they cannot justify withdrawal from all such questions, unless the doubter is willing to go the full distance with Learned Hand and give up most of the residue of modern judicial review.

VI. The Disappearing Double Standard

In the light of the inadequacies that seem to afflict all of the arguments for judicial abdication of the field of economic rights, we are perhaps justified in concluding that the policy of abstention was never really thought through. It seems to have been a kind of reflex, arising out of indignation against the excesses of the Old Court, and resting on the vague, uncritical idea that "personal rights" are "O.K." but economic rights are "Not O.K." Thus are fashioned the decisions about the shape of our constitutional polity.

This conclusion gains strength when we note from time to

time certain signs of uneasiness with the "double standard." The most familiar such manifestation appears in the judicial and extra-judicial remarks of jurists like Learned Hand, Robert Jackson,[85] and Felix Frankfurter. Their misgivings center around the problem of justifying judicial activism in any field where the Court's only guideposts are the inexplicit "moral adjurations" [86] of the Bill of Rights. They have doubts about a judge's capacity to enforce such adjurations in the economic realm, and their modesty is not altogether dissipated when they turn to the field of personal rights; for they are unsatisfied by easy phrases like "preferred position." Hand, as has been said, carried his doubts somewhat further than the others, perhaps because he was speaking non ex cathedra in semiretirement. Jackson and Frankfurter have expressed themselves more restrainedly and therefore less clearly, but the broad drift of their qualms has been plain enough. They would partly resolve the dilemma of the double standard by adopting a modest approach to both economic rights and personal rights, though still retaining perhaps some distinction between them.

The other possibility of course would be, not to protect both kinds of rights less, but to protect both equally, i.e., to reassert the Court's power to disallow economic legislation that lacks a rational basis. It would be too much to say that such a development is portended by a few sporadic judicial pronouncements in recent years, but they may indicate a measure of disquiet with the prevailing dichotomy. From the first the modern Court has been troubled by a recurring problem: how does the dichotomy stand up when economic matters and personal rights are involved in a single governmental action? Examples abound: statutes that strike at picketing, which may be both free speech and an economic activity; [87] State-supported professional dues-paying requirements, and other restrictions with a secular purpose, that regulations that impinge on freedom of religion; [89] license requirements, and other restrictions with a secular purpose ,that nevertheless impose burdens on religious practice,[90] to name only

[85] Jackson, The Supreme Court in the American System of Government 57–58 (1955).

[86] Hand, op. cit. supra note 50, at 163.

[87] Thornhill v. Alabama, 310 U.S. 88 (1940).

[88] 367 U.S. 820 (1961).

[89] Prince v. Massachusetts, 321 U.S. 158 (1944).

[90] Murdock v. Pennsylvania, 319 U.S. 105 (1943); and cases cited in note 91 infra.

a few. It is no help to the judge faced by these hybrid problems to tell him that the economic order is Caesar's affair while personal rights are the Constitution's affair, for the twain have met and he must decide between one or the other. One solution is to hold that a law primarily "secular" in purpose must stand even if it operates incidentally to infringe personal rights; that the law or an application of it will fall only if it was aimed at or discriminates against personal rights as such.[91] Leaving aside the very real difficulty of determining what a law's primary purpose is, the trouble with this formula is that it does permit the state to impose de facto burdens on the exercise of personal rights, and this has disturbed some of the Justices. A Court that has resolved to protect personal rights because of their indispensability to democracy is not likely to be content with a doctrine that allows them to be frittered away, even though an otherwise legitimate secular purpose can be descried. Another imaginable solution is to filter out the personal-rights elements in the law and insist on their protection; the economic-rights residue being left, as usual, to the chance of legislative judgment. But this can involve very nettling problems of discrimination and remedy, as is demonstrated by the arguments in such recent decisions as Lathrop v. Donohue [92] and the Sunday Law cases.[93]

Moreover this last solution is likely to strain the logic of the Court's position more than it can perhaps bear. In the situation presented by the Lathrop case, for example, the Court would have to say that a lawyer has a "right" to practice his profession free from the kinds of restrictions to which the First Amendment refers, that he has under these circumstances a constitutional "right to work," but that the right somehow vanishes when the statute is cured of its First Amendment defects. The State can be as arbitrary as it likes in regulating my occupational freedom just so long as the regulations do not touch on my speech (or religion, or race, or perhaps national origin [94]). The logical strain inherent in such a position has been suggested above. The Court's dilemma is reminiscent of the 1920's, when constitutional history

[91] Braunfeld v. Brown, 366 U.S. 599 (1961); Gallagher v. Crown Kosher Super Market, 366 U.S. 617 (1961); McGowan v. Maryland 366 U.S. 420 (1961); Two Guys from Harrison-Allentown, Inc. v. McGinley, 366 U.S. 582 (1961).

[92] Note 88 supra.

[93] Note 91 supra.

[94] But see State of Ohio ex rel. Clarke v. Deckebach, 274 U.S. 392 (1927).

was moving in the opposite direction. A Court that had enshrined economic liberty in the Constitution under the due-process rubric found it increasingly difficult to maintain that the Due Process Clause did not protect other liberties that men might deem important. In spite of the flat statement to the contrary in 1922,[95] within three years thereafter freedom of expression was acknowledged as a constitutional right enforceable against State action.[96]

Perhaps an analogous restlessness helps account for hints about economic freedom, especially the right to work, that have turned up here and there in recent years. In *Barsky v. Board of Regents* [97] in 1954, the Court sustained the suspension of a physician's license against a charge of unreasonableness. The majority was willing to allow the license-revoking authority virtually unlimited discretion and would not conclude that whim and caprice had guided the authority's decision even though the evidence to that effect seemed fairly strong. This is the standard, extreme presumption of validity, that has effectively barred judicial review in the economic field. But the dissenters used language that may point in a rather different direction. Mr. Justice Frankfurter, while conceding that the Court must presume the validity of the State agency's action in the absence of evidence to the contrary, nevertheless argued that such evidence should be considered if it does appear on the record. And, in considering it, the Court should ask whether the revocation has "some rational relation to the qualifications required of a practitioner" in the profession. "If a State licensing agency lays bare its arbitrary action, or if the State law explicitly allows it to act arbitrarily, that is precisely the kind of State action which the Due Process Clause forbids." [98] True, the case involved the possibility that the agency here had been influenced by the appellant's supposed left-wing connections, so that this might be regarded as merely another example of special judicial sensitivity when personal rights and economic rights are mixed. But Frankfurter's words do not suggest that he would be any less hostile to an irrelevant standard because it lacked First Amendment undertones. And Douglas, also dissenting, described the right to work in terms that hardly suggest a niggardly interpretation of its range: [99]

[95] Prudential Insurance Co. v. Cheek, 259 U.S. 530 (1922).
[96] Gitlow v. New York, 268 U.S. 652 (1925).
[97] 347 U.S. 442.
[98] *Id.* at 470 (dissenting opinion).
[99] *Id.* at 472.

The right to work, I had assumed, was the most precious liberty that man possesses. Man has indeed as much right to work as he has to live, to be free, to own property. . . . To work means to eat. It also means to live. For many it would be better to work in jail, than to sit idle on the curb. The great values of freedom are in the opportunities afforded man to press to new horizons, to pit his strength against the forces of nature, to match skills with his fellow man.

It would be a little hard to laud a right so fully in one breath and in the next to say that judicial review has no concern with it except insofar as another right like freedom of speech is also involved.

In view of such pronouncements it is not surprising that the Court a few years later struck down such a restraint on occupational freedom. In *Schware* v. *Board of Bar Examiners*,[100] petitioner had been refused permission to take the State bar examination on the ground that he lacked "good moral character." Again First Amendment problems were mingled with the right-to-work issue, but again the language of the Justices suggested a standard that would forbid arbitrary determinations in general. Mr. Justice Black for the Court declared that State-imposed qualifications "must have a rational connection with the applicant's fitness or capacity" to practice the occupation, and continued: "Even in applying permissible standards, officers of a State cannot exclude an applicant when there is no basis for their finding that he fails to meet these standards, or when their action is invidiously discriminatory." [101] This language is potentially far-reaching, for it suggests (as does the body of the opinion) that the Court is prepared to review and evaluate the administration of licensing requirements in the professions and trades in general. If its potentiality were realized, it would mean that licensing boards were now constitutionally required to show that their findings had a basis in evidence, and that would go far to bring economic rights back under the shelter of the Constitution.

This is probably too much to wring from the decision, although it is easy to believe that Black would be quite prepared to carry it thus far. Mr. Justice Frankfurter's concurring opinion for himself and two others was much more careful. He would, as in his *Barsky* opinion, allow the Board wide discretion in judg-

[100] 353 U.S. 232 (1957).
[101] *Id.* at 239.

ing "moral character" and would not question individual determinations simply because they involve intuitions, impressions, and other "subjective factors," rather than hard, objective evidence. But even he would overthrow a determination based on "avowed considerations" that were inadmissible under appropriate doctrines of due process.[102] This in itself would establish a modest but significant degree of judicial surveillance in the economic field. Nor is there anything in a trio of 1961 "right-to-work" decisions [103] to suggest that the Court was backtracking on this point. To be sure the majority found in each case that the State restriction was rationally justified. But Mr. Justice Harlan, who spoke for the Court in all three, went to considerable lengths to find and evaluate that rational basis. However unsatisfactory his conclusions were to the dissenters, the process of reaching them did not have the perfunctory quality of cases like Olsen [104] and Queenside Realty,[105] where the rational-basis terminology seemed to be recited for rhetorical purposes only. Here, on the contrary, a real inquiry was being made.

VII. REQUIESCAT IN PACE

It appears then that the Court has at least taken the preliminary steps for re-establishing judicial review of laws infringing occupational freedom. Whether the operative doctrine should be the rather strict one suggested by Mr. Justice Black in Schware [106] or the more tolerant one implied in Mr. Justice Frankfurter's concurrence,[107] the fact is that some genuine review of laws in this field does seem plausible. The doctrinal road is open. Of course, the opening of that road with respect to the right to work does not necessarily clear the way for review of other governmental inroads on economic freedom. As has been intimated, there may be special reasons for protecting the right to work: the primacy of the right to the affected individual, the difficulty of protecting it through ordinary political processes. Indeed, there is no assurance that the apparently new attitude toward occupational freedom will itself be translated into the actuality of constitutional

[102] Id. at 249. (Emphasis added).
[103] Cohen v. Hurley, 366 U.S. 117; In re Anastaplo, 366 U.S. 82; Konigsberg v. State Bar, 366 U.S. 36.
[104] Olsen v. Nebraska, 313 U.S. 236 (1941).
[105] Queenside Hills Realty Co. v. Saxl, 328 U.S. 80 (1946).
[106] Note 100 supra.
[107] Id. at 247.

limitation. The Court's present position is somewhat similar to the position of 1925–1930 when a doctrinal basis had been laid for protecting speech against State action, but no State law had actually been struck down. Only the Justices themselves could tell us whether the guilds are going to have their comfortable world disturbed by the *deus ex machina* of the Constitution. And perhaps even they could not enlighten us, for there is little in the preceding survey to suggest that they are prone to think a course of action out before embarking on it.

Nevertheless it is legitimate, and perhaps timely, for an observer of the Court's work to ask whether constitutional law *should* move down that road again, whether the Court should reassert its claim to examine the reasonableness of economic legislation. To reiterate a point that has perhaps already been sufficiently made, this is not a question whether the Justices should return to the dogmatics of *Adkins* [108] and *Ribnik*,[109] or to the delusions of grandeur that prompted the judicial crusade against the New Deal, or to the tangled thickets of *Smyth* v. *Ames*.[110] The Court could not re-establish "laissez faire" even if it wanted to; some economic matters are too big for the Court to handle and some are too intricate. The question is simply whether the Court should begin to apply a modest but real version of the rational-basis standard in economic fields that are not intrinsically inaccessible to the judicial power.

As has been argued earlier, none of the usual justifications for saying "no" to this question will quite do. Some of the rights involved, such as occupational freedom, are not unimportant, nor are they necessarily any more beyond the reach of judicial capacity than other rights which the Justices have chosen to protect. If this were 1937, if the Court were poised on the brink of the modern constitutional era, the case for retaining some constitutional limits in the economic field might be strong. Those who planned the course of future events might well feel that the objective of a just society would be best served by a judicial policy in which economic rights held a respected place. But the year is not 1937, it is 1962; and modern constitutional policy has developed, not by plan but by impulse, not as a coherent body of doctrine but as a congeries of *ad hoc* responses. These circumstances raise a point that takes us back to the opening paragraphs

[108] Adkins v. Children's Hospital, 261 U.S. 525 (1923).
[109] Ribnik v. McBride, 277 U.S. 350 (1928).
[110] 169 U.S. 466 (1898).

of this essay. They may constitute in themselves a compelling reason for leaving economic due process in repose.

The reason has to do with what might be called judicial economy. The Court's personal-rights decisions in the past twenty-five years have involved constitutional law in some of the most difficult and emotion-charged issues that modern American government faces. The problem of defining and defending the legal rights of Negroes, in a society that has long shamefully neglected their rights, is alone formidable enough to tax the intellectual and power resources of a single tribunal. Yet this is only the beginning of the lofty assignments the Justices have set for themselves. They have undertaken to evaluate governmental encroachments on political and artistic expression, to supervise, in increasing degree, State administration of criminal law. And each of these major personal-rights categories is replete with subcategories, each of which poses ample problems of its own. Nor is there any sign that the rate of accretion is slowing down. In 1962, the Court, in one opinion, brought the jungle of electoral apportionment under judicial scrutiny [111] and, in another, reasserted its willingness to act as a national school board in the field of church-state relationships.[112]

Even if there were no practical, political limitations on the range of Court power, this multitude of self-imposed tasks would be intimidating. The lines between liberty and authority, between justice and injustice, between the necessary and the intolerable, are not easy to draw in a single field: to lay them down in such a variety of fields requires a whole series of painstaking evaluations in which not only intuition, but hard, searching analysis must play its part. It is a common and just complaint that the modern Court has so far failed to develop reasoned formulations for many of its judgments in the personal-rights area.[113] This means that important work is left undone each time the Court gathers to itself a new subject for review. Having spent the last twenty-five years assuming new tasks, the Justices could easily spend the next twenty-five working out the problem

[111] Baker v. Carr, 369 U.S. 186 (1962). See Neal, *Baker v. Carr: Politics in Search of Law,* [1962] *Supreme Court Review, infra.*

[112] Engel v. Vitale, 370 U.S. 421 (1962). See Kurland, *The Regents' Prayer Case: "Full of Sound and Fury, Signifying . . ."* [1962] *Supreme Court Review* 1, *supra.*

[113] See Wechsler, *Toward Neutral Principles of Constitutional Law,* 73 Harv. L. Rev. 1 (1959); Kurland, *op. cit. supra* note 6.

of how those tasks should be done. These considerations in themselves might argue against taking on any further assignments for the time being, leaving the question of practical power out of account.

In the long run, however, that issue cannot be left out of account. The Supreme Court is an agency of government and, like other agencies of government, must work within the limits of political possibility. It has been suggested above that a revival of economic due process in connection with a subject like occupational freedom would not by itself overstrain the Court's power. But when the prospect of such a devolpment is considered against the background of other recent assumptions of authority, the calculus may be very different. Various personal-rights decisions during that period have taxed not only the "time-chart" [114] and the reasoning power of the Justices but their effective prestige as well. In the summer of 1958, an accumulation of political resentment led to one of the most serious—and most nearly successful—congressional counterattacks in judicial history.[115] No one yet knows whether *Baker* v. *Carr* will make more friends for the Court than it makes enemies, but there seems at this writing to be little question about *Engel* v. *Vitale* on this score.[116] Doubtless it is regrettable that factors like these must be brought into an assessment of judicial capacities. A world in which the ethical-legal mandates of the Court were accepted without question by those affected would be a comfortable world for the Justices and perhaps not a bad one for the United States as a whole. But it is not, and never has been, the world the Court lives in; and in the real world a friend of the Court quails at the thought of seeing it assume still another politically delicate task.

All things considered, then, it seems best that the cause of economic rights be left by the Supreme Court to lie in its uneasy grave. This need not mean that the legislatures of the nation are warranted in ignoring them, nor that the State courts, applying their own constitutions, should be indifferent to plausible due-

[114] See Hart, *Foreword: The Time Chart of the Justices*, 73 *Harv. L. Rev.* 84 (1959).

[115] See Murphy, *Congress and the Court* (1962).

[116] See Lewis, *Supreme Court's Term Viewed As One of Most Significant in Its History*, N.Y. Times, July 2, 1962, p. 12; *The Court Decision —and the School Prayer Furor*, 60 *Newsweek* 43 (July 9, 1962); Kurland, *supra* note 112.

process claims.[117] These rights, or some of them, do have a bearing on the justness of a society and on the happiness and well-being of the people who live in it. If the Supreme Court of today had a free hand in choosing the subjects of judicial review, there might well be an argument for choosing the right to work over some of the other subjects that engage Court attention. But it does not have a free hand; its liberty of choice has been considerably foreclosed by the episodic course of constitutional law since 1937. The Supreme Court, like the American political system of which it is a part, proceeds by impulse rather than by design, pragmatically rather than foresightedly. Like the United States, the Court derives advantages from this approach; but like the United States, the Court, too, is bound by its limitations.

[117] But see Hoskins & Katz, *Substantive Due Process in the States Revisited,* 18 *Ohio St. L. J.* 384 (1952).

6. The Problems of Yesteryear — Commerce and Due Process

ROBERT L. STERN

EDITORIAL NOTE. Dissenting in 1936 from a majority opinion which completely sealed off the entire realm of agriculture from the reaches of the national commerce power, Justice Stone declared, "Courts are not the only agency of government that must be assumed to have the capacity to govern." Elsewhere in the same dissent, he added, "the only check upon our own exercise of power is our own sense of self restraint." Within a decade the situation respecting the national commerce power had totally changed, and nothing has since altered the new dispensation. It may now be said of that power that Congress is the only agency of government that is assumed to have the capacity to govern, or, to put the point another way, that the Court has no capacity whatever. The only check now on Congress's exercise of the commerce power is Congress's own sense of self-restraint.

For all practical purposes the scope of the national commerce power is a political question; it is no longer a constitutional question nor even a subject of constitutional law. By definition constitutional law in the American sense means that limitations which are derived from some higher authority, and are policed by a supreme court, circumscribe the exercise of governmental authority. But there are no longer any meaningful constitutional limitations on the national commerce power. Congress may do as it wishes; policy is politically determined, without constitutional restraints. There is now only a constitutional law of the commerce clause as a source of limitations upon state authority.

In Wickard v. Filburn, a 1942 case which opened the entire realm of agriculture to the national commerce power, the Court, in describing that power with a breadth never exceeded, asserted that Chief Justice Marshall, when deciding Gibbons v. Ogden— the mainstay of modern commerce decisions—had described the power "with a breadth never yet exceeded. He made emphatic the embracing and penetrating nature of this power by warning that effective restraints on its exercise must proceed from political rather than judicial processes." Marshall in fact compared the national commerce power to the power of declaring war, and expressly cautioned that the wisdom and discretion of Congress plus the influence of the people in elections, constituted "the sole restraints" which guard against abuse of either power. One may of course imagine some reprehensible, far-fetched legislation, passed under the guise of the commerce clause, which would provoke the Court to a declaration of unconstitutionality—such as an act of Congress barring the New York Times from the channels of commerce. The commerce power must be exercised in subordination to the principles of the First Amendment and procedural requirements of due process. But tortured examples drawn from nightmares prove nothing.

The commerce clause is Congress's authority to regulate every aspect of the nation's economy, should it wish to do so. It is a power "commensurate with national needs," to use the language of a 1946 decision. Its limitations may be formally stated, but they have no realistic application. For the record, those limitations were described as recently as 1964 in one of the cases sustaining the constitutionality of the public accommodations section of the Civil Rights Act of that year. The activities that are beyond the reach of Congress, said the Court, quoting Gibbons v. Ogden, are "those which are completely within a particular State, which do not affect other States, and with which it is not necessary to interfere, for the purpose of executing some of the general powers of government." This rule, added the Court, is as good today as when Marshall laid it down nearly a century and a half ago. But it is a rule which means nothing for practical purposes. One cannot imagine a legitimate economic regulation by Congress which the Court might void as a violation of the commerce clause. Whenever a case raises a question of the constitutionality of Congressional exercise of this power, the only thing in doubt is the size of the Court majority. No act of Congress, needless to add, has been struck down on commerce grounds, since 1936.

Has the Court construed the clause too generously, even promiscuously? Marshall's description of its meaning in Gibbons and his warning that its "sole restraints" were to be found in the ballot box, suggest that the modern Court has fulfilled the intentions of the framers of the Constitution. The records of the Federal Convention support this view. As John P. Roche pointed out in the first essay in this volume, the Virginia Plan proposed a strong, autonomous central government with undefined, sweeping powers; opponents concentrated their fire on the institutional structure rather than on the proposed scope of national authority. When a draft constitution in the form of resolutions was unanimously sent to the Committee on Detail, one resolution authorized Congress "to legislate in all cases for the general interests of the union" as well as in the cases in which the separate states were incompetent or disrupted the harmony of the United States. The Committee on Detail simply enumerated or broke down these vast powers into component parts without diminishing them. The comerce clause was then adopted unanimously, without discussion. The delegates apparently believed that the clause differed only in phrasing but not in spirit or meaning from the unanimous resolution instructing the Committee on Detail.

The power to regulate "interstate commerce" is not the power vested by the Constitution. Shortened or popularized phrases are sometimes used in place of the correct phrase of the document itself, and such phrases often come to have a life of their own with a meaning that differs from the original. The right against self-incrimination, for example, is much narrower than the right guaranteed in the Constitution, the right not to be a witness against oneself. Interstate commerce, literally, is commerce between the states, signifying movement across state lines. But the constitutional phrase is commerce "among" the states, which Marshall in Gibbons understood as much broader than "between." "Among," he said, meant "intermingled with," or commerce "which concerns more States than one." Commerce completely within a state's borders, he noted, may "affect other States." This reading of the commerce clause, which comports with the framers' intent and the document itself, results in the limitless scope given to the clause since 1936.

Perhaps the most important reason for the scope of the

clause, as construed by the Court, is economic. As Robert L. Stern observes in the following essay, industry is nationally organized and its operations, like the economy itself, are interrelated and integrated. Commerce is a process not divisible into formal or artificial boundaries, one labeled "interstate" and the other "intrastate." The power must follow the process without respect to the artificial boundaries. Chief Justice Hughes, when still mesmerized by legalistic formulas that ignored economic realities, declared in a case of 1935, that if the national commerce power were construed to reach any economic activity that had an effect upon "interstate" commerce, the national authority would embrace practically all economic activity and the authority of the states over their domestic concerns "would exist only by sufferance of the federal government." Hughes's statement was prophetic. In the same case, Justice Cardozo remarked, "Motion at the outer rim is communicated perceptibly, though minutely, to recording instruments at the center. A society such as ours is an elastic medium which transmit all tremors throughout its territory." Cardozo understood what Hughes later learned the hard way about the nature of our economy and its necessary impact on the commerce power. The small farmer who consumes his own crops in the form of seed, feed, and food comes within the national commerce power, even though his activity is admittedly local and may not even be "commerce." So ruled the Court in Wickard v. Filburn. The farmer's activity was like a spit in the commercial ocean, only a spit, but it had a ripple effect, a tremor in Cardozo's word, which affected interstate commerce.

The essay by Stern, who is perhaps the nation's foremost student of the history of the commerce clause, succinctly describes and interprets the single most important development in modern constitutional history, the emancipation of the national commerce power. Nothing has occurred since the publication of this essay which in any way outdates it. The most notable commerce clause cases since 1951 were the companion cases of 1964 in which the Court upheld the provisions of the Civil Rights Act outlawing segregation in motels and restaurants. Yet no new doctrines emerged in those decisions. The "principles which we apply today," said the Court, "are those first formulated by Chief Justice Marshall in Gibbons v. Ogden." But the Court did not fail to quote also from modern precedents which Stern discusses, including the Wickard case mentioned above. In sum the Court has abdicated its power of judicial review when passing on the constitutionality of Congressional exercises of the commerce power.

Holmes, in a famous statement, once said that he did not think the Union would be imperiled if the Court had no power to declare acts of Congress unconstitutional, but that the loss of judicial review over state acts would imperil the country. "For one in my place," he added, "sees how often a local policy prevails with those who are not trained to national views and how often action is taken that embodies what the Commerce Clause was meant to end." The clause remains a significant limitation on the power of the states to tax and regulate their economies as the second section of Stern's essay shows. But his stress on the Southern Pacific, Morgan, Hood and Dean Milk cases gives the somewhat misleading impression that much state legislation affecting interstate commerce is struck down. Such cases are in fact few in number, and it is surprising that Stern, who writes with a strong nationalist bias, should not criticize the Court for its excessive tolerance when reviewing state acts. In some states, state property and franchise taxes on railroads exceed the earnings attributable to their business in those states. There are many state acts that discriminate against interstate commerce and encroach on national authority with impunity. For example, permitting Illinois to tax interstate trucking at rates that go as high as $1,580 for large trucks permits a burden on interstate commerce, although the Court ruled otherwise. But as Hughes prophesied, state authority exists at the sufferance of Congress. Stone best summed up the matter in the Southern Pacific case when he said, "Congress has undoubted power to redefine the distribution of power over interstate commerce. It may either permit the state to regulate the commerce in a manner which would otherwise not be permissible, or exclude state regulation even of matters of peculiarly local concern which nevertheless affect interstate commerce." If it be asked how Congress can delegate to the states a power which is not only vested in Congress but in some cases may be prohibited to the states as a matter of constitutional law, the answer is as Marshall, once again, said, that the power to regulate is the power to prescribe the rule by which commerce is to be governed. Such is the very remarkable state of constitutional law in our time.

THE PROBLEMS OF YESTERYEAR— COMMERCE AND DUE PROCESS

Less than fifteen years ago, there were constitutional problems important enough to stir the country, to threaten the sanctity of the Supreme Court. These were the culmination of at least three decades of judicial controversy, in which the pressure of events brought criticism of the Court's decisions, both in noteworthy dissenting opinions and outside, to a new height. Fifteen years later, there still are difficult and important constitutional problems, and there still is criticism of the Supreme Court's decisions—though on a relatively minor scale. But the issues which rocked more than the legal world in the 1930's and in the period preceding have disappeared. A glance backwards to see what happened to them may help give perspective to the significance of the problems of the current day.

The crucial issue prior to 1937 was whether the Constitution prohibited government—state and Federal—from interfering with the free play of economic forces (outside of the field of public utilities)—no matter how great the public need. Federal legislation dealing with other phases of national or interstate industry than transportation was on important occasions found to invade the powers reserved to the states.[1] State laws were frequently found invalid because they impinged on the field of interstate commerce committed by the Constitution to the Federal Congress.[2] And the due process clauses of the Fifth and Fourteenth

[1] Carter v. Carter Coal Co., 298 U.S. 238, 56 Sup. Ct. 855, 80 L. Ed. 1160 (1936); United States v. Butler, 297 U.S. 1, 56 Sup. Ct. 312, 80 L. Ed. 477 (1936); Railroad Retirement Board v. Alton R.R., 295 U.S. 330, 55 Sup. Ct. 758, 79 L. Ed. 1468 (1935); Schechter Corp. v. United States, 295 U.S. 495, 55 Sup. Ct. 651, 79 L. Ed. 1570 (1935); United Mine Workers v. Coronado Coal Co., 259 U.S. 344, 42 Sup. Ct. 570, 66 L. Ed. 975 (1922); Hammer v. Dagenhart, 247 U.S. 251, 38 Sup. Ct. 529, 62 L. Ed. 1101 (1918); Hopkins v. United States, 171 U.S. 578, 19 Sup. Ct. 40, 43 L. Ed. 290 (1898); United States v. E. C. Knight Co., 156 U.S. 1, 15 Sup. Ct. 249, 39 L. Ed. 325 (1895).

[2] E.g., DiSanto v. Pennsylvania, 273 U.S. 34, 47 Sup. Ct. 267, 71 L. Ed. 524 (1927); Leisy v. Hardin, 135 U.S. 100, 10 Sup. Ct. 681, 34 L. Ed. 128 (1890). The cases up to 1932 are collected in Gavit, The Commerce Clause 551–6, Appendix E (1932).

Amendments were held to bar both state and federal governments from regulating such economic factors as prices, wages, and labor relations in businesses "not affected with a public interest." [3]

There were, of course, cases which ran counter to these general trends [4] and which seemed to offer hope that the Court would relax its restrictions. But as late as 1936 the Court was still holding that labor relations in the coal industry only affected interstate commerce "indirectly," and therefore were not subject to the power of Congress,[5] that the amount of cotton produced in the United States was only of local concern and therefore not subject to federal control; [6] and that the fixing of minimum wages for women violated the due process clause.[7] These decisions, and the doctrines for which they stand, now seem antediluvian. Although they hardly can be said to be of great antiq-

---

[3] Morehead v. New York ex rel. Tipaldo, 298 U.S. 587, 56 Sup. Ct. 918, 80 L. Ed. 1347 (1936); New State Ice Co. v. Liebmann, 285 U.S. 262, 52 Sup. Ct. 371, 76 L. Ed. 747 (1932); Williams v. Standard Oil Co., 278 U.S. 235, 49 Sup. Ct. 115, 73 L. Ed. 287 (1929); Ribnik v. McBride, 277 U.S. 350, 48 Sup. Ct. 545, 72 L. Ed. 913 (1928); Tyson & Brother v. Banton, 273 U.S. 418, 47 Sup. Ct. 426, 71 L. Ed. 718 (1927); Adkins v. Children's Hospital, 261 U.S. 525, 43 Sup. Ct. 394, 67 L. Ed. 785 (1923); Charles Wolff Packing Co. v. Court of Industrial Relations, 262 U.S. 522, 43 Sup. Ct. 630, 67 L. Ed. 1103 (1923); Adams v. Tanner, 244 U.S. 590, 37 Sup. Ct. 662, 61 L. Ed. 1336 (1917); Coppage v. Kansas, 236 U.S. 1, 35 Sup. Ct. 240, 59 L. Ed. 441 (1915); Adair v. United States, 208 U.S. 161, 28 Sup. Ct. 277, 52 L. Ed. 436 (1908); Lochner v. New York, 198 U.S. 45, 25 Sup. Ct. 539, 49 L. Ed. 937 (1905).

[4] Commerce cases: Local 167 v. United States, 291 U.S. 293, 54 Sup. Ct. 396, 78 L. Ed. 804 (1934); Coronado Coal Co., v. United Mine Workers, 268 U.S. 295, 45 Sup. Ct. 551, 69 L. Ed. 963 (1925); Chicago Board of Trade v. Olsen, 262 U.S. 1, 43 Sup. Ct. 470, 67 L. Ed. 839 (1923); Stafford v. Wallace, 258 U.S. 495, 42 Sup. Ct. 397, 66 L. Ed. 735 (1922); Standard Oil Co. v. United States, 221 U.S. 1, 31 Sup Ct. 502, 55 L. Ed. (1911); Swift & Co. v. United States, 196 U.S. 375, 25 Sup. Ct. 276, 49 L. Ed. 519 (1905). Due process cases: Nebbia v. New York, 291 U.S. 502, 54 Sup. Ct. 92, 78 L. Ed. 940 (1934); O'Gorman & Young v. Hartford Fire Ins. Co. 282 U.S. 251, 51 Sup. Ct. 130, 75 L. Ed. 324 (1931); Texas & New Orleans R. R. v. Brotherhood of Railway Clerks, 281 U.S. 548, 50 Sup. Ct. 427, 74 L. Ed. 1034 (1930).

[5] Carter v. Carter Coal Co., 298 U.S. 238, 56 Sup. Ct. 855, 80 L. Ed. 1160 (1936).

[6] United States v. Butler, 297 U.S. 1, 56 Sup. Ct. 312, 80 L. Ed. 477 (1936).

[7] Morehead v. New York ex rel. Tipaldo, 298 U.S. 587, 56 Sup. Ct. 918, 80 L. Ed. 1347 (1936).

uity, they have a much less modern ring and infinitely less authority than *Gibbons* v. *Ogden*,[8] decided in 1824.

As all who remember the spring of 1937 in the Supreme Court will recall, the great reversal in constitutional adjudication took place prior to any change in the personnel of the Court—shortly after President Roosevelt announced his plan to add six new Justices to the Supreme Court. This is not the occasion to explore the details of that fascinating period, a story which has often been told elsewhere.[9] Suffice it to say that as new Justices began ascending the bench during the following terms, the principles of the 1937 decisions came to be firmly entrenched. The four original dissenters—Justices Van Devanter, Sutherland, Butler, and McReynolds—were quickly reduced to the latter two by voluntary retirement, and then to none. And although the new Court in turn has divided into groups sometimes labeled—accurately or inaccurately—as "conservative" and "liberal," there has seldom been any difference of opinion as to any of the old fighting issues. For a time, cases requiring interpretation of the doctrines finally accepted in 1937 continued to reach the Court. These cases enabled the Court to flesh out the content of the newly accepted—if not newly invented[10]—doctrines. But in recent years fewer and fewer such cases have been heard by the Court, both because most lawyers have probably realized the futility of waging the useless battle any longer, and because, except in very unusual situations, the Court refuses to hear most such cases when attorneys do attempt to bring them up. Only cases on the periphery of the "new" doctrines are now likely to arouse the interest of the Court.

A brief discussion of the principles which the Court now applies, and of the cases since 1937, will indicate both the extent to which the subjects are no longer regarded as controversial and the locality of the present borderline of uncertainty.

I. SUBSTANTIVE DUE PROCESS

In a series of decisions prior to 1930, the Supreme Court had held that the "liberty" guaranteed by the due process clause in-

[8] 9 Wheat. 1, 6 L. Ed. 23 (1824).

[9] E.g., Jackson, *The Struggle for Judicial Supremacy* (1941); Stern, The Commerce Clause and the National Economy, 1933–1946, 59 Harv. L. Rev. 645, 883 (1946).

[10] Some of the "new" doctrines can be traced back to ohn Marshall. See p. 171 *infra*.

cluded liberty to contract, and that except in "business affected
with a public interest," governmental interference with such essential economic relationships as prices and wages was an infringe-
ment of that liberty.[11] Since the validity of many restrictions
upon the freedom of business men was sustained,[12] the only
general rule which could be drawn from the decisions was that
types of regulation of which the Court sufficiently disapproved
were unconstitutional.

Although the Nebbia case in 1934,[13] in which Mr. Justice
Roberts joined Chief Justice Hughes and Justices Brandeis, Stone,
and Cardozo in sustaining a New York statute fixing minimum
prices for milk, seemed to presage a departure from this rule,
Morehead v. Tipaldo,[14] in 1936, saw Mr. Justice Roberts joining
the conservative Justices to nullify the New York minimum wage
law, on the disputable ground that overruling of Adkins v. Children's Hospital [15] had not been specifically requested. In 1937,
however, he rejoined the liberal Justices to overrule the Adkins
case and uphold the validity of the Washington minimum wage
legislation in West Coast Hotel v. Parrish.[16] On the same day
and two weeks later the provisions of the Railway Labor Act
and the National Labor Relations Act, requiring employers to
bargain exclusively with the representatives chosen by a majority
of the employees, were held not to violate the due process
clause [17]—decisions clearly inconsistent with Adair v. United
States [18] and Coppage v. Kansas [19] decided in 1908 and 1915.

The 1937 decisions declared that regulatory legislation would
not be found to violate the due process clause merely because
it restricted economic liberty. Only restrictions which were in
fact arbitrary, or not reasonably related to a proper legislative
purpose, it was suggested, would be held unconstitutional in the

[11] See cases cited in note 3 supra.

[12] E.g., the antitrust laws, zoning laws, banking and insurance laws,
laws relating to conservation, workmen's compensation, health and safety,
laws designed to protect the public against deception and fraud.

[13] Nebbia v. New York, 291 U.S. 502, 54 Sup. Ct. 505, 78 L. Ed. 940
(1934).

[14] 298 U.S. 587, 56 Sup. Ct. 918, 80 L. Ed. 1347 (1936).

[15] 261 U.S. 525, 43 Sup. Ct. 394, 67 L. Ed. 785 (1923).

[16] 300 U.S. 379, 57 Sup. Ct. 578, 81 L. Ed. 703 (1937).

[17] Virginian Ry v. System Federation No. 40, 300 U.S. 515, 57 Sup.
Ct. 592, 81 L. Ed. 789 (1937); National Labor Relations Board v. Jones
& Laughlin Steel Corp., 301 U.S. 1, 57 Sup. Ct. 615, 81 L. Ed. 893 (1937).

[18] 236 U.S. 1, 35 Sup. Ct. 240, 59 L. Ed. 441 (1915).

[19] 208 U.S. 161, 28 Sup. Ct. 277, 52 L. Ed. 436 (1908).

future. Subsequently, in the Carolene Products case, the Court, through Mr. Justice Stone, stated:

[T]he existence of facts supporting the legislative judgment is to be presumed, for regulatory legislation affecting ordinary commercial transactions is not to be pronounced unconstitutional unless in the light of the facts made known or generally assumed it is of such a character as to preclude the assumption that it rests upon some rational basis within the knowledge and experience of the legislators. . . .

[B]y their very nature such inquiries, where the legislative judgment is drawn in question, must be restricted to the issue whether any state of facts either known or which could reasonably be assumed affords support for it. . . .[20]

Since it is difficult to conceive of any statute for which some rational basis may not be found, this test means that the due process barrier to substantive legislation as to economic matters has been in effect removed—although it still stands in theory against completely arbitrary legislative action.

As might be expected, under this doctrine no statutes have been held violative of the due process clause on grounds of substantive irrationality since 1937. In 1939 and 1940, the Court sustained federal statutes fixing prices of milk and coal,[21] in 1941 the minimum wage provisions of the Fair Labor Standards Act,[22] and in 1944 the general price and rent provisions of the Emergency Price Control Act.[23] *Olsen* v. *Nebraska*,[24] which upheld a state law regulating the fees fixed by employment agencies, explicitly repudiated "the philosophy and approach of the majority" of the Court in the pre-Nebbia price fixing cases. And *Lincoln Union* v. *Northwestern Iron Co.*,[25] in sustaining state laws prohibiting the closed shop, made it clear that this principle would be applied to laws restricting the freedom to contract of

[20] United States v. Carolene Products Co., 304 U.S. 144, 152, 154, 58 Sup. Ct. 778, 82 L. Ed. 1234 (1938).

[21] United States v. Rock Royal Co-Op., 307 U.S. 533, 59 Sup. Ct. 993, 83 L. Ed. 1446 (1939); Sunshine Anthracite Coal Co. v. Adkins, 310 U.S. 381, 60 Sup. Ct. 907, 84 L. Ed. 1263 (1940).

[22] United States v. Darby, 312 U.S. 100, 61 Sup. Ct. 451, 85 L. Ed. 609 (1941).

[23] Yakus v. United States, 321 U.S. 414, 64 Sup. Ct. 660, 88 L. Ed. 834 (1944); Bowles v. Willingham, 321 U.S. 503, 64 Sup. Ct. 641, 88 L. Ed. 892 (1944).

[24] 313 U.S. 236, 61 Sup. Ct. 862, 85 L. Ed. 1305 (1941).

[25] 335 U.S. 525, 69 Sup. Ct. 251, 93 L. Ed. 212 (1949).

employees as well as employers. In other cases, the Court has disposed summarily of the contention that statutes were in violation of the due process clause because they interfered with economic freedom or were otherwise unreasonable.[26]

Although there is no longer doubt as to how the Court will decide cases of this sort, it cannot be said that the Court has limited the due process clause to procedural matters and repudiated the concept of due process as a bar to sufficiently arbitrary or irrational substantive legislation—although Mr. Justice Black's opinion in the Lincoln Union case looks strongly in that direction. The Court has certainly not so stated in express terms, and the opinions still continue to examine legislation under attack to see whether it has a rational basis or is "substantially related to a legitimate end sought to be attained." [27] But, as the Court recently declared, "a pronounced shift of emphasis . . . has deprived the words 'unreasonable' and 'arbitrary' of the content" which they formerly held.[28] The self-abnegation with which the Court now applies the rationality test may, as a practical matter, make it unnecessary for the Court to decide whether it must reconsider the basic doctrine.

Recent decisions have given the due process clause broad scope in protecting against state action the rights guaranteed by the First Amendment and also other "fundamental" rights contained in the first eight amendments.[29] Certainly the rights to freedom of speech, press, and religion are not "procedural" in the ordinary sense. The due process clause would thus seem still to be interpreted as embodying a restriction which is substantive rather than procedural—but in an orbit entirely different

[26] Cities Service Oil Co. v. Peerless Oil & Gas Co., 340 U.S. 179, 186, 71 Sup. Ct. 215 (1950); Railway Express Agency v. United States, 336 U.S. 106, 109, 69 Sup. Ct. 463, 93 L. Ed. 533 (1949); Sage Stores v. Kansas, 323 U.S. 32, 36, 65 Sup. Ct. 9, 89 L. Ed. 25 (1944); Carolene Products Co. v. United States, 323 U.S. 18, 29, 65 Sup. Ct. 1, 89 L. Ed. 15 (1944); Railroad Commission v. Rowan & Nichols Oil Co., 311 U.S. 570, 61 Sup. Ct. 343, 85 L. Ed. 358 (1941); Railroad Commission v. Rowan & Nichols Oil Co., 310 U.S. 573, 60 Sup. Ct. 613, 84 L. Ed. 1368 (1940), as amended, 311 U.S. 614, 61 Sup. Ct. 66, 85 L. Ed. 390 (1940); Mayo v. Lakeland Highlands Canning Co., 309 U.S. 310, 318, 60 Sup. Ct. 517, 84 L. Ed. 774 (1940).

[27] E.g., Cities Service Oil Co. v. Peerless Oil & Gas Co., 340 U.S. 179, 186, 71 Sup. Ct. 215 (1950).

[28] Daniel v. Family Security Life Ins. Co., 336 U.S. 220, 225, 69 Sup. Ct. 550, 93 L. Ed. 632 (1949).

[29] For an apt exposition of this, see Freund, On Understanding the Supreme Court, c. 1 (1949).

from that of the older cases. Significantly, in the field of civil liberties, the test is not whether there is a rational basis for legislation. Instead, since the due process clause is held to embody the content of the First Amendment, the legislation may be required to sustain the heavier burden imposed upon laws restricting First Amendment freedoms.[30] These problems are beyond the scope of this paper. They are suggested here only because of their bearing upon the presently unanswerable question as to the extent to which the due process clauses have been deprived of force as restrictions upon substantive law.

II. STATE POWER TO REGULATE INTERSTATE COMMERCE [31]

Since *Gibbons* v. *Ogden*,[32] and *Cooley* v. *Board of Wardens*,[33] it has been established that under the commerce clause some subjects of regulation are within the exclusive power of Congress, and that even in the absence of a showing of congressional intention some types of state laws are invalid. This has not meant that the states were deprived by the commerce clause of all power to enact measures affecting, or even directly regulating, interstate commerce. But at some point, when the national, as compared to the local, interest in the subject was sufficiently great, when the practical burden on interstate commerce became sufficiently clear, the Court has always drawn a line beyond which the states could not go.

The test applied in drawing this line has been expressed in various ways. In the Cooley case, the first authoritative formulation of the accepted doctrine, the Court declared:

> Now the power to regulate commerce, embraces a vast field, containing not only many, but exceedingly various subjects, quite unlike in their nature; some imperatively demanding a single uniform rule, operating equally on the commerce of the United States in every port; and some, like the subject now in question, as imperatively demanding that diversity, which alone can meet the local necessities of navigation.
>
> Either absolutely to affirm, or deny that the nature of this

[30] See Nietmotko v. Maryland, 340 U.S. 268, 71 Sup. Ct. 325 (1951); Kunz v. New York, 340 U.S. 290, 71 Sup. Ct. 312 (1951); Feiner v. New York, 340 U.S. 315, 71 Sup. Ct. 303 (1951); Kovacs v. Cooper, 336 U.S. 77, 69 Sup. Ct. 448, 93 L. Ed. 513 (1949); Saia v. New York, 334 U.S. 558, 68 Sup. Ct. 1148, 92 L. Ed. 1574 (1948), 2 Vand. L. Rev. 113, Thomas v. Collins, 323 U.S. 516, 65 Sup. Ct. 315, 89 L. Ed. 430 (1945), in which the prior authorities are collected and discussed.

[31] [This footnote omitted—ed.]

[32] 9 Wheat. 1, 6 L. Ed. 23 (1824).

[33] 12 How. 299, 13 L. Ed. 996 (1852).

power requires exclusive legislation by Congress, is to lose sight of the nature of the subjects of this power, and to assert concerning all of them, what is really applicable but to a part. Whatever subjects of this power are in their nature national, or admit only of one uniform system, or plan of regulation, may justly be said to be of such a nature as to require exclusive legislation by Congress.[34]

In some cases, this doctrine is regarded as "predicated upon the implications of the commerce clause itself," in others "upon the presumed intention of Congress, where Congress has not spoken." [35] Whatever the theory, the result is the same.

In the years preceding 1937, the Court, without ever openly abandoning the Cooley test, used many other expressions—such as whether the state law was a "burden," or a "substantial" or "undue" burden, on commerce, whether the effect on commerce was "direct" or "indirect," whether the regulation was or was not imposed "on" interstate commerce itself. It was difficult, if not impossible, to tell—at least with any certainty—whether these expressions merely constituted different methods of stating the Cooley doctrine, or whether the Court was applying different tests. The only generalization which could be drawn from the numerous decisions and expressions was, approximately in the words of my mentor on this subject,[36] that the states may regulate interstate commerce some, but not too much. Under this not very definite test, a great many state laws were held invalid.[37]

The principal change since 1937 has not yet been in the formula but in its application. For a number of years thereafter no nondiscriminatory [38] state regulations fell afoul of the commerce clause. Justice Black expressed the view that the Cooley doctrine itself went too far in limiting state power; he preferred the theory of Chief Justice Taney that only Congress, and not

[34] 12 How. at 319.

[35] Southern Pacific Co. v. Arizona, 325 U.S. 761, 768, 65 Sup. Ct. 1515, 89 L. Ed. 1915 (1945), citing cases; California v. Zook, 336 U.S. 725, 728, 69 Sup. Ct. 841, 93 L. Ed. 1005 (1949).

[36] Professor Thomas Reed Powell of Harvard Law School.

[37] See the compilation in Appendix E to Gavit, The Commerce Clause 550–56 (1932). This tabulation shows that during the decade 1921–1930, 38 state laws (both tax and regulatory) were found invalid under the commerce clause. Between 1941 and 1950 there were ten such decisions, of which five involved state taxes. Of the remaining five cases, three were concerned with statutes which would be regarded as discriminating against interstate commerce (see p. 162 infra). The remaining two cases are the southern Pacific and Morgan cases, discussed immediately below in the text.

[38] As to laws discriminating against interstate commerce, see p. 162 et seq.

the courts, could invalidate state legislation.[39] There was doubt as to whether the Court would find any nondiscriminatory state law in conflict with the commerce clause itself.

Southern Pacific Co. v. Arizona,[40] decided in 1945, and *Morgan v. Virginia,*[41] in 1946, not only resolved the doubt, but marked a definite reassertion of the principle of the Cooley case. In doing so, the Court speaking through Chief Justice Stone and following the thoughts expressed in his earlier opinions,[42] made explicit the considerations which would guide it in applying that principle. The test was a practical one, in which the actual effect upon interstate or national interests was weighed against the local or state interest involved. State laws limiting the number of cars on railroal trains and requiring the segregation of passengers in interstate busses were found to impinge upon commerce in fields in which national uniformity was essential. In the one instance the make-up of trains, and in the other the seating arrangement in busses was subject to disturbance at every state line if differing state regulations were permissible. On the other hand, state laws having a lesser impact upon interstate transportation, such as a requirement that cabooses be placed at the end of freight trains,[43] were upheld. The competing national interest has not been deemed sufficiently clear to prevent the states from fixing prices for natural gas and milk sold within a state for outside consumption, even though the direct effect was to raise prices for extrastate consumers.[44] Whether the decisions last cited would be applied to commodities generally, which did not present the problems peculiar to natural gas and milk, cannot be foretold.

The recent cases seem to integrate the "need for uniformity"

[39] See opinions of Mr. Justice Black, dissenting in Southern Pacific Co. v. Arizona, 325 U.S. 761, 784, 65 Sup. Ct. 1515, 89 L. Ed. 1915 (1945); concurring in Morgan v. Virginia, 328 U.S. 373, 386, 66 Sup. Ct. 1050, 90 L. Ed. 1317 (1946); dissenting in Hood & Sons v. DuMond, 336 U.S. 525, 545, 553, 69 Sup. Ct. 657, 93 L. Ed. 865 (1949). For Taney's views, see Frankfurter, *The Commerce Clause Under Marshall, Taney and Waite,* c. 2 (1937).

[40] 325 U.S. 761, 65 Sup. Ct. 1515, 89 L. Ed. 1915 (1945).

[41] 328 U.S. 373, 66 Sup. Ct. 1050, 90 L. Ed. 1317 (1946).

[42] E.g., DiSanto v. Pennsylvania, 273 U.S. 34, 44, 47 Sup. Ct. 267, 71 L. Ed. 524 (1927) (dissent).

[43] Terminal Railroad Ass'n v. Brotherhood of Railroad Trainmen, 318 U.S. 1, 63 Sup. Ct. 420, 87 L. Ed. 571 (1943).

[44] Cities Service Oil Co. v. Peerless Oil & Gas Co. 340 U.S. 179, 71 Sup. Ct. 215 (1950); Milk Control Board v. Eisenberg, 306 U.S. 346, 59 Sup. Ct. 528, 83 L. Ed. 752 (1939).

principle of the Cooley case and the "undue burden" formula appearing in later decisions with the statements requiring the weighing of conflicting local and national interests. In some sentences in the opinions, the first two concepts are stated in the alternative. Thus, in the Southern Pacific case, the Court declared that the states lack "authority to impede substantially the free flow of commerce from state to state, or to regulate those phases of the national commerce which, because of the need of national uniformity, demand that their regulation, if any, be prescribed by a single authority." [45] In the Morgan case, these two ideas—if they are two—are interwoven in Mr. Justice Reed's statement that "state legislation is invalid if it unduly burdens that commerce in matters where uniformity is necessary." [46] In California v. Zook,[47] the balancing of state and national interests is treated as a more accurate statement of the Cooley rule: "if a case falls within an area in commerce thought to demand a uniform national rule, state action is struck down. If the activity is one of predominantly local interest, state action is sustained. More accurately, the question is whether the state interest is outweighed by a national interest in the unhampered operation of interstate commerce." [48] These cases—and others [49] —recognize that the Court exercises a practical judgment in balancing the national interest against the local interest in each case.

Most recently, in December 1950, a unanimous Court, speaking through Mr. Justice Clark in Cities Service Gas Co. v. Peerless Oil & Gas Co.,[50] restated the governing principle as follows:

> It is now well settled that a state may regulate matters of local concern over which federal authority has not been exercised, even though the regulation has some impact on interstate commerce. . . . The only requirements consistently recognized have been that the regulation not discriminate against or place an embargo on interstate commerce, that it safeguard an obvious state

[45] 325 U.S. at 767.
[46] 328 U.S. at 377.
[47] 336 U.S. 725, 69 Sup. Ct. 841, 93 L. Ed. 1005 (1949).
[48] 336 U.S. at 728.
[49] Bob-Lo Excursion Co. v. Michigan, 333 U.S. 28, 37–40, 68 Sup. Ct. 358, 92 L. Ed. 455 (1948); Union Brokerage Co. v. Jensen, 322 U.S. 202, 211, 64 Sup. Ct. 967, 88 L. Ed. 1227 (1944); Illinois Natural Gas Co. v. Central Ill. Pub. Serv. Co., 314 U.S. 498, 506, 62 Sup. Ct. 384, 86 L. Ed. 371 (1942).
[50] 340 U.S. 179, 71 Sup. Ct. 215 (1950).

interest, and that the local interest at stake outweigh whatever national interest there might be in the prevention of state restrictions.[51]

It is likely—though not at all certain—that the Court will apply the same test whether the direct impact of the state law burdening interstate commerce is upon interstate or intrastate transactions. In *Parker* v. *Brown*,[52] the question presented was whether California regulation of the intrastate marketing of the bulk of the national crop of raisins before they were processed for interstate sale and shipment was prohibited by the commerce clause. The Court, speaking through Mr. Justice Stone, held that whether the proper rule was the "mechanical test" applied in some earlier cases, under which a state law was invalid if it regulated interstate—but not intrastate—commerce, or the balance of interest rule based upon an "accommodation of the competing demands of the state and national interest involved," [53] the state law was valid. But the reference to the first test as "mechanical" strongly suggests that the Court though such an approach an artificial one, which it would not favor if forced to a choice. The Parker decision cannot properly be appraised without reference to the fact that California's program had been approved and financed by the Secretary of Agriculture pursuant to congressional agricultural policy. The Court has subsequently cast some doubt as to whether, apart from this factor, the decision would have been the same.[54] And indeed, it is certainly arguable that the national commercial interest should prevent a state producing most of a commodity distributed throughout the nation from limiting the quantity produced or marketed in order to raise the price to consumers.[55] But, at least where the state is seeking to conserve a limited national resource, the state's authority seems to be definitely established.[56]

Both the Southern Pacific and the Morgan cases significantly rejected the contention that a state may avoid the limitations of

[51] 340 U.S. at 186–87.

[52] 317 U.S. 341, 63 Sup. Ct. 307, 87 L. Ed. 315 (1943).

[53] 317 U.S. at 362.

[54] Hood & Sons v. DuMond, 336 U.S. 525, 537, 69 Sup. Ct. 657, 93 L. Ed. 865 (1949), 3 Vand. L. Rev. 113.

[55] See p. 163 *infra*.

[56] Cities Service Gas Co. v. Peerless Oil & Gas Co. 340 U.S. 179, 71 Sup. Ct. 215 (1950); Champlin Refining Co. v. Corporation Commission, 286 U.S. 210, 52 Sup. Ct. 559, 76 L. Ed. 1062 (1932); see Note, 64 Harv. L. Rev. 642 (1951).

the general doctrine of the Cooley case by "simply invoking the convenient apologetics of the police power," [57] in the former as a means of preventing accidents, and in the latter to avert possible friction between races. Although a great many cases have upheld state laws relating to safety, even as applied to interstate transportation,[58] the Court pointed to other safety regulations held invalid when the burden upon interstate commerce became unduly great.[59] State regulation of the weight and width of motor trucks on interstate highways, which concededly "materially interfered with interstate commerce," [60] was differentiated on the ground that the highways were built, maintained, and policed by the states and were, therefore, of peculiar local concern, or, more accurately, constituted a subject over which "the state has exceptional scope for the exercise of its regulatory power." [61]

The conclusion to be drawn from these recent cases is that the Court has returned to the historical Cooley doctrine, but has articulated more candidly than in the older cases what it takes into consideration in applying that principle. It is probably also true that, with respect to most subjects, a heavier burden than formerly is placed upon the party seeking to establish that the state legislation improperly burdens interstate commerce.

The discussion up to this point has assumed that the state legislation involved does not discriminate against interstate commerce. Even Mr. Justice Black seems to agree that a state law imposing greater burdens on interstate commerce than on local commerce is repugnant to the commerce clause.[62] State

---

[57] Southern Pacific case, 325 U.S. at 780; Morgan case, 328 U.S. at 380; quoting from Mr. Justice Holmes in Kansas City Southern Ry. v. Kaw Valley Drainage Dist., 233 U.S. 75, 79, 34 Sup. Ct. 564, 58 L. Ed. 857 (1914).

[58] See cases collected in Southern Pacific, 325 U.S. at 779, and in Morgan, 328 U.S. at 378–9.

[59] Ibid.

[60] Southern Pacific Co. v. Arizona, 325 U.S. 761, 783, 65 Sup. Ct. 1515, 89 L. Ed. 1915 (1945).

[61] Ibid. The leading cases distinguished were South Carolina Highway Dep't v. Barnwell Bros., 303 U.S. 177, 58 Sup. Ct. 510, 82 L. Ed. 734 (1938); and Maurer v. Hamilton, 309 U.S. 598, 60 Sup. Ct. 726, 84 L. Ed. 969 (1940).

[62] See his dissent in Hood & Sons v. DuMond, 336 U.S. 525, 549, 556, 69 Sup. Ct. 657, 93 L. Ed. 865 (1949), in which he refers to Best & Co. v. Maxwell, 311 U.S. 454, 61 Sup. Ct. 334, 85 L. Ed. 275 (1940), an opinion in which he joined, and his earlier dissent in Gwin, White & Price v. Henneford, 305 U.S. 434, 446, 455, 59 Sup. Ct. 325, 83 L. Ed. 272 (1939). But

laws designed to keep a resource or to favor a business within the state, to benefit that state at the expense of other states, have also consistently been held invalid, at least when the injury to other states was substantial.[63] A recent example is the South Carolina statute held invalid in *Toomer v. Witsell*,[64] which required vessels catching shrimp in South Carolina waters to unload, pack and stamp their catch at a South Carolina port before shipment to other states. A California law designed to exclude indigent immigrants from other states would also seem to fall in the same category.[65] Such statutes can be regarded as discriminatoryt—hough the results in the cases are also justifiable under the "uniformity" or "undue burden" theories discussed above.

In *Hood & Sons v. Du Mond*,[66] decided in 1949, the Court divided sharply as to whether in order to prevent depletion of the supply available within the state, and to avoid destructive competition, New York could refuse to permit a Massachusetts local distributor to open an additional receiving plant from which milk could be taken from New York. The majority treated the case as one in which a state was favoring home consumers and competitors against those in other states, and thus condemned the New York regulation as discriminating against, as well as burdening, interstate commerce. The majority opinion of Mr. Justice Jackson declares that the basic historical purpose of the commerce clause was to prevent each state from seeking economic advantage at the expense of the other states.[67] The four dissenting Justices asserted that the Court's decision was a departure from the fundamental principle of the Cooley case. Mr. Justice Black thought the decision a reinvigoration of the Court's former tendency improperly to restrict the authority of the states to regulate business.[68] Mr. Justice Frankfurter believed that

---

cf. his dissents in Toomer v. Witsell, 334 U.S. 385, 407, 68 Sup. Ct. 1157, 92 L. Ed. 1460 (1948); and Dean Milk Co. v. Madison, 340 U.S. 349, 357, 71 Sup. Ct. 295 (1951).

[63] See cases cited in Hood & Sons v. DuMond, 336 U.S. 535–37, 69 Sup. Ct. 657, 93 L. Ed. 865 (1949).

[64] 334 U.S. 385, 403, 68 Sup. Ct. 1157, 92 L. Ed. 1460 (1948).

[65] Edwards v. California, 314 U.S. 160, 62 Sup. Ct. 164, 86 L. Ed. 119 (1941).

[66] 336 U.S. 525, 69 Sup. Ct. 657, 93 L. Ed. 865 (1949), 3 Vand. L. Rev. 113.

[67] 336 U.S. at 532–39.

[68] See *id.* at 562–64, particularly.

further inquiry into the facts was essential to determine how the
competing state and national interests should be balanced.[69]

It is true that the opinion of Mr. Justice Jackson, for the
Court, does not follow the Cooley approach, or even cite any
of the cases in which the doctrine has been approved and applied.
But since he himself, along with most of the Justices who joined
with him, had joined in the leading opinions accepting the
Cooley principle, it is doubtful if he, or they, regarded the Hood
decision as an abandonment of the basic doctrine. It seems much
more likely, in view of the language of the opinion and the facts
of the case, that the majority believed that the case came within
the exceptional category for discriminatory state regulations, and
also that such an assertion of state power, from its very nature,
imposed a burden on interstate commerce which was necessarily
"undue," since it was precisely the type of regulation which the
framers meant most clearly to prohibit.[70] Although the case
may have been a close one on its facts, it seems clear that it was
not meant to be the forerunner of any new general doctrine. The
subsequent Cities Service case, decided in the following year by

[69] *Id.* at 576.
[70] "The material success that has come to inhabitants of the states
which make up this federal free trade unit has been the most impressive
in the history of commerce, but the established interdependence of the states
only emphasizes the necessity of protecting interstate movement of goods
against local burdens and repressions. We need only consider the consequences
if each of the few states that produce copper, lead, high-grade iron ore,
timber, cotton, oil, or gas should decree that industries located in that state
shall have priority. What fantastic rivalries and dislocations and reprisals
would ensue if such practices were begun! Or suppose that the field of
discrimination and retaliation be industry. May Michigan provide that auto-
mobiles cannot be taken out of that State until local dealers' demands are
fully met? Would she not have every argument in the favor of such a statute
that can be offered in support of New York's limiting sales of milk for
out-of-state shipment to protect the economic interests of her competing
dealers and local consumers? Could Ohio then pounce upon the rubber-tire
industry, on which she has a substantial grip, or retaliate for Michigan's
auto monopoly?

"Our system, fostered by the Commerce Clause, is that every farmer and
every craftsman shall be encouraged to produce by the certainty that he will
have free access to every market in the Nation, that no home embargoes
will withhold his exports, and no foreign state will by customs duties or
regulations exclude them. Likewise, every consumer may look to the free
competition from every producing area in the Nation to protect him from
exploitation by any. Such was the vision of the Founders; such has been
the doctrine of this Court which has given it reality." 336 U.S. at 538–9.

a unanimous Court, including, of course, Mr. Justice Jackson, reaffirms the Cooley doctrine and states:

> The vice in the regulation invalidated by Hood was solely that it denied facilities to a company in interstate commerce on the articulated ground that such facilities would divert milk supplies needed by local consumers; in other words, the *regulation discriminated against interstate commerce*.[71]

The most recent case on the subject is both interesting and significant. Madison, Wisconsin, required all milk consumed within the city to be pasteurized within five miles of the center of the town. This excluded milk from the Dean Milk Company's pasteurization plants in Illinois, 65 and 85 miles away. Although the ordinance doubtless favored local business, its avowed and undenied purpose was to facilitate inspection by the local health department; it was certainly more convenient and economical for Madison not to send its inspectors far afield. In *Dean Milk Co. v. Madison*,[72] decided January 15, 1951, the Court, speaking through Mr. Justice Clark, held the ordinance to be an unlawful discrimination against interstate commerce. The Court assumed that, apart from the discrimination, the subject lay within the sphere of state regulation, despite its effect upon interstate commerce. But it concluded that, "an economic barrier protecting a major local industry against competition from without the state" was not permissible "even in the exercise of [a city's] unquestioned power to protect the health and safety of its people, if reasonable non-discriminatory alternatives, adequate to conserve legitimate local interests, are available."[73] The Court then found that "reasonable and adequate alternatives are available,"[74] since Madison could charge the cost of inspection of distant milk plants to the pasteurizer, or could rely on inspection by local officials in other areas whose standards of inspection were so graded by the United States Public Health Service as to enable Madison to determine whether its own standards were satisfied. Both Madison and Wisconsin health officials had testified in the case that this system gave consumers adequate protection. The court concluded that to permit Madison to adopt

---

[71] Cities Service Gas Co. v. Peerless Oil & Gas Co. 340 U.S. 179, 188, 71 Sup. Ct. 215 (1950). [Italics supplied.]

[72] 340 U.S. 349, 71 Sup. Ct. 295 (1951).

[73] 340 U.S. at 354.

[74] *Ibid.*

a regulation of this sort when "not essential for the protection of local health interests . . . would invite a multiplication of preferential trade areas destructive of the very purpose of the Commerce Clause." [75]

Mr. Justice Black, with Justices Douglas and Minton concurring, dissented on the grounds that a good faith health regulation applicable both to interstate and intrastate pasteurizers was not a discrimination against interstate commerce, and that in any event, the Court should not "strike down local health regulations unless satisfied beyond a reasonable doubt" that the available substitutes "would not lower health standards." [76]

The Dean Milk decision, seemingly for the first time, applies to a local law found to discriminate against interstate commerce the technique of balancing the respective local and national interests employed in other cases in which local regulations are said to burden commerce, though with a reversed presumption. In the absence of discrimination, the Court tends to sustain the state action unless interference with commerce is clear and the local interest not very substantial; where there is discrimination, the Dean case holds, it must appear that there is no other reasonable method of safeguarding a legitimate local interest. [77] Where a state law has no other purpose than to favor local industry, this balancing of interest approach probably will not be used, inasmuch as the purpose of the state regulation would be illegitimate.

The early cases invalidating state laws requiring local inspection in such a way as to exclude products from distant sources —Minnesota v. Barber [78] and Brimmer v. Rebman [79]—had adopted a less flexible approach. But where no discriminatory purpose is apparent, and where both interstate and intrastate imports from over five miles away are excluded, it is not too clear whether the regulation can properly be said to "discriminate" against interstate commerce. And even if such a regulation be properly classified as discriminatory for commerce clause purposes, the local need might be so overpowering as to completely outweigh, for the particular situation, the national interest in a

[75] Id. at 356.

[76] Id. at 357, 359.

[77] See Braden, Umpire to the Federal System, 10 U. of Chi. L. Rev. 27, 30 (1942).

[78] 136 U.S. 313, 10 Sup. Ct. 862, 34 L. Ed. 455 (1890).

[79] 138 U.S. 78, 11 Sup. Ct. 213, 34 L. Ed. 862 (1891).

market not restricted by state lines.[80] It is thus reasonable in such cases to employ the same practical approach as when a state law interferes with but does not technically discriminate against interstate commerce. The justification for shifting the burden is that an actual prohibition of all interstate but not of all local trade is, on its face, what the commerce clause was designed to prevent, and therefore to be countenanced only when the local need in the particular case can plainly be shown to be greater than the interest in nation-wide free trade upon which the economy and welfare of this nation largely rest.

Basic to the Court's premise is the view, with which the minority seem to disagree, that a local regulation which prohibited both interstate and intrastate trade—shipments from pasteurization plants more than five miles from the city—discriminated against interstate commerce. With respect to this, the majority merely stated, "It is immaterial that Wisconsin milk from outside the Madison area is subjected to the same proscription as that moved in interstate commerce. Cf. Brimmer v. Rebman, 138 U.S. 78, 82–83 (1891)." [81] Brimmer v. Rebman does appear to be directly in point, since the state law there involved prohibited the sale of all meat slaughtered more than one hundred miles from the place of sale, unless locally inspected, while not requiring the inspection of other meat. As a matter of semantics, however, it cannot be said with certainty that a state regulation of this sort is "discriminatory." It excludes some intrastate trade, along with the interstate; on the other hand, it excludes all interstate. Nevertheless, the purpose of the commerce clause would be effectively frustrated by a multitude of municipal trade barriers of this sort, even though they discriminated against some intrastate trade along with the interstate. Accordingly, it seems reasonable for the Court to treat such regulations as discriminatory—or at least to require their proponents to justify them by proof of actual and serious local necessity, as distinct from local economic advantage and convenience.

The principles and cases heretofore discussed have been concerned with the effect of the commerce clause itself upon state

---

[80] Thus, if pasteurized milk should become unsafe for human consumption in the time necessary to transport it more than a specified distance, the local interest in protecting the health of its people would seem to overbalance, even from the standpoint of the nation as a whole, the advantages of interstate trade in milk from more distant points.

[81] 340 U.S. at 354 n. 4.

laws, in the absence of any federal regulation. Since the Constitution vests the power to regulate interstate commerce in the Congress, there cannot be—or at least there should not be [82]— any doubt as to the overriding authority of Congress to determine what the states may or may not regulate in the field subject to congressional control. The Southern Pacific case states in express terms that Congress "may either permit the states to regulate the commerce in a manner which would otherwise not be permissible . . . or exclude state regulation even of matters of peculiarly local concern which nevertheless affect interstate commerce" (citing cases).[83] In 1949, in California v. Zook,[84] the Court reiterated that "despite theoretical inconsistency with the rationale of the Commerce Clause as a limitation in its own right, the words of the Clause—a grant of power [to Congress] —admit of no other result." [85] These statements as to the supremacy of the congressional will when Congress breaks its silence were amplified in the exhaustive opinion of Mr. Justice Rutledge, speaking for a unanimous Court, in Prudential Insurance Co. v. Benjamin,[86] which sustained the authority of Congress to permit the states to regulate interstate commerce in insurance.

This paper will not deal with the problem of supersedure or "occupancy of the field"—that is, when state regulation is invalidated or superseded by congressional action under the commerce clause (or any other clause). Although this is often regarded as a constitutional question, since there is no doubt as to the supremacy of federal legislation the issue in each case relates to the intention of Congress, actual or presumed. The problem is thus more akin to statutory construction than to the constitutional matters considered in this symposium. In each case the

---

[82] Writers have found logical difficulty in reconciling the conception of the commerce clause as forbidding state action by its own force with the power of Congress to consent to otherwise invalid state regulation. See Biklé, The Silence of Congress, 41 Harv. L. Rev. 200 (1927); Powell, The Validity of State Legislation Under the Webb-Kenyon Law, 2 So. L.Q. 112 (1917); Dowling, Interstate Commerce and State Power—Revised Version, 47 Col. L. Rev. 547, 552–60 (1947). But "The Supreme Court has not been concerned in its opinions with the theoretical difficulties." Rutledge, A Declaration of Legal Faith 64 n. 26 (Univ. of Kan. Press, 1947).

[83] 325 U.S. at 769.

[84] 336 U.S. 725, 69 Sup. Ct. 841, 93 L. Ed. 1005 (1949).

[85] 336 U.S. at 728.

[86] 328 U.S. 408, 66 Sup. Ct. 1142, 90 L. Ed. 1342 (1946).

question to be determined is whether a state law is inconsistent with what Congress has said, or with the accomplishment of the purpose of Congress, or with what can be deduced as to what Congress intends when the federal statute is not explicit. It seems sufficient here to cite the leading recent cases on the subject for the reader who might wish to explore the matter further.[87]

III. The Commerce Power of Congress

The burning issue of the 1930's was the extent of the regulatory power of Congress under the commerce clause. Long prior to that time, in the Shreveport Rate case [88] and many others, the Court had recognized that under the commerce power, Congress could regulate intrastate transactions which were sufficiently related to interstate commerce, which affected it "directly" but not "indirectly." [89] But the development of this principle was blocked by an opposing doctrine that certain activities, notably those occurring in the process of producing commodities to be shipped in commerce, were "local" by their very nature, and thus exclusively subject to state authority under the Tenth Amend-

[87] International Union of Automobile Workers v. O'Brien, 339 U.S. 454, 70 Sup. Ct. 781, 94 L. Ed. 978 (1950); United Automobile Workers v. Wisconsin Employment Relations Board, 336 U.S. 245, 69 Sup. Ct. 516, 93 L. Ed. 651 (1949); California v. Zook, 336 U.S. 725, 69 Sup. Ct. 841, 93 L. Ed. 1005 (1949); Bethlehem Steel Co. v. New York State Labor Board, 330 U.S. 767, 67 Sup. Ct. 1026, 91 L. Ed. 1234 (1947); Rice v. Santa Fe Elevator Co., 331 U.S. 218, 67 Sup. Ct. 1146, 91 L. Ed. 1447 (1947); First Iowa Hydro-Electric Co-op v. Federal Power Commission, 328 U.S. 152, 66 Sup. Ct. 906, 90 L. Ed. 1143 (1946). See note, "Occupation of the Field" in Commerce Clause Cases, 1936–1946: Ten Years of Federalism, 60 Harv. L. Rev. 262 (1946). And see Amalgamated Ass'n. of Street, Elec. Ry., & M.C. Employees v. Wisconsin Employment Relations Board, 340 U.S. 383, 71 Sup. Ct. 359 (1951).

[88] Houston E. & W. T. Ry v. United States, 234 U.S. 342, 34 Sup. Ct. 833, 58 L. Ed. 1341 (1914).

[89] Local 167 v. United States, 291 U.S. 293, 54 Sup. Ct. 396, 78 L. Ed. 804 (1934); Coronado Coal Co. v. United Mine Workers, 268 U.S. 295, 45 Sup. Ct. 551, 9 L. Ed. 963 (1925); Chicago Board of Trade v. Olsen, 262 U.S. 1, 43 Sup. Ct. 70, 67 L. Ed. 839 (1923); Stafford v. Wallace, 258 U.S. 495, 42 Sup. Ct. 397, 66 L. Ed. 735 (1922); Railroad Comm'n of Wisconsin v. Chicago B. & Q. R.R., 257 U.S. 563 42 Sup. Ct. 232, 66 L. Ed. 373 (1922); United States v. Patten, 226 U.S. 525, 33 Sup. Ct. 141, 57 L. Ed. 333 (1913); Southern Ry. v. United States, 222 U.S. 20, 32 Sup. Ct. 2, 56 L. Ed. 72 (1911); Swift & Co. v. United States, 196 U.S. 375, 25 Sup. Ct. 276, 49 L. Ed. 518 (1905).

ment.[90] The Court reconciled this theory with the "affecting commerce" doctrine by finding that no matter how close the actual factual relationship, production affected commerce only "indirectly." This line of decisions reached its climax, and conclusion, in the Carter Coal case in 1936,[91] which held that labor relations in the coal industry only had an indirect effect upon interstate commerce, even though a coal strike might halt not only all interstate shipments of coal but a large proportion of the interstate movement of everything else as well.

The well-known story of how, in the following term, the Court abandoned this approach and has since given full scope to the power of Congress to regulate intrastate activities which in fact had a substantial relationship to interstate commerce has been told elsewhere.[92] There is no occasion for repeating it here.

The test presently applied has been stated in various ways. *Wickard* v. *Filburn* [93] declared that "even if appellee's activity be local and though it may not be regarded as commerce, it may still whatever its nature, be reached by Congress if it exerts a *substantial economic effect* on interstate commerce, and this irrespective of whether such effect is what might at some earlier time have been defined as 'direct' or 'indirect.' " [94] Mr. Justice Jackson's opinion also quotes from the opinion of Mr. Justice Stone in *United States* v. *Wrightwood Dairy Co.*, that "the reach of that power extends to those intrastate activities which *in a substantial* way interfere with or obstruct the exercise of the granted

[90] See cases cited in note 1, supra; Utah Power and Light Co. v. Pfost, 286 U.S. 165, 52 Sup. Ct. 548 76 L. Ed. 1038 (1932); Industrial Ass'n v. United States, 268 U.S. 64, 45 Sup. Ct. 403, 69 L. Ed. 849 (1925); Oliver Iron Mining Company v. Lord, 262 U.S. 172 43 Sup. Ct. 526, 67 L. Ed. 929 (1923); Heisler v. Thomas Colliery Co., 260 U.S. 245, 43 Sup. Ct. 83, 67 L. Ed. 237 (1922); Kidd v. Pearson, 128 U.S. 1, 9 Sup. Ct. 6, 32 L. Ed. 346 (1888); Veazie v. Moor, 14 How. 567, 14 L. Ed. 545 (1852). Although many of these cases involve state legislation, they were treated as authoritative with respect to the power of Congress during the period in question.

[91] Carter v. Carter Coal Co., 298 U.S. 238, 56 Sup. Ct. 855, 80 L. Ed. 1160 (1936).

[92] See particularly, the discussion in Mandeville Island Farms v. American Crystal Sugar Co., 334 U.S. 219, 229–35, 68 Sup Ct. 996, 92 L. Ed. 1328 (1948); Wickard v. Filburn, 317 U.S. 111, 119–25, 63 Sup. Ct. 82, 87 L. Ed. 122 (1942); Stern, The Commerce Clause and the National Economy, 1933–1946, 59 Harv. L. Rev. 645, 883 (1946).

[93] 317 U.S. 111, 63 Sup. Ct. 82, 87 L. Ed. 122 (1942).

[94] 317 U.S. at 125. [Italics supplied.]

power." [95] The Mandeville Farms case refers to "practical imped-
ing effects" upon commerce,[96] and also declared that: "The
essence of the affectation doctrine was that the exact location
of this line made no difference, if the forbidden effects flowed
across it to the injury of interstate commerce or to the hindrance
or defeat of congressional policy regarding it." [97]

These statements still appear to treat the test as one of
degree, which does not substantially differ in terms from the
former "direct-indirect" formula, except that the standard of
judgment is not the same and all non-factual artificial restrictions
upon application of the test have been removed. But in these
opinions, as well as others, the Court has not relied primarily
on these quantitative formulas but has gone back to basic constitutional principles first enunciated by Chief Justice Marshall.
In the Mandeville case, Mr. Justice Rutledge pointed out that
"the 'affectation' approach was actually a revival of Marshall's
'necessary and proper' doctrine," [98] that is, of the necessary and
proper clause of the Constitution itself. The classical expression
in McCulloch v. Maryland,[99] that "let the end be legitimate, let
it be within the scope of the Constitution, and all means which
are appropriate, which are plainly adapted to that end, which are
not prohibited, but consistent with the letter and spirit of the
Constitution, are constitutional," is plainly the source of the statement by Mr. Justice Stone in the Darby [100] and Wrightwood
Dairy cases,[101] reiterated by Mr. Justice Jackson in Wickard v.
Filburn,[102] that the commerce power "extends to those activities
intrastate which so affect interstate commerce, or the exertion
of the power of Congress over it, as to make regulation of them
appropriate means to the attainment of a legitimate end, the
effective execution of the granted power to regulate interstate
commerce."

Other leading decisions have returned to the language of

[95] Id. at 125, quoting from United States v. Wrightwood Dairy Co.,
315 U.S. 110, 119, 62 Sup. Ct. 523, 86 L. Ed. 726 (1942). [Italics supplied.]
[96] 334 U.S. 219, 233, 68 Sup. Ct. 996, 92 L. Ed. 1328 (1948).
[97] 334 U.S. at 232.
[98] Id. at 232.
[99] 4 Wheat. 316, 421, 4 L. Ed. 579 (1819).
[100] United States v. Darby, 312 U.S. 100, 121, 61 Sup. Ct. 451, 85
L. Ed. 609 (1941).
[101] United States v. Wrightwood Dairy, 315 U.S. 110, 119, 62 Sup.
Ct. 523, 86 L. Ed. 126 (1942).
[102] 317 U.S. 111, 124, 63 Sup. Ct. 82, 87 L. Ed. 122 (1942).

Chief Justice Marshall in *Gibbons* v. *Ogden*,[103] and have emphasized the function of the commerce clause as the practical instrument by which multi-state problems, not susceptible of solution
by any single state, were to be subjected to the authority of the
only governmental agency capable of dealing with them. In the
insurance case, *United States* v. *South-Eastern Underwriters*[104]
the Court, speaking through Mr. Justice Black,[105] declared, quoting from *Gibbons* v. *Ogden*, that "Commerce is interstate, he
said, when it 'concerns more States than one.' . . . No decision
of this Court has ever questioned this as too comprehensive a
description of the subject matter of the Commerce Clause."[106]

In the case sustaining the validity of the so-called death sentence provision for public utility holding companies, *North American Co.* v. *SEC*,[107] the Court reaffirmed this practical concept,
saying—

> This broad commerce clause does not operate so as to render
> the nation powerless to defend itself against economic forces that
> Congress decrees inimical or destructive of the national economy.
> Rather it is an affirmative power commensurate with the national
> needs. . . . And in using this great power, Congress is not bound
> by technical legal conceptions. Commerce itself is an intensely
> practical matter. *Swift & Co.* v. *United States*, 196 U.S. 375, 398.
> . . . To deal with it effectively, Congress must be able to act in
> terms of economic and financial realities. The commerce clause
> gives it authority so to act. . . . Once it is established that the evil
> concerns or affects commerce in more states than one, Congress
> may act. . . .[108]

Since the North American opinion also states that the commerce "power permits Congress to attack an evil directly at its
source provided that the evil bears a *substantial* relationship to
interstate commerce,"[109] it is apparent that the Court does not
regard the general principle enunciated in that case as inconsistent with the need for determining the question of degree referred
to in some of the other recent cases—whether or not the relation-

---

[103] 9 Wheat. 1, 6 L. Ed. 23 (1824).

[104] 322 U.S. 533, 64 Sup. Ct. 1162, 88 L. Ed. 1440 (1944).

[105] Although this was a 4 to 3 decision, the dissents did not relate to
the constitutional issue, or to the constitutional principles set forth in the
majority opinion. See Polish National Alliance *v.* NLRB, 322 U.S. 643, 64
Sup. Ct. 1196, 88 L. Ed. 1509 (1944).

[106] 322 U.S. at 551.

[107] 327 U.S. 686, 66 Sup. Ct. 784, 90 L. Ed. 945 (1946).

[108] 327 U.S. at 705–06.

[109] *Id.* at 705.

ship of the intrastate transaction or regulation to interstate commerce is sufficiently substantial. Indeed, no formulation of a test which requires the exercise of judgment in drawing a line can avoid the necessity for determining such questions of degree. But the cases since 1937 demonstrate not only that the Court will examine the question before it pragmatically, but that it will accord the greatest of weight to the congressional determination that the relationship to interstate commerce is sufficiently close.

The relationship between the intrastate transaction and interstate commerce may take a number of forms. The simplest is actual interference with the physical movement of goods interstate, such as may result from a strike caused by an unfair labor practice or a boycott in violation of the Sherman Act.[110] A physical effect may be that of floods in a nonnavigable tributary upon navigation, or other commercial activities, downstream.[111] Where there is a physical commingling of interstate and intrastate products and activities, the whole may be regulated.[112] And the same is true of economic commingling in a market in which interstate and intrastate transactions are inseparable.[113] The effect may be upon interstate competition, by diverting the interstate flow from one competitor to another as through unlawful restraint in violation of the antitrust laws,[114] or substandard labor conditions forbidden by the Fair Labor Standard Act,[115] or where an intrastate price cutter could take business away from an interstate competitor whose prices were fixed.[116] The relationship between the supply of a commodity available for interstate shipment and

[110] *Consolidated Edison Co.* v. *NLRB*, 305 U.S. 197, 221–22, 59 Sup. Ct. 206, 83 L. Ed. 126 (1938); *NLRB* v. *Jones & Laughlin Steel Corp.*, 301 U.S. 1, 57 Sup. Ct. 615, 81 L. Ed. 893 (1937); *Local 167* v. *United States*, 291 U.S. 293, 54 Sup. Ct. 396, 78 L. Ed. 804 (1934).

[111] Oklahoma ex rel. *Phillips* v. *Guy F. Atkinson Co.*, 313 U.S. 508, 61 Sup. Ct. 1050, 85 L. Ed. 1487 (1941).

[112] *Currin* v. *Wallace*, 306 U.S. 1, 59 Sup. Ct. 379, 83 L. Ed. 441 (1939); *Mulford* v. *Smith*, 307 U.S. 38, 59 Sup. Ct. 648, 83 L. Ed. 1092 (1939).

[113] *United States* v. *Wrightwood Dairy Co.*, 315 U.S. 110, 62 Sup. Ct. 523, 86 L. Ed. 726 (1942); *Houston, E. & W. T. Ry.* v. *United States*, 234 U.S. 342, 34 Sup. Ct. 833, 58 L. Ed. 1341 (1914).

[114] *Federal Trade Commission* v. *Morton Salt Co.*, 334 U.S. 37, 68 Sup. Ct. 822, 92 L. Ed. 1196 (1948); *International Salt Co.* v. *United States*, 332 U.S. 392, 68 Sup. Ct. 12, 92 L. Ed 20 (1947); *Local 167* v. *United States*, 291 U.S. 293, 54 Sup. Ct. 396, 78 L. Ed. 804 (1934).

[115] *United States* v. *Darby*, 312 U.S. 100, 122, 61 Sup. Ct. 451, 85 L. Ed. 609 (1941).

[116] *United States* v. *Wrightwood Dairy Co.* 315 U.S. 110, 62 Sup. Ct. 523, 86 L. Ed. 726 (1942).

the amount produced permits regulation of the quantity manufactured or grown, as in the statutes fixing agricultural quotas.[117] Intrastate practices affecting interstate prices, such as the cornering of a market or the control of the intrastate price for raw materials or processes, are proper objects of federal regulation.[118] Intrastate acts which result in interstate shipments of noxious or unsafe articles,[119] or of products which will cause economic or other injury in the state of destination, may be controlled.[120] The Public Utility Holding Company Act is in part justified as a means of preventing evils which are spread and perpetuated through the channels of interstate commerce.[121] More generally, intrastate transactions may be regulated when reasonably necessary to the control of interstate movements,[122] or to the effectuation of the purpose for which such movements may be controlled.[123]

A brief reference to some of the recent decisions will show how these principles have been applied.

The original Labor Board cases of 1937 [124] established the power of Congress to regulate labor relations in factories which receive raw materials and ship the goods they produce into other

[117] *Wickard v. Filburn*, 317 U.S. 111, 63 Sup. Ct. 82, 87 L. Ed. 122 (1942).

[118] *United States v. Women's Sportswear Ass'n*, 336 U.S. 460, 69 Sup. Ct. 714, 93 L. Ed. 805 (1949); *Mandeville Island Farms v. American Crystal Sugar Co.*, 334 U.S. 219, 68 Sup. Ct. 996, 92 L. Ed. 1328 (1948); *Chicago Board of Trade v. Olsen*, 262 U.S. 1, 43 Sup. Ct. 470, 67 L. Ed. 839 (1923); *United States v. Patten*, 226 U.S. 525, 33 Sup. Ct. 141, 57 L. Ed. 333 (1913).

[119] E.g., Meat Inspection Act, 34 Stat. 1260 (1908, 21 U.S.C.A. § § 71 et seq. (1927).

[120] *United States v. Darby*, 312 U.S. 100, 61 Sup. Ct. 451, 85 L. Ed. 609 (1941); *Kentucky Whip & Collar Co. v. Illinois Cent. R.R.*, 299 U.S. 334, 57 Sup. Ct. 277, 81 L. Ed. 270 (1937).

[121] *North American Co. v. SEC*, 327 U.S. 686, 66 Sup. Ct. 784, 90 L. Ed. 945 (1946); *American Power & Light Co. v. SEC*, 329 U.S. 90, 67 Sup. Ct. 133, 91 L. Ed. 103 (1946).

[122] *United States v. Darby*, 312 U.S. 100, 61 Sup. Ct. 451, 85 L. Ed. 609 (1941).

[123] *United States v. Sullivan*, 332 U.S. 689, 68 Sup. Ct. 331, 92 L. Ed. 297 (1948); *McDermott v. Wisconsin*, 228 U.S. 115, 33 Sup. Ct. 431, 57 L. Ed. 754 (1913).

[124] *NLRB v. Jones & Laughlin Steel Corp.*, 301 U.S. 1, 57 Sup. Ct. 615, 81 L. Ed. 893 (1937); *NLRB v. Fruehauf Trailer Co.*, 301 U.S. 49, 57 Sup. Ct. 642, 81 L. Ed. 918 (1937); *NLRB v. Friedman-Harry Marks Clothing Co.*, 301 U.S. 58, 57 Sup. Ct. 642, 81 L. Ed. 921 (1937).

states. Subsequent cases held the Act applicable to processors of products grown within the state but shipped outside [125] and to a small manufacturer who delivered finished products within the state to their owner for shipment.[126] The Sherman Act has also been held to reach combinations of contractors in a single city who raised prices for manufacturing operations on goods assembled and shipped interstate by local jobbers.[127] It was in this case that Mr. Justice Jackson stated: "If it is interstate commerce that feels the pinch, it does not matter how local the operation which applies the squeeze." [128]

The leading case under the Fair Labor Standards Act held it applicable to a manufacturer of a raw material for sale in interstate commerce, both on the ground that the regulation of wages at the factory helped keep goods made under substandard conditions out of commerce and because such conditions in themselves affect interstate competition.[129] The statute was subsequently held to extend to employees in a building tenanted principally by corporations producing for interstate commerce,[130] to watchmen and window cleaners in factories producing for commerce even when employed by an independent contractor,[131] to a contractor who drilled oil wells for others with knowledge that any oil produced would move interstate,[132] to employees of a small newspaper with a regular circulation of 45 copies, or one half of one per cent, outside the state.[133]

Perhaps the most sweeping of all the cases holding activity in the field of production subject to the commerce power is

[125] *Santa Cruz Fruit Packing Co. v. NLRB*, 303 U.S. 58 Sup. Ct. 656, 82 L. Ed. 954 (1938).

[126] *NLRB v. Fainblatt*, 306 U.S. 601, 59 Sup. Ct. 668, 83 L. Ed. 1014 (1939).

[127] *United States v. Women's Sportswear Manufacturers Ass'n*, 336 U.S. 460, 69 Sup. Ct. 714, 93 L. Ed. 805 (1949).

[128] 336 U.S. at 464.

[129] *United States v. Darby*, 312 U.S. 100, 61 Sup. Ct. 451, 85 L. Ed. 609 (1941).

[130] *Kirschbaum Co. v. Walling*, 316 U.S. 517, 62 Sup. Ct. 1116, 86 L. Ed. 1638 (1942).

[131] *Martino v. Michigan Window Cleaning Co.* 327 U.S. 173, 66 Sup. Ct. 379, 90 L. Ed. 603 (1946); *Walton v. Southern Package Corp.*, 320 U.S. 540, 64 Sup. Ct. 320, 88 L. Ed. 298 (1944).

[132] *Warren-Bradshaw Drilling Co. v. Hall*, 317 U.S. 88, 63 Sup. Ct. 125, 87 L. Ed. 83 (1942).

[133] *Mabee v. White Plains Publishing Co.*, 327 U.S. 178, 66 Sup. Ct. 511, 90 L. Ed. 607 (1946).

Wickard v. *Filburn*,[134] which sustained the allocation of wheat quotas even to farmers who consumed their own crops in the form of food, livestock feed and seed. More recently, the Sherman Act was held to reach a scheme by manufacturers in a single state to fix the prices paid farmers in the same state for their beets, on the ground that the prices so fixed would inevitably affect the interstate price of refined sugar.[135]

All of these cases involved transactions occurring before commerce began. The Court has also held that the federal power extends to intrastate acts after commerce has ceased. When, in *United States* v. *Sullivan*,[136] a retail druggist was prosecuted for selling improperly labeled pills which, though previously shipped in interstate commerce, had been purchased by him within the state and held for nine months, the court disposed of the commerce question summarily by reference to the early case of *McDermott* v. *Wisconsin*.[137] That case had barred Wisconsin from substituting for the federal interstate label its own label for use by the retail store, on the ground that the purpose of the regulation of interstate labeling would be frustrated if the label were removed before the product reached the ultimate consumer. The National Labor Relations Act has also been held to reach large retail stores; [138] for reasons of policy the Board has refrained from bringing cases against smaller retail outlets.[139] At the time this was written, the Supreme Court had before it the application of the Taft-Hartley Act to union restraints in local building operations where some of the building materials have come from without the state.[140] The antitrust laws have

[134] 317 U.S. 111, 63 Sup. Ct. 82, 87 L. Ed. 122 (1942).

[135] *Mandeville Island Farms Co.* v. *American Crystal Sugar Co.*, 334 U.S. 219, 68 Sup. Ct. 996, 92 L. Ed. 1328 (1948).

[136] 332 U.S. 689, 68 Sup. Ct. 331, 92 L. Ed. 297 (1948).

[137] 228 U.S. 115, 33 Sup. Ct. 431, 57 L. Ed. 754 (1913).

[138] *Loveman, Joseph & Loeb* v. *NLRB*, 146 F.2d 769 (5th Cir. 1945); *J. L. Brandeis & Sons* v. *NLRB*, 142 F.2d 977 (8th Cir. 1944), *cert. denied*, 323 U.S. 751 (1944); *NLRB* v. *M. E. Blatt Co.*, 143 F. 2d 268 (3d Cir. 1943), *cert. denied*, 323 U.S. 774 (1944); *NLRB* v. *J. L. Hudson Co.*, 135 F.2d 380 (6th Cir. 1943), *cert. denied*, 320 U.S. 740 (1943); *NLRB* v. *Kudile*, 130 F.2d 615 (3d Cir. 1942), *cert. denied*, 317 U.S. 694 (1943); *NLRB* v. *Suburban Lumber Co.*, 121 F.2d 829 (3d Cir. 1941), *cert. denied*, 314 U.S. 693 (1941).

[139] See NLRB announcement, October 3, 1950, 19 U.S.L. Week 2147 (1950).

[140] *NLRB* v. *Local 74*, 181 F.2d 126 (6th Cir. 1950), *cert. granted*, 340 U.S. 902 (1950); *International Brotherhood of Electrical Workers* v.

also been held to reach a scheme to fix retail prices when the means adopted reach beyond state boundaries.[141]

The courts have also recognized the inseparability of interstate industry by sustaining regulatory provisions which in isolation seem to have little to do with interstate commerce. An extreme example is *Egan v. United States*,[142] which upheld the provision of the Public Utility Holding Company Act prohibiting registered holding companies (by which is meant companies engaged in interstate commerce, *inter alia*) from making contributions to persons running for state or local political office. The court of appeals reasoned that Congress could rationally conclude that such expenditures might affect or burden interstate commerce through their impact upon rates, and might also demonstrate a lack of economy in management and operation which would be injurious to investors and consumers; [143] the Supreme Court denied certiorari.[144] The Court has also removed the pre-existing barrier—or at least what many persons thought was a barrier—to the exercise of the commerce power over the world of finance by holding that insurance companies were engaged in interstate commerce.[145]

These cases, which indicate roughly the present scope of the power of Congress under the commerce clause, justify two general observations. Industry organized on a national scale, all the operations of which are inevitably economically interrelated, will not be compartmentalized into interstate and local segments, the former subject exclusively to federal control and the latter exclusively to state regulation. The Court no longer construes the Constitution as requiring a division for governmental purposes of what is in fact inseparable.[146]

NLRB, 181 F.2d 34 (2d Cir. 1950), cert. granted, 340 U.S. 902 (1950); NLRB v. Denver Building & Construction Trades Council, 186 F.2d 326 (D.C. Cir. 1950), cert. granted, 340 U.S. 902 (1950). All of these cases were argued on February 26 and 27, 1951.

[141] *United States v. Frankfort Distilleries*, 324 U.S. 293, 65 Sup. Ct. 661, 89 L. Ed. 951 (1945).

[142] 137 F.2d 369 (8th Cir. 1943), cert. denied, 320 U.S. 788 (1943).

[143] *Id.* at 374–75.

[144] 320 U.S. 788 (1943).

[145] *United States v. South-Eastern Underwriters*, 322 U.S. 533, 64 Sup. Ct. 1162, 88 L. Ed. 1440 (1944); *Polish National Alliance v. NLRB*, 322 U.S. 643, 64 Sup. Ct. 1196, 88 L. Ed. 1509 (1944).

[146] See particularly, *Mandeville Island Farms v. American Crystal Sugar Co.*, 334 U.S. 219, 68 Sup. Ct. 996, 92 L. Ed. 1328 (1948); *Wickard v. Filburn*, 317 U.S. 111, 63 Sup. Ct. 82, 87 L. Ed. 122 (1942).

The cases also demonstrate that it is unnecessary to judge merely the effect on commerce of the individual transaction or person involved in the particular case. The amount of wheat produced by a single farmer, or a single sale of drugs by a retailer, obviously would not affect interstate commerce substantially, or even noticeably. But Congress is entitled to take into account the total effect of many small transactions. "The total effect of the competition of many small producers may be great." [147] In *Wickard* v. *Filburn*,[148] the Court noted: "That appellee's own contribution to the demand for wheat may be trivial by itself is not enough to remove him from the scope of federal regulation where, as here, his contribution, taken together with that of many others similarly situated, is far from trivial."

It may be true that the application of the principles now approved by the Supreme Court may leave only minor aspects of our economy free from the regulatory power of Congress. The reason for this, however, is not legal but economic. If, in fact, the interstate and intrastate features of American business are inseparable, it would be crippling to require an artificial separation for purposes of governmental control. This was the vice of the older, now discarded, authorities.

The expansion of the power of Congress does not mean that there is nothing left for the states to regulate. Congress need not exercise its authority over all aspects of our national economy, and, of course, it has not done so. Some of its legislation is in aid of the authority of the states. It is not at all unlikely— if a guess may be ventured—that the amount of state commerce regulation has expanded along with the federal, rather than the reverse. For along with the growth of federal power has come a greater reluctance to find state legislation in conflict with the commerce clause. In his lectures before the University of Kansas in 1947, Mr. Justice Rutledge concluded:

> [J]ust as in recent years the permissible scope for congressional commerce action has broadened, returning to Marshall's conception, the prohibitive effect of the clause has been progressively narrowed. The trend has been toward sustaining state regulation formerly re-

[147] *United States* v. *Darby*, 312 U.S. 100, 123, 61 Sup. Ct. 451, 85 L. Ed. 609 (1941).

[148] 317 U.S. 111, 127–28, 63 Sup. Ct. 82, 87 L. Ed. 122 (1942). See also *Polish National Alliance* v. *NLRB*, 322 U.S. 643, 648, 64 Sup. Ct. 1196, 88 L. Ed. 1509 (1944); *North American Co.* v. *SEC*, 327 U.S. 686, 710, 66 Sup. Ct. 784, 90 L. Ed. 945 (1946).

garded as inconsistent with Congress' unexercised power of commerce. . . .

Nevertheless, the general problem of adjustment remains. It has only been transferred to a level more tolerant of both state and federal legislative action. On this level a new or renewed emphasis on facts and practical considerations has been allowed to work. . . .

But the scope of judicial intervention has been narrowed by the more recent trends, affecting both the affirmative and the prohibitive workings of the clause. Greater leeway and deference are given for legislative judgments, national and state, formally expressed. Larger emphasis is put on scrutiny of particular facts and concrete consequences, with an eye on their practical bearing for creating the evils the commerce clause was designed to outlaw. Correspondingly, less stress . . . is placed upon large generalizations and dogmatism inherited from levels of debate time has lowered. More and more the controlling considerations of policy implicit in thinking, judgment, and decision are brought into the open.[149]

These principles have also governed the application of the due process clause to the regulation of economic relationships. It is because of the greater leeway given legislative judgments that the commerce and due process clauses have ceased to arouse as much controversy as formerly. There are, of course, and presumably always will be, peripheral issues, some of undoubted importance, for the courts to decide. But, apart from these, in this vital field of constitutional adjudication, there is seldom any longer much doubt as to what the Court will do. As a consequence, many of the problems of yesteryear are hardly problems today.

[149] Rutledge, A Declaration of Legal Faith, 68–70 Univ. of Kan. Press (1947).

7. The Supreme Court: Temple and Forum

ALPHEUS THOMAS MASON

EDITORIAL NOTE. Unlike the Roman god Janus, the Supreme Court cannot face in two directions at once. But its special burden is not that its members must in every case shake off the Hamlet-complex and decide, one way or another—for there is no escape from the necessity of making a final judgment. The greater and often agonizing problem is that judgment must almost invariably be made in cases which have compelling arguments and persuasive considerations on both sides. As Wallace Mendelson said, cases that reach the Court "usually represent conflicts between highly commendable principles none of which can fully prevail in life on earth. Each is apt to have impressive legal backing. In such conflicts 'the law' is far from clear. Yet the judges must somehow decide cases." And since the cases will often involve such volatile issues as race or religion, money or politics, it is even less surprising that the losing parties may burst into public denunciation and no surprise at all that there is more than a smidgen of truth to some of their charges. Regrettably the example of Lincoln, who blasted the Dred Scott decision without attacking the integrity of the Court, is not followed more often than it is. Criticism of the justices, whatever its temper or nature, is to be expected when they defend against a majority the rights of individuals or minorities, and such criticism is a sign that the Court is doing its job. Public disinterest in the work of the Court might mean that it is taking the path of least resistance by dodging issues or is drifting with the popular tides which the Constitution sometimes requires it to dam. Jefferson once said that a court of able, independent judges enforcing bills of rights would not buckle before the "civium ardor prava jubentium"—the frenzy of

222

citizens commanding wrong. But no one would expect that a court decision against them would still their frenzy.

In the following essay, Alpheus T. Mason brings the perspective of history to the criticism which the Court has had to endure in our generation. More important he soberly evaluates the reasons for it and judges its merits. Mason defends the Court, but is by no means uncritical. His defense, however, has a special quality; it is the defense of a liberal and is as interesting for what it reflects about liberal scholarship as for its analysis of the work of the modern court. His distinction between judicial supremacy and judicial review is at the core of his interpretation. Its theme is in the following passage:

> It is still relevant to ask whether a politically irresponsible body, such as the Supreme Court, can block the will of the majority in the name of minorities and still remain a democratic institution. When the minority rights protected are those of property, the answer is probably 'no.' . . . When, on the other hand, judicial review serves to give a minority, otherwise barred, access to the political process, it implements rather than limits free government . . . Judicial hands-off in economic matters is perfectly consistent with judicial activism to preserve the integrity and effective operation of the political process.

This view of the matter may seem to many to be as doctrinaire as the absolutism of Justices Black and Douglas which Mason calls, rightly, doctrinaire. That the Constitution incorporates no particular economic philosophy by no means implies that property rights should not be protected or that their protection is a necessary characteristic of judicial supremacy. Mason comes close to the crude proposition that the protection of civil liberties is good, democratic judicial review, while protection of property rights is bad, undemocratic judicial supremacy. In an essay that appears elsewhere in this volume, Robert G. McCloskey broke a lance for property rights and questioned the very position that Mason champions, making repetition needless. Readers might refer once again to section four, in particular, of McCloskey's essay. Even if one thinks that Mason is on the side of the better argument, one may question his simple distinction between property rights and civil liberties. He writes as if they are unrelated categories, each requiring an opposite judicial response. He would have the Court sustain social and economic legislation by exercising self-restraint, but to strike down statutes abridging civil liberties by exercising judicial activism. There are too many cases, however, in which social reform or economic regulation cuts athwart a guarantee of the Bill of Rights or of the Fourteenth Amendment's insurance of "liberty" or "equal protection." Mason offers no guidance in such cases when in effect he calls simultaneously for judicial self-restraint and judicial activism. If, for example, the Court came to the right decision, as Mason alleges, in the Second Flag Salute case, did it come to the wrong decision in Prince v. Massachusetts where it permitted a statute outlawing child labor to infringe on the religious freedom of Jehovah's Witnesses' children? And how useful are Mason's categories in the frequent cases that pit one provision of the Bill of Rights against another?

In other writings, where Mason has greater space to develop his argument he does not, as in this essay, slight the democratic theory that underlay Justice Frankfurter's self-restraint in the flag salute and other civil liberty cases. In this essay one might scarcely realize that Frankfurter, at any rate, deeply believed that his position advanced the cause of free government far more than the activist review that Mason supports.

Frankfurter's views are all the more relevant because they were a source of principled and quite vigorous dissension among the justices, despite Mason's contention that activism in civil liberties cases did not provoke much telling criticism within the Court. Justice Clark's outburst in the Jencks case was by no means typical of the quality of dissenting opinions, nor was the Court quite as united as Mason indicates. Indeed, it was not even as united as he says in the cases which he uses to make his point. The positions depicted by Mason as mustering large majorities in the Yates and Sweezy cases actually represented the views of only four justices; there were significant, separate concurrences. Even in Jencks, two justices dissented in part, in addition to Clark's dissent en toto. In Trop v. Dulles, which Mason refers to, the Court divided 5 to 4. The Butler Bill, which he mentions, would have nullified Cole v. Young and Pennsylvania v. Nelson, as well as Watkins and Yates. In Cole, where the Court held that the federal loyalty program did not extend to non-sensitive positions, the vote was 6 to 3; so too in Nelson, where the holding was that Congressional legislation, by preempting the field, disabled the states from enforcing their own anti-subversive legislation. The state chief justices in their formal protest of August 1958 described Koningsberg v. State Bar of California as "a high water mark" by the Supreme Court in "overthrowing the action of a state." There too the Court split 6 to 3; in three related cases, criticized by the state chief justices, where disqualification for employment by reason of subversive activity was similarly involved, the Court divided 5 to 4. The same vote decided Griffin v. Illinois, which the state chief justices singled out as "probably the most far reaching decision of recent years on state criminal procedure." In the years immediately following the appearance of Mason's article, dissent, bickering, and strained relationships among the justices reached a new high, yet the quality of dissenting opinions bears comparison with any, short of the classic dissents in the Court's history.

The Warren Court deserves Mason's praise and the gratitude of the citizenry. It is substantially accurate to say as he does that libertarian results have been achieved and that they have come about, as to Congressional legislation, largely through statutory construction. In its review of state legislation, however, the Court has necessarily achieved the same results by way of constitutional interpretation. In the cases which have provoked the greatest public controversy, perpetuating the storm of criticism beyond the period covered by Mason, the Court has struck down state legislation and state criminal procedures. The Bible reading and school prayer cases and the legislative apportionment cases, like racial segregation cases, have turned on constitutional interpretation, as have the many public offender cases. Judicial review is by no means dead, despite the dominance of concepts of self-restraint in commerce clause cases and state regulatory cases. In the 1964 Term of the Court even two acts of Congress were held unconstitutional, one as a bill of attainder and the other as an abridgement of the First Amendment—the first such decision in our history. But if the Court is "showing us what free government means," as Mason concludes, it is a profoundly melancholy fact, certainly not one to cheer. The "third legislative chamber," to use Learned Hand's words, composed of a "bevy of Platonic Guardians" should not have to lead the way.

THE SUPREME COURT: TEMPLE AND FORUM

Since May 17, 1954, when the Supreme Court electrified the nation by outlawing racial segregation in public schools, the judiciary has been a storm center. Public response was immediate, provoking controversy and action of the most portentous nature. The brush fire started in 1954 has continued to smolder and sometimes to flare. Tinder was added on June 17, 1957, when the Court handed down a series of rulings in the so-called political offender cases.

The result has been to thrust the Justices into a no-man's land of public condemnation. Hot-tempered accusations are hurled; clear abuse of judicial power is charged; individual members of the Court are singled out for impeachment. Measures have been introduced in Congress modifying particular decisions and imposing drastic curbs on the Court's power and jurisdiction. On March 12, 1956, nineteen United States Senators and seventy-seven Representatives, all from the South and many of them lawyers, issued a "manifesto" urging reversal of the segregation decision. The attack was broadened in August 1958, when the Chief Justices of thirty-six States issued a report declaring that there is "at least considerable doubt" whether "we have a government of laws and not of men." Early in 1959 the American Bar Association's House of Delegates, speaking through a committee on Communist tactics, strategy, and objectives, approved a report charging that many cases have been decided in "such a manner as to encourage or increase Communist activity." The report went on to blame "the paralysis of our internal security" on "construction and interpretation centering around technicalities emanating from our judicial process." These are serious charges from highly respectable sources.

Criticism of the Supreme Court is, of course, not new in our history, and to certain observers these latest outcries merely echo old rumblings of discontent, reminiscent of those heard in 1803, 1857, 1895, and 1937. These earlier skirmishes left no permanent scar, and the Hughes Court repulsed F.D.R.'s bold assault of 1937 by simply reversing its embattled decisions. Is this a probable or feasible way out of present difficulties? Or do the Court's controversial decisions have such firm support as to make them impregnable?

It is easy to forget, especially when, as now, the Court is the focus of criticism, that the judiciary occupies vis-à-vis the public a position not unlike that of the British crown. Monarchy sweetens politics with "nice and pretty events." The Court performs a similar function in making the Constitution appear like a vehicle of inspired revelation. The king on the throne stimulates interest and imagination, but he does not govern. Parliament and the Cabinet are the working parts of the British Constitution. In England distinct roles are played by different institutions. In America these functions are blended. The Court is both symbol and instrument of power; it is both temple and forum. It is the American counterpart of the British crown, but there is a difference—and a big one. The Court has real power; it can bring Congress, President, State governors and legislators to heel. The occult ways customarily employed in doing so have evoked critical comment from judges themselves. Writing in 1958, Judge Learned Hand noted:

> Judges are seldom content to annul the particular solution before them; they do not, indeed may not say that, taking all things into consideration, the legislator's solution is too strong for the judicial stomach. On the contrary, they wrap up their veto in a protective veil of adjectives such as 'arbitrary', 'artificial', 'normal', 'reasonable', 'inherent', 'fundamental', or 'essential', whose office usually, though quite innocently, is to disguise what they are doing and impute to it a derivation far more impressive than their personal preferences, which are all that in fact lie behind the decision. If we do need a third chamber it should appear for what it is, and not as the interpreter of inscrutable principles.

Others would not only preserve the mythology that surrounds the judging process, but would hamper understanding by shielding it from the public gaze. The workings of the Court are supposed to require "a degree of privacy incomparably stricter than is fitting in the legislature or executive process."

This mingling of the occult and power aspects of governing in a single instrument leads to confusion. The Court has been called the most venerated and the least understood of all our political institutions. In our tripartite constitutional system, it is the Holy of Holies. "I reckon him one of the worst enemies of the community," Charles Evans Hughes once remarked, "who will talk lightly of the dignity of the Bench." Yet criticism, much of it irresponsible and uninformed, continues unabated. Today's headlines are just as tall as ever. The traditional reverence nevertheless remains. A critic may lash out at particular decisions and still venerate the Court as an institution. Virginia's Congressman, Burr P. Harrison, signer of the Southern Manifesto, criticized the segregation decision, but objected to the proposal that the Chief Justice of the United States be formally requested to report from time to time on "the state of the federal judiciary." The effect would be, the Congressman explained, "to inject our Judges into politics." "An air of detachment," he insisted, "is precisely what is to be prized in the men who run our Courts. Let us leave our Chief Justice on the cool height of Olympus." One recalls Edmund Burke's caveat as to the proper attitude toward the British Constitution: "We ought to understand it according to our measure, and to venerate where we are not able to comprehend."

The Court as a revered symbol stems in part from the effort to resolve what the late Robert H. Jackson once described as "a basic inconsistency between popular government and judicial supremacy." The founding fathers proclaimed that just governments derive their powers from the consent of the governed. At the same time, they apparently sanctioned the much quoted observation that "The Constitution is what the Judges say it is." To render more palatable this oligarchic element in our politics, the Court evolved the theory that judges exercise only judgment, not will. "Judicial power is never exercised for the purpose of giving effect to the will of the judge," Chief Justice Marshall commented, "always for the purpose of giving effect to the will of the law." "The thrill is irresistible," Judge Cardozo remarked on this passage in 1931. "We feel the mystery and awe of inspired revelation."

To preserve this magic, however, the Court is confronted with the well-nigh insuperable task of maintaining close identity between the Constitution and the judicial version of it. In his book of 1928 on the Supreme Court Charles Evans Hughes singled out three instances—Dred Scott, Legal Tender and Pollock—in which the Court signally failed to achieve this coincidence and, as a consequence, it "suffered severely from self-inflicted wounds." The Dred Scott ruling of 1857 inflicted injury by making the Supreme Court seem like a citadel of slavocracy. The Legal Tender decision of 1870 was damaging because it overturned a precedent of only two years' standing by only one vote and as a direct result of the appointment of two new judges after the first decision came down. The third wound was perhaps the most serious, for a single judge's change of mind after reargument resulted in voiding a federal income tax by vote of five to four. "Stability in judicial opinion," Hughes commented on this record, "is of no little importance in maintaining respect for the Court's work."

It is ironical, in light of the value Mr. Hughes placed on the Court as a symbol of stability, that the lawmakers who, in 1930, debated his nomination for the Chief Justiceship should have made it seem so much like a political forum. Believing that Supreme Court Justices are molders of policy rather than vehicles of revealed truth, more Senators vetoed Hughes's confirmation in 1930 than voted against Brandeis in 1916. This irony was heightened when it became Chief Justice Hughes's fate to preside over the most serious crisis in the Court's history. Under his leadership, "self-inflicted wounds" rose to an all-time high. In a single term, 1935–36, thirteen acts of Congress were set aside as invalid. A judicial blockage was declared on government action at all levels. At the term's end, Justice Stone remarked: "We seem to have tied Uncle Sam up in a hard knot."

The high-level political struggle that ensued between President Franklin D. Roosevelt and the Court obscures the fact that the Justices, without exception, regarded the New Deal with a jaundiced eye. On this point they were unanimous. The sharp differences dividing them had to do with the Court's role in a free society. These were clearly revealed in *United States* v. *Butler* outlawing the Agricultural Adjustment Act.

Speaking for a majority which included Hughes, Justice Roberts contended that upholding the AAA would mean "legislative powers without restriction or limitation." Congress might become "a parliament of the whole people, subject to no restrictions save such as are self-imposed." Turning the tables, Justice Stone, joined by Brandeis and Cardozo, countered by asking the majority to consider the status of its own power. The Executive and Congress were restrained, Stone pointed out, by "the ballot box and the process of democratic government," and "subject to judicial restraint; the only check on our own power is our own sense of self-restraint." The three dissenters went on to suggest that judicial preëminence had now been carried to such lengths that the Court had come to think of itself as "the only agency of government that must be assumed to have the power to govern."

The battle among the Justices in the AAA case highlights the distinction between judicial review and judicial supremacy. Under the guise of interpreting fundamental law, the Court had, in fact, made itself a super-legislature; it had denied Congress a power conferred by the Constitution. Underscored also is the "basic inconsistency" between popular government and judicial supremacy. Justice Roberts' opinion demonstrates the limits to which this oligarchic element in our politics can be carried; Justice Stone's urgent plea for judicial self-restraint shows how this element might be reduced to a minimum. When it became clear that dissenting views redounded to the advantage of the President, he exploited these for all they were worth. Finally, in face of the President's threat to pack it, the Court retreated. Indeed, even as the storm over F.D.R.'s packing proposal raged, and before any new appointments were made, the Court, discrediting its own precedents, and ignoring the "stability" Hughes valued so highly, upheld State and Federal legislation recently suspect on constitutional grounds. The impasse was thus resolved by the Justices themselves.

The secret was out, Max Lerner wrote. "Americans learned that judges are human, and that the judicial power need be no more sacred in our scheme than any other power. . . . They dared look upon the judicial Medusa-head, and lo! they were not turned to stone. It was then that the symbol of divine right began to crumble."

Like the opposition party that finally wins an election, Supreme Court Justices after 1937 were faced with the necessity of probing for the limits of the now dominant philosophy of judicial self-restraint. "Self-restraint" had been recognized as to commercial regulations. Would the same narrow concept of judicial power apply to enactments infringing freedom of speech, thought, and religion? An answer to this question was soon forthcoming. In an otherwise obscure opinion of 1938 Justice Stone appended a now famous footnote, suggesting that for legislation regulating the economy, judicial laissez-faire would henceforth be the rule, but in the orbit of civil rights the Court's responsibility was less confined. There would be narrower scope for presumption of constitutionality when legislation infringed specific prohibitions outlined in the so-called Bill of Rights. Moreover, any legislation restricting those political processes which could ordinarily be expected to bring about repeal of undesirable legislation, any statutes directed against particular religious or national or racial minorities, would require "more exacting judicial scrutiny."

Less than two years after these propositions were formulated, war clouds hung threateningly over the United States. Once more the question of national security began to loom large in public and private discussions. Unlike Woodrow Wilson during the First World War, F.D.R. did not recommend restrictive legislation as a security measure. Rather, he continued to stress fundamental rights, seeming confident that national safety would not be endangered by continuing along our normal political paths. Nor is there evidence that any large segment of the people disagreed with him. The nation was considerably shocked, therefore, when, on April 21, 1940, Justice Felix Frankfurter read the majority opinion for the Supreme Court in the first Flag Salute case, upholding the state's power to require school children to salute the flag.

Ignoring a tendency the Court had already manifested toward assuming special guardianship of the so-called "preferred freedoms," Frankfurter declared that the "precise issue" in this case was "whether the legislatures of the various states and the authorities in a thousand counties and school districts of this country [were by judicial action to be] barred from determining the appropriateness of various means to evoke that unifying sentiment without which there can ultimately be no liberties, civil or religious." Apparently convinced, as Wilson had been, that conformity was essential in wartime, he held that the States must not be barred from requiring the flag salute, in spite of the specific words of the First Amendment enjoining legislation abridging freedom of speech, press, and religion. A free society, he thought, rests on the binding tie of cohesive sentiment; national unity is the basis of national security and such unity may, if necessary, be achieved by legislative coercion, even to the extent of forcing little school children to salute the flag in violation of their family's religious beliefs. All this was considered within the confines of the Constitution.

Justice Stone, later Chief Justice, alone dissented. To his mind, the school board had not merely chosen an ineffective means of evoking unity and inspiring patriotism; it had struck at the very heart of a basic constitutional guarantee. It had destroyed the religious freedom of Jehovah's Witnesses. That destruction the Supreme Court could not ignore, and no cautious hesitation to use judicial power should keep the Court from saying so. Stone recognized the necessity of making reasonable accommodation between exertions of governmental power and a specific constitutional guarantee of religious freedom—whenever possible. Indeed, he declared, "It is the function of the courts to determine whether such accommodation is really possible." But wherever they found accommodation impossible, they had no alternative but to rule in favor of freedom.

For the time being, Stone's dissenting views were ignored. The ruthlessness of the European dictators impressed the Court as it impressed the people. Looking ahead to the imminent probability of war, and remembering the social confusion following the First World War, the majority felt that considerations of national unity and security must have precedence.

Before long, however, opinions began to change. The impact of adverse public reaction to the Flag Salute decision revealed itself three years later, when three Justices, dissenting, took the unusual step of announcing that they now believed that the Flag Salute case had been wrongly decided. The scales were finally tipped altogether against the Frankfurter point of view in 1943, when the late Justice Jackson, speaking for the Court, adopted Stone's position. "If there is any fixed star in our constitutional constellation," Jackson wrote, "it is that no official, high or petty, can prescribe what shall be orthodox in politics, nationalism, religion, or other matters." "The very purpose of a Bill of Rights was to withdraw certain subjects from the vicissitudes of political controversy, to place them beyond the reach of majorities and officials and to establish them as legal principles to be applied by the courts." Said Jackson:

> We act in these matters not by authority of our competence but by the force of our commissions. We cannot, because of modest estimates of our competence in such specialties as public education, withhold the judgment that history authenticates as the function of this Court when liberty is infringed.

Like Thomas Jefferson, Jackson believed that freedom increased our national strength. "Government of limited power," the Justice asserted, "need not be anemic government. Assurance that rights are secure tends to diminish fear and jealousy of strong government, and by making us feel safe to live under it makes for its better support. Without promise of a limiting Bill of Rights it is doubtful if our Constitution could have mustered enough strength to enable ratification. To enforce those rights today is not to choose weak government over strong government. It is only to adhere as a means of strength to individual freedom of mind in preference to officially disciplined uniformity for which history indicates a disappointing and disastrous end."

Jackson's position seems to be in accord with the best in our tradition, but disagreement with it also fits our tradition. Underlying the judicial cleavage are basic differences as to the meaning and requirements of free government, and of the role of the Court with respect to those requirements. Justice Frankfurter believes that liberty is best maintained when instilled in the habits of the people and left to the "forum of public opinion."

Judicial review is regarded as a limitation on "popular government." Overlooked is the fact that the framers planned it that way. They insisted that the dependence of the government on the people must not be carried to such point that individual rights are left unprotected. Judicial review was "American democracy's way of covering its bet." Far from being at war with the principles of "free government," judicial review is essential to its implementation.

That fundamental disagreement can exist among men of high intelligence and unquestioned patriotism emphasizes the complexity of the civil rights issue in this day of national power and unsettled world conditions. The divergent points of view expressed on the Court have not yet been reconciled. Indeed, recent events have exacerbated the split. Experience, since the Second World War, with Communist aggression abroad and suspected infiltration at home has greatly increased the drive toward conformity for security's sake and has catapulted the question to top position among the political puzzles of our time. Although there has not been a "Big Red Scare," there has certainly been a little one. Many of the devices used between 1918 and 1920 to coerce opinion and stifle discussion have been reëmployed, and new ones added. If the net result of their use has not been as serious as the consequences of their earlier employment, the fact that they have been resorted to at all suggested persistence in the belief that coerced conformity is an appropriate method of achieving national security.

Substitution of judicial *supremacy* for judicial *review*, as in the AAA case, reversal of the subordinate position of judicial restraints in relation to political restraints created, as we have seen, the crisis of 1937. The corrective was found in returning to the wisdom of the framers, to judicial humility. Once political controls had been reëstablished as the primary check on government, it seemed logically to follow that the Court must shoulder a corresponding responsibility for the effective functioning of the political process. But cases involving such responsibility have evoked a variety of responses from the Justices. For certain of them, First Amendment freedoms are "preferred." More sacred than those of property and contract, these freedoms are protected from legislative encroachment not only by the due process requirement but also by the injunction that "Congress shall make no law . . . abridging the freedom of speech, or of the press; or the right of the people peaceably to assemble. . . ." The thought of the so-called activists (notably Justices Black and Douglas) seems to be that though the Constitution does not embody, as Holmes said, any particular economic philosophy, it does incorporate a particular political theory. Central to that theory are the freedoms listed in the First Amendment. As to these, judicial self-restraint does not mean that the Court is paralyzed. "It simply conserves its strength," as Attorney-General Jackson put it, "to strike more telling blows in the case of a working democracy."

Except for occasional deviations, especially those occurring during Fred Vinson's Chief-Justiceship, the Court since 1937 has subjected legislative and administrative infringements on civil rights to more exacting scrutiny. When, in 1955, Justice Frankfurter observed, "as no constitutional guarantee enjoys preference, so none should suffer subordination or deletion," Justice Reed wrote a cryptic concurrence solely to take exception to Justice Frankfurter's repudiation of the "preferred freedoms" doctrine.

Evidence mounts that the "self-restraint" banner raised in 1937 has not blinded Chief Justice Warren's Court to certain positive responsibilities which his predecessors had, on occasion, shunned. His Court began to discharge these on May 17, 1954, that historic day when the Justices handed down their unanimous judgment in the school segregation cases. The anxiously awaited opinion was short and incisive. The Chief Justice found neither history nor precedent an adequate guide. Special studies of the intention of the framers of the Fourteenth Amendment were inconclusive. "In approaching this problem," the Chief Justice remarked, "we must consider public education in the light of its full development and its present place in American life throughout the Nation." Segregation, he said, may affect hearts and minds in a way unlikely ever to be undone.

Certain observers marked the case as statesmanship of the first order. For others the decision opened a Pandora's box of criticism and recrimination, not only among Southerners but also among thoughtful people elsewhere. The Governor of Georgia naturally predicted "dark days ahead" and in his anguish, cried out, "Georgia belongs to Georgians—not to the U.S. Supreme Court and not to the NAACP." A sober student of constitutional law concluded that the Court had displayed a "missionary zeal in behalf of . . . underprivileged . . . Negroes," that "is not compatible with [the] true function of democratic leadership."

Nor is racial segregation the only field in which the Warren

Court has responded to a larger responsibility. At a single sitting, June 17, 1957, the Justices shouldered other tasks in the civil rights orbit. In the Yates case the Court upheld the right of anyone to advocate overthrow of the government, so long as the preaching does not openly advocate specific action. In the Watkins case, it qualified the power of congressional committees to make investigations and require witnesses to testify. In Sweezy v. New Hampshire, it limited the State's power to require witnesses to testify in investigations authorized by State law. In the Jencks case earlier in the term, the Justices held that the FBI and other government agency reports must be made available to defendants in criminal trials if the persons who made the report are called as witnesses. In Trop v. Dulles, decided in 1958, the Court declared unconstitutional a section of the Nationality Act of 1941 which expatriates the wartime deserter dishonorably discharged after conviction by court-martial. In all these cases the Court took the position that government action restricting or taking away fundamental rights of citizenship should be examined with special diligence, that "the Judiciary has the duty of implementing the constitutional safeguards that protect individual rights."

"We cannot simply assume," Chief Justice Warren commented in the Watkins case, "that every congressional investigation is justified by a public need that overbalances any private rights affected. To do so would be to abdicate the responsibility placed by the Constitution upon the judiciary to insure that the Congress does not unjustifiably encroach upon an individual's right of privacy nor abridge his liberty of speech, press, religion or assembly." Even Justice Frankfurter, the most persistent exponent of judicial laissez-faire, regardless of the area involved, now recognizes that the Court must balance the contending claims of a citizen to political privacy and the right of the state to self-protection. "This is the inescapable judicial task," Frankfurter wrote, concurring in the Sweezy decision, "and it is a task ultimately committed to this Court."

Because of these decisions and of others in this genre, the Warren Court finds itself the focus of public controversy. Are its troubles like those in which the Hughes Court was embroiled?

The adverse criticism directed against Warren and his Court comes mainly from outsiders, many of them lawyers. The most telling blasts against the Hughes Court of 1935-36 came from the Justices themselves. Dissenting opinions in the Warren Court are less significant both quantitatively and qualitatively than those directed against the majority on Hughes's Bench. The segregation decision was unanimous. The *Yates* decision was six to one, *Jencks*, seven to one, *Sweezy*, six to two, *Watkins*, six to one. In quality, the dissents tend to drop to the level of Justice Clark's outburst in the *Jencks* case. The majority had, he said, opened FBI files "to the criminal and thus afforded him a Roman holiday for rummaging through confidential information as well as vital national secrets." Justice Clark's complaint is reminiscent of McReynolds' frenzied outcry in the Gold Clause case of 1935—"The Constitution is gone"—rather than of Stone's trenchant analysis of the majority opinion in the AAA case. Though certain of the Warren Court's decisions are open to valid criticism and may be in for trimming (some has already occurred), one finds little in the dissents likely to qualify them as future majority opinions.

The Warren Court, while responding to the positive responsibility committed to it by the Constitution, has not been unmindful of the bounds set by the principle of judicial self-restraint. Since 1937, the Constitution has been seldom invoked as a barrier against congressional action. Statutory interpretation rather than constitutional interpretation is involved. Here contrast with the Hughes Court is sharp. The Justices of 1935–36 met the constitutional issue with alacrity. The Hughes Court vitalized old constitutional barriers and refashioned new ones against the power to govern. Even the well-worn principle of presumption of constitutionality was sometimes ignored. This flouting of judicial self-restraint, this destruction of a national legislative program having strong popular support meant the raising of bars that could be removed only by constitutional amendment, or by reversal of judicial decisions. The Warren Court, on the other hand, has achieved libertarian objectives largely by statutory interpretation. Thus the ill-effects and shortcomings of momentous decisions like *Yates*, *Watkins* and *Jencks*, can be removed by an ordinary act of Congress. It thus seems improbable that some future commentator will be able to write as an epitaph on Warren's Chief-Justiceship the words Samuel Hendel used to describe Hughes's strategy during the 1937 crisis:

> When the pressure for innovation became great, and the risks to the nation and to the Court itself apparent, reluctantly at first, but increasingly he went along with change. Having sedulously sought to protect the precedents of the Court, sometimes at the risk of offending logic, he witnessed and often participated in the shattering of one precedent after another. He stood thus as a kind

of heroic and in a sense, tragic figure, torn between the old and the new, seeking at first to stem the tide, but then ruthlessly caught up and moving with it.

The Hughes Court precipitated a crisis by blocking legislation which the Constitution itself did not enjoin. The Warren Court is under attack in responding to popular aspirations, perhaps in moving ahead of them, as in the segregation decisions. In repudiating the separate but equal doctrine and thus bringing the law of the American Constitution into line with the social conscience of the world, it has aroused strong protest in certain Southern States. The Court has also evoked criticism from less localized quarters. By curbing legislation designed to achieve national security in a time of unprecedented peril, it finds itself in the awkward posture of frustrating government effort to stave off the Communist threat. Little wonder the Court is under fire. Like that headed by John Marshall, the Warren Court is damming a powerful current in our politics. Just as Marshall's fervent nationalism stirred violent criticism among Democratic Republicans, so the Warren Court's defense of our basic freedoms rouses bitter denunciation from those inclined to equate security with repression.

Can a rationale be fashioned justifying greater judicial alertness to infringements on civil liberties than to legislation regulating the economy? The Justices, in attempting to supply it, have reached different results. There is, for example, the doctrinaire formula of Justices Black and Douglas, which elevates First Amendment freedoms practically to an absolute. There is the more restrained position of Justice Stone which suggests that legislation infringing speech, thought, and religion, and legislation so restrictive of the political process as to make it impossible for minorities to resort to it effectively, must be subjected to more careful judicial scrutiny. In applying Stone's formula, the Warren Court has the sanction of tradition, as well as the support of such eminent jurists as Brandeis, Cardozo, Holmes, and Hughes.

Those who won our independence and framed the Constitution believed that the only security worth having is built on freedom. By 1790, American society had already reached a degree of stability sufficient to prompt the first Congress to write into the Constitution provisions protecting the right of political disagreement. In piloting the Bill of Rights through the first Congress, Madison observed:

The prescriptions in favor of liberty ought to be levelled against that quarter where the greatest danger lies, namely, that which possesses the highest prerogative of power. But this is not found in either the Executive or Legislative departments of Government, but in the body of the people, operating by the majority against the minority. . . . If they [the bill of rights] are incorporated into the Constitution, independent tribunals of justice will consider themselves in a peculiar manner the guardians of those rights; they will be an impenetrable bulwark against every assumption of power in the Legislative or Executive; they will be naturally led to resist every encroachment upon rights, expressly stipulated for in the Constitution by the declaration of rights.

A century and a half later the late Justice Robert H. Jackson echoed Madison's sentiments:

There is nothing covert or conflicting in the recent judgments of the Court on social legislation and on legislative repressions of civil rights. The presumption of validity which attaches in general to legislative acts is frankly reversed in the case of interferences with free speech and free assembly, and for a perfectly cogent reason. Ordinarily, legislation whose basis in economic wisdom is uncertain can be redressed by the processes of the ballot box or the pressures of opinion. But when the channels of opinion or of peaceful persuasion are corrupted or clogged, these political correctives can no longer be relied on, and the democratic system is threatened at its most vital point. In that event the Court, by intervening, restores the processes of democratic government; it does not disrupt them.

Despite the apparent strength of the Warren Court's position, its defenders are small in number compared to the host that rallied around Hughes's when F.D.R. launched his abortive crusade to "reform" the Court. The 1937 crisis represented a conflict between the Court and the President. The current battle is between the Court and Congress, the President being a somewhat confused spectator. Among the Warren Court's most vigorous defenders are the Justices themselves. On November 8, 1958, Justice Douglas bluntly announced that the Court would not "take a back seat." "The courts as an institution are too deeply fixed in our society," he said. "There is no sturdier element in our democratic system than an independent judiciary." On November 25, Justice Harlan, mindful of the poison in the Butler-Jenner bill limiting the Supreme Court's appellate jurisdiction in a wide assortment of cases involving civil rights, stressed the seriousness of the attack. At the peak of his power F.D.R. could muster the support of only 30 Senators in favor of Court packing. The Butler-Jenner bill went down in the Senate by the narrow margin of 49 to 41. F.D.R. proposed to increase the Court's membership, leaving its power untouched. The Butler-Jenner bill goes far beyond these bounds. By withdrawing appellate jurisdiction in an important group of national security cases, it makes the Court, in this extremely crucial area, something less than supreme.

Why should defense of the Court against F.D.R.'s attempt to pack it have been so spontaneous, and the Warren Court's outside support, including that of President Eisenhower, have been so ambiguous? There are, of course, various possible reasons; one may be the inroads which the Warren Bench has made on the Court as a powerless symbol of justice. Four short years have witnessed the shattering of judicial axioms of the most sacred character. The legal profession's mighty principle of *stare decisis* has been rudely shaken; the notion that sociological and other extra-legal data are meet for the legislature but not for courts has been ignored; the venerable fiction that courts exercise judgment and not will, always tenuous, has been honored only in the breach. Chief Justice Warren himself has slighted the symbolic aspects of our jurisprudence. "Our judges are not monks or scientists," the Chief Justice wrote in 1955, "but participants in the living stream of our national life, steering the law between the dangers of rigidity on the one hand and formlessness on the other. . . ." As Thurman Arnold has observed, the Court under Chief Justice Warren is becoming "unified," "a Court of inspired choice and policy, . . . rather than a Court of law as we used to know it."

Though the Court in playing its positive role in support of civil liberties may not have inflicted any major wound on itself, it has on occasion, as in *Jencks* and *Watkins*, been guilty of something less than good craftsmanship. "The real concern," Paul Freund has observed, "is with the Court's tendency to make broad principles do service for specific problems that call for differentiation." In preparing an exhaustive treatise on Administrative Law, Kenneth Culp Davis was prompted to make five "constructive suggestions":

(1) The Court probably should write fewer general essays in its opinions and it should give more meticulous care to the ones

it does write. (2) The Court should take greater advantage of the values of case-to-case development of law. (3) The Court should make further effort to reduce the frequency of contradictory holdings, and it should check its apparently growing tendency to indulge in easy generalizations that are misleading if read literally. (4) The Court should have greater respect for its own holdings and for its own opinions; without restricting its freedom to overrule, it should restrict its freedom to violate its own doctrine. (5) The Court should inquire whether it is often too lighthearted about the manipulation of technical doctrine in order to produce desired substantive results in particular cases.

Professor Davis leaves open the question whether these suggestions would apply to other fields of law, but students of the Court will perhaps find little difficulty in citing recent Supreme Court cases illustrative of the points he finds applicable in Administrative Law.

It is still relevant to ask whether a politically irresponsible body, such as the Supreme Court, can block the will of the majority in the name of minorities and still remain a democratic institution. When the minority rights protected are those of property, the answer is probably "no." Between 1890 and 1937, the Supreme Court actually retarded the growth of democracy. When, on the other hand, judicial review serves to give a minority, otherwise barred, access to the political process, it implements rather than limits free government. The Court's function is not to determine what decisions can be made by political processes, but to prevent the mechanism from breaking down. Under this theory the legislature can control the wages and hours of workers; it cannot limit the right to vote with respect to race or color. Congress can regulate agricultural production; it cannot control the content of newspapers. The state can demand that children attend school; it cannot compel them to participate in ceremonies that violate their religious convictions. Judicial hands-off in economic matters is perfectly consistent with judicial activism to preserve the integrity and effective operation of the political process.

An appointive body, such as the Supreme Court, exercising political control in a system of government whose powers are supposed to derive from the people, has, as we have seen, sometimes been considered an alien offshoot from an otherwise democratic polity. The dilemma was once resolved by invoking the fiction that the Court had no power—that it merely applied the

Constitution which, in some mystical way, is always the highest expression of the people's will. Though this ancient theory still shows signs of vitality, it is not altogether satisfying. The real problem is to protect individuals and minorities without thereby destroying capacity in the majority to govern. Majorities—and this is the key point of democratic theory—are always in flux. To-morrow's majority may have a different composition as well as different goals. Defense of the political rights of minorities thus becomes, not the antithesis of majority rule, but its very foundation. The Supreme Court can contribute toward realization of free government by guaranteeing all minority groups free access to the political process and the instruments of political change, while at the same time allowing the majority government—as long as the political process is open and untrammeled—to rule.

In a free society, no organ of government can be defended solely in terms of its symbolic value. The Supreme Court is but one among several agencies empowered, within limits, to govern. The suggestion that any organ of government is beyond public scrutiny, more particularly that the judiciary should enjoy free-dom from critical examination greater than any other agency can claim, is to be deplored. Nothing of the sort was envisioned by the framers of the Constitution. Implicit in the system of government they established is the basic premise that unchecked power in any hands whatsoever is intolerable. The freedom the judiciary has from political responsibility and control makes its processes more rather than less appropriate for critical exploration.

The Supreme Court is a forum. Its contribution consists in what it does, in the deliberative process that precedes judgment. An act of judgment based on reason can have a moral force far exceeding that of the purse or sword. Thus the Court's worth consists not only in its restraining power, but also in the part it plays in making vocal and audible the ideals and values that might otherwise be silenced. The Court explores and passes judgment on living issues, on complexities which are at any given moment puzzling and dividing us. By precept and example the Court now, as in the past, is showing us what free government means.

Contributors and Sources

JOHN P. ROCHE. "The Founding Fathers: A Reform Caucus in Action," *The American Political Science Review*, vol. LV (December, 1961), pp. 799–816. Copyrighted by the American Political Science Association; reprinted by permission. Mr. Roche is Morris Hilquit Professor of Labor and Social Thought in the Politics Department, Brandeis University. His books include *The Dynamics of Democratic Government; Courts and Rights; The Quest for the Dream;* and *Shadow and Substance.*

MAX LERNER. "John Marshall and the Campaign of History," *Columbia Law Review*, vol. 39 (March, 1939), 396–431. Copyrighted by the *Columbia Law Review;* reprinted by permission. Mr. Lerner is a columnist for the New York Post and Max Richter Professor of American Civilization and Institutions in the Politics Department, Brandeis University. His books include *The Mind and Faith of Justice Holmes; Ideas Are Weapons; The Unfinished Country;* and *America as a Civilization.*

ROBERT J. HARRIS. "Chief Justice Taney: Prophet of Reform and Reaction," *Vanderbilt Law Review*, vol. 10 (February, 1957), 227–257. Copyrighted by the Vanderbilt Law Review; reprinted by permission. Mr. Harris is Dean of Faculty and Professor of Political Science, University of Virginia. His books include *The Judicial Power of the United States;* and *The Quest for Equality: the Constitution, Congress, and the Supreme Court.*

WALTON H. HAMILTON. "The Path of Due Process," *Ethics*, vol. XLVIII (April, 1938), 269–296. Reprinted from *Ethics* by permission of the University of Chicago Press. Mr. Hamilton was Southmayd Professor of Law, Yale Law School. His books included *Price and Price Policies; Antitrust in Action;* and *The Pattern of Competition,* in addition to many articles on constitutional law.

ROBERT G. MC CLOSKEY. "Economic Due Process and the Supreme Court: an Exhumation and Reburial," *The Supreme Court Review* (1962), ed. by Philip B. Kurland, pp. 34–62. Reprinted from *The Supreme Court Review* by permission of the University of Chicago Press. Mr. McCloskey is Professor of Government, Harvard University. His books include *American Conservatism in the Age of Enterprise; The American Supreme Court;* and *Essays in Constitutional Law.*

ROBERT L. STERN. "The Problems of Yesteryear—Commerce and Due Process," *Vanderbilt Law Review,* vol. 4 (March, 1951), 446–468. Copyrighted by the *Vanderbilt Law Review;* reprinted by permission. Mr. Stern was First Assistant and then Acting Solicitor General, United States Department of Justice; he is currently a partner in the firm of Mayer, Friedlich, Spiess, Tierney, Brown, and Platt, Chicago, Ill. He is co-author of *Supreme Court Practice* and in many articles established himself as the foremost expert on the commerce clause.

ALPHEUS T. MASON. "The Supreme Court: Temple and Forum," *The Yale Review,* vol. XLVIII (Summer, 1959), 524–540. Copyrighted by *The Yale Review;* reprinted by permission. Mr. Mason is McCormick Professor of Jurisprudence in the Department of Government, Princeton University. His books include *Brandeis: a Free Man's Life; Harlan Fiske Stone: Pillar of the Law; The Supreme Court: Palladium of Freedom;* and *William Howard Taft: Chief Justice.*

LEONARD W. LEVY is Earl Warren Professor of Constitutional Law and History, Brandeis University. His books include *The Law of the Commonwealth and Chief Justice Shaw; Legacy of Suppression: Freedom of Speech and Press in Early American History;* and *Jefferson and Civil Liberties: the Darker Side.*

Bibliography

This is a selected bibliography of the best articles that have appeared in the journals in the field of American Constitutional history. All are worthy of inclusion in this anthology. Many, regrettably, were much too long for consideration but merit the attention of students. Articles dealing with the subject of judicial review are excluded from the list. They will appear in a companion volume in this series on the subject of judicial review and the Supreme Court.

Chester James Antieau, "Judicial Delimitation of the First Amendment Freedoms," *Marquette Law Review*, XXXIV (Fall 1950), 57–89.

Arthur Bestor, "The American Civil War as a Constitutional Crisis," *American Historical Review*, LXIX (January 1964), 327–52.

—— "State Sovereignty and Slavery," *Journal of the Illinois State Historical Society*, LIX (Summer 1961), 117–80.

Alexander Bickel, "The Original Understanding and the Segregation Decision," *Harvard Law Review*, LXIX (November 1955), 1–65.

Louis Boudin, "The Sherman Act and Labor Disputes," *Columbia Law Review*, XXXIX (December 1939), 1283–1337 and XL (January 1940), 14–51

—— "Truth and Fiction about the Fourteenth Amendment," *New York University Law Quarterly Review*, XVI (November 1938), 19–82.

Henry S. Commager, "The Constitution: Was It an Economic Document?" *American Heritage, The Magazine of History*, X (December 1958), 58–61, 100–103.

Edward S. Corwin, "The Basic Doctrine of American Constitutional Law," *Michigan Law Review*, XII (February 1914), 247–76.

—— "The Doctrine of Due Process before the Civil War,"

Harvard Law Review, XXIV (March 1911), 366–85 and (April 1911), 460–79.

―――― "The Passing of Dual Federalism," Virginia Law Review, XXXVI (February 1950), 1–24.

―――― "The Progress of Constitutional Theory between the Declaration of Independence and the Meeting of the Philadelphia Convention," American Historical Review, XXX (April 1925), 511–536.

Thomas I. Emerson, "Toward a General Theory of the First Amendment," Yale Law Journal, LXXII (April 1963), 877–956.

Charles Fairman, "Does the Fourteenth Amendent Incorporate the Bill of Rights? The Original Understanding," Stanford Law Review, II (December 1949), 5–139.

John P. Frank and Robert F. Munro, "The Original Understanding of 'Equal Protection of the Laws,' " Columbia Law Review, L (February 1950), 131–69.

Felix Frankfurter, "The Supreme Court in the Mirror of Justices," University of Pennsylvania Law Review, CV (April 1957), 781–96.

Paul A. Freund, "Civil Rights and the Limits of Law," Buffalo Law Review, XIV (Winter 1964), 199–207.

―――― "The Supreme Court and Civil Liberties," Vanderbilt Law Review, IV (April 1951), 533–554.

―――― "The Supreme Court and Fundamental Freedoms," Harvard Law School Association of New Jersey Annual Lecture Series, 1957, pp. 3–22.

Howard J. Graham, "The Conspiracy Theory of the Fourteenth Amendment," Yale Law Journal, XLVII (January 1938), 371–403 and XLVIII (December 1938), 171–194.

―――― "Our 'Declaratory' Fourteenth Amendment," Stanford Law Review, VII (December 1954), 3–39.

―――― "The Early Antislavery Backgrounds of the Fourteenth Amendment," Wisconsin Law Review, Vol. 1950 (May 1950), 479–507 and (July 1950), 609–61.

―――― "Procedure to Substance—Extra-Judicial Rise of Due Process, 1830–1860," California Law Review, XL (Winter 1952–1963), 483–500.

John Raeburn Green, "Liberty under the Fourteenth Amendment," Washington University Law Quarterly, XXVII (Summer 1942), 497–562.

―――― "The Supreme Court, the Bill of Rights and the States,"

University of Pennsylvania Law Review, XCVII (April 1949), 608–40.

Charles Grove Haines, "Judicial Review of Legislation in the United States and the Doctrine of Vested Rights," Texas Law Review, II (June 1924), 387–421 and III (December 1924), 1–43.

Robert L. Hale, "The Supreme Court and the Contract Clause," Harvard Law Review, LVII (April 1944), 512–57; (May 1944), 621–74; and (July 1944), 852–92.

John A. C. Hetherington, "State Economic Regulation and Substantive Due Process of Law," Northwestern University Law Review, LII (March 1958), 13–32, and (April 1958), 226–51.

Alfred H. Kelly, "The Fourteenth Amendment Reconsidered," Michigan Law Review, LIV (June 1956), 1049–86.

Phillip B. Kurland, "Of Church and State and the Supreme Court," University of Chicago Law Review, XXIX (Autumn 1961), 1–96.

Max Lerner, "Constitution and Court as Symbols," Yale Law Journal, XLVI (June 1937), 1290–1319.

——— "The Supreme Court and American Capitalism," Yale Law Journal, XLII (February 1933), 668–701.

Andrew C. McLaughlin, "The Court, the Corporation, and Conkling," American Historical Review, XLVI (October 1940), 45–63.

Alexander Meiklejohn, "The First Amendment and Evils That Congress Has a Right to Prevent," Indiana Law Journal, XXVI (Summer 1951), 477–93.

——— "What Does the First Amendment Mean?" University of Chicago Law Review, XX (Spring 1953), 461–80.

Stanley Morrison, "Does the Fourteenth Amendment Incorporate the Bill of Rights? The Judicial Interpretation," Stanford Law Review, II (December 1949), 140–173.

Roscoe Pound, "Liberty of Contract," Yale Law Journal, XVIII (May 1909), 454–87.

Thomas Reed Powell, "The Logic and Rhetoric of Constitutional Law," Journal of Philosophy, Psychology, and Scientific Methods, XV (November 1918).

John P. Roche, "Civil Liberty in the Age of Enterprise," University of Chicago Law Review, XXXI (Autumn 1963), 103–135.

——— "Entrepreneurial Liberty and the Commerce Power," University of Chicago Law Review, XXX (Summer 1963), 680–703.

——— "Entrepreneurial Liberty and the Fourteenth Amendment," *Labor History*, IV (Winter 1963), 3–31.

Eugene V. Rostow, "The Supreme Court and the People's Will," *Notre Dame Lawyer*, XXXIII (August 1958), 573–96.

Henry Rottschaefer, "The Constitution and a 'Planned Economy,'" *Michigan Law Review*, XXXVIII (June 1940), 1133–64.

Robert L. Stern, "The Commerce Clause and the National Economy, 1933–1946," *Harvard Law Review*, LIX (May 1946), 645–693 and (July 1946), 883–947.

——— "The Scope of the Phrase Interstate Commerce," *American Bar Association Journal*, XLI (September 1955), 823–26 and 871–74.

Joseph Tussman and Jacobus tenBroek, "The Equal Protection of the Laws," *California Law Review*, XXXVII (September 1949), 341–81.

Selected titles: revised June, 1966

harper ✲ torchbooks

American Studies: General

CARL N. DEGLER, Ed.: Pivotal Interpretations of American History   TB/1240, TB/1241

A. S. EISENSTADT, Ed.: The Craft of American History: Recent Essays in American Historical Writing   Vol. I   TB/1255;   Vol. II   TB/1256

MARCUS LEE HANSEN: The Immigrant in American History   TB/1120

JOHN HIGHAM, Ed.: The Reconstruction of American History △   TB/1068

ROBERT H. JACKSON: The Supreme Court in the American System of Government   TB/1106

JOHN F. KENNEDY: A Nation of Immigrants. △ Illus.   TB/1118

RALPH BARTON PERRY: Puritanism and Democracy   TB/1138

ARNOLD ROSE: The Negro in America   TB/3048

American Studies: Colonial

BERNARD BAILYN, Ed.: The Apologia of Robert Keayne: Self-Portrait of a Puritan Merchant   TB/1201

BERNARD BAILYN: The New England Merchants in the Seventeenth Century   TB/1149

JOSEPH CHARLES: The Origins of the American Party System   TB/1049

LAWRENCE HENRY GIPSON: The Coming of the Revolution: 1763-1775. † Illus.   TB/3007

PERRY MILLER & T. H. JOHNSON, Eds.: The Puritans: A Sourcebook   Vol. I   TB/1093;   Vol. II   TB/1094

EDMUND S. MORGAN, Ed.: The Diary of Michael Wigglesworth, 1653-1657   TB/1228

EDMUND S. MORGAN: The Puritan Family   TB/1227

RICHARD B. MORRIS: Government and Labor in Early America   TB/1244

WALLACE NOTESTEIN: The English People on the Eve of Colonization: 1603-1630. † Illus.   TB/3006

American Studies: From the Revolution to 1860

JOHN R. ALDEN: The American Revolution: 1775-1783. † Illus.   TB/3011

MAX BELOFF, Ed.: The Debate on the American Revolution, 1761-1783: A Sourcebook △   TB/1225

RAY A. BILLINGTON: The Far Western Frontier: 1830-1860. † Illus.   TB/3012

EDMUND BURKE: On the American Revolution. ‡ Edited by Elliott Robert Barkan   TB/3068

WHITNEY R. CROSS: The Burned-Over District: The Social and Intellectual History of Enthusiastic Religion in Western New York, 1800-1850   TB/1242

GEORGE DANGERFIELD: The Awakening of American Nationalism: 1815-1828. † Illus.   TB/3061

FELIX GILBERT: The Beginnings of American Foreign Policy: To the Farewell Address   TB/1200

FRANCIS GRIERSON: The Valley of Shadows: The Coming of the Civil War in Lincoln's Midwest   TB/1246

JAMES MADISON: The Forging of American Federalism. Edited by Saul K. Padover   TB/1226

JOHN C. MILLER: Alexander Hamilton and the Growth of the New Nation   TB/3057

RICHARD B. MORRIS, Ed.: The Era of the American Revolution   TB/1180

R. B. NYE: The Cultural Life of the New Nation: 1776-1801. † Illus.   TB/3026

FRANCIS S. PHILBRICK: The Rise of the West, 1754-1830. † Illus.   TB/3067

TIMOTHY L. SMITH: Revivalism and Social Reform: American Protestantism on the Eve of the Civil War   TB/1229

American Studies: Since the Civil War

THOMAS C. COCHRAN & WILLIAM MILLER: The Age of Enterprise: A Social History of Industrial America TB/1054

W. A. DUNNING: Reconstruction, Political and Economic: 1865-1877   TB/1073

ROBERT GREEN MCCLOSKEY: American Conservatism in the Age of Enterprise: 1865-1910   TB/1137

ARTHUR MANN: Yankee Reformers in the Urban Age   TB/1247

VERNON LANE WHARTON: The Negro in Mississippi: 1865-1890   TB/1178

A. RUSSELL BUCHANAN: The United States and World War II. † Illus.   Vol. II   TB/3044;   Vol. II   TB/3045

FOSTER RHEA DULLES: America's Rise to World Power: 1898-1954. † Illus.   TB/3021

JOHN D. HICKS: Republican Ascendancy: 1921-1933. † Illus.   TB/3041

SIDNEY HOOK: Reason, Social Myths, and Democracy   TB/1237

WILLIAM E. LEUCHTENBURG: Franklin D. Roosevelt and the New Deal: 1932-1940. † Illus.   TB/3025

ARTHUR S. LINK: Woodrow Wilson and the Progressive Era: 1910-1917. † Illus.   TB/3023

GEORGE E. MOWRY: The Era of Theodore Roosevelt and the Birth of Modern America: 1900-1912. † TB/3022

RUSSEL B. NYE: Midwestern Progressive Politics: 1870-1958   TB/1202

JACOB RIIS: The Making of an American. ‡ Edited by Roy Lubove   TB/3070

PHILIP SELZNICK: TVA and the Grass Roots: A Study in the Sociology of Formal Organization   TB/1230

IDA M. TARBELL: The History of the Standard Oil Company: Briefer Version.‡ Edited by David M. Chalmers   TB/3071

GEORGE B. TINDALL, Ed.: A Populist Reader ‡   TB/3069

History: Ancient

A. ANDREWES: The Greek Tyrants △   TB/1103

---

† The New American Nation Series, edited by Henry Steele Commager and Richard B. Morris.
‡ American Perspectives series, edited by Bernard Wishy and William E. Leuchtenburg.
* The Rise of Modern Europe series, edited by William L. Langer.
¶ Researches in the Social, Cultural, and Behavioral Sciences, edited by Benjamin Nelson.
§ The Library of Religion and Culture, edited by Benjamin Nelson.
Σ Harper Modern Science Series, edited by James R. Newman.
° Not for sale in Canada.
△ Not for sale in the U. K.